SHIFTING THE DEBATE

Public/Private Sector Relations in the Modern Welfare State

Edited by

Susan A. Ostrander and Stuart Langton

(1987)

Transaction Books
New Brunswick (U.S.A.) and Oxford (U.K.)

Library of Congress Catalog Number: 87-19078
ISBN 0-88738-185-5
Printed in the United States of America

Library of Congress Cataloging-in-Publication Data

Shifting the debate.

  1. Social service.   2. Voluntarism.   3. Corporations, Nonprofit.   4. Social policy.
5. Welfare state.
I. Ostrander, Susan A.   II. Langton, Stuart.
HV40.S583   1987   361.2   87-19078
ISBN 0-88738-185-5

Contents

Preface

The dance between government and voluntary sector organizations is always intricate and complex, and the steps change quickly. The contributors to this volume have "caught the rhythm" of a difficult and often stormy partnership.

The articles in this book were initially published as a Special Issue of the *Journal of Voluntary Action Research*, the official journal of the Association of Voluntary Action Scholars. Supported by a grant from Aid Association for Lutherans, the Special Issue addressed a number of questions that have moved to centrality in the field of voluntary action research.

It soon became apparent that the contributions in this volume merited the widest possible distribution. The editors, authors, and members of the Association of Voluntary Action Scholars were all gratified when Transaction Publishers invited the publication of this book.

It seems particularly appropriate that this book is principally co-edited by faculty members at Tufts University, the new home of the Executive Office of the Association of Voluntary Action Scholars (AVAS). For 16 years, AVAS has provided a professional home for the nearly 400 practicing researchers and scholars who make the voluntary sector a major focus of their research. Early in 1987, AVAS's Executive Office was moved to the Lincoln Filene Center at Tufts University.

Susan Ostrander, whose vision initiated this volume, and whose leadership and hard work made it possible, is an associate professor in the Sociology Department at Tufts. Stuart Langton, who lent his experience and commitment to the project, directs the Lincoln Filene Center at Tufts. My own listing as the third co-editor signifies the role of the *Journal of Voluntary Action Research* in presenting the best research available on voluntarism, citizen participation, philanthropy, and nonprofit organizations.

The Association of Voluntary Action Scholars welcomes readers of this book to join with them in developing and presenting significant research in this field. Its members are pleased with the opportunity presenting this book provides to signify their commitment to research on voluntary action, and look forward to presenting in a similar manner future issues of such general interest as this one.

Jon Van Til
Urban Studies and Public Policy,
Rutgers University, Camden College
Editor-in-Chief, *Journal of Voluntary Action Research*

Shifting the Debate: Public/Private Sector Relations in the Modern Welfare State

Susan A. Ostrander

Current scholarly literature on nongovernmental nonprofits recognizes that the line between the "private" nongovernmental sector and the "public" governmental sector has become increasingly blurred. The public/private dichotomy is no longer seen as a useful or accurate conceptualization of social reality. The papers in this collection take this principle of blurred boundaries as a premise and begin to build new theoretical directions in public/private sector relations in the modern welfare state. The papers set out to develop new ways of thinking about the existence and interpenetration of what has now come to be seen as three interrelated sectors in contemporary Western societies: the governmental or state sector, the for-profit business or corporate sector, and the nongovernmental nonprofit or voluntary sector.

This now recognized ambiguity and intermingling between public and private has profound implications for theory and practice in all three sectors. Perhaps of greatest current import, it shifts the grounds of the debate about whether services should be provided by government or by "private" agencies and organizations. If public and private are no longer separate and distinct entities, then dichotomously framed questions about which sector is more appropriate or more desirable no longer makes sense. New questions arise about when and how and under what social and economic and political circumstances various patterns of relations between public and private arise. When public and private cease as terms to be identified with particular organizational entities in the society, they come to be seen rather as kinds of relations characteristic to greater or lesser degrees of activity in all kinds of organizations. The patterns of these relations come to be seen as dynamic, as historically changing, as actively created by subjects in everyday life as well as by macro-historical forces in the larger political economy.

The papers here are new theories in the sense that they lay out new conceptual schemes. They map out a domain of study, a scientific project. The papers articulate assumptions and lay bare their consequences; and they contrast claims and realities about the social world.

The first of these papers, that by Peter Dobkin Hall, articulates three crises in the contemporary United States that caused a shift in thinking needed to address what Lester Salamon has called a "weakness of theory"—a weakness which, as Hall shows, has worked against the interest of nonprofits. It was not until the first of these

Susan A. Ostrander, Department of Sociology, Tufts University, Medford, MA 02155.

crises, the Reagan challenge to nonprofits to fill gaps in services left by government cuts, that researchers did the empirical studies that demonstrated the dependence of nonprofits on government support. The three overlapping crises—Reagan, nonprofits management, and nonprofit scholarship—converged to demand new theory that locates nonprofits in the total organizational universe connected to other sectors of social, economic, political, and intellectual activity. Hall suggests three broad characteristics of this new theory. It should be multidisciplinary; it should abandon the rhetoric of independence in regard to the nonprofit sector; and it should move the debate from whether services should be organized on a for-profit, governmental, or nonprofit basis to looking at the interdependence among these three in the larger organizational and societal context of which they are all a part.

The second paper, by Urban Institute researcher Lester Salamon, documents the historic and current "partnership" between government and voluntary organizations, arguing that this is by no means a recent innovation though it has varied in scope and depth. He calls for a reorientation of both our theories of the voluntary sector and of the modern welfare state to more accurately take account of the relations between them, and to explain why the nonprofit sector is strong and why government relies on nonprofits. He claims that the mutual reliance of these two sectors has been beneficial to both, and points out that conventional theories have contributed to creating a vision of antagonistic rather than cooperative relations between them. He proposes the beginnings of a new theory of voluntarism and government which recognizes the strengths and weaknesses of each and the mutual advantages of cooperation. In this new theory the voluntary sector is seen not as secondary to government, but as a kind of "third party government" enabling public action without expansion of the public bureaucracy. He sees this theory as a way to reconcile conflicts about public demands for services at the same time the public is hostile to government. Also part of this new theory is a turning on its head of the more conventional view of the voluntary sector as a residual for government, as performing roles government fails to do. Salamon poses a "voluntary failure" theory where government is seen as doing what voluntarism cannot do or does not do well.

The paper by Jon Van Til echoes this point by arguing for the development of a view of business, government, and the nonprofit sector that sees these sectors as part of a larger political economy. As Van Til conceptualizes this political economy, it would recognize the public nature of what have been defined as private organizations, both business and nonprofit. Van Til repeats Robert Bellah's call for bringing "citizenship and civic association more centrally into the economic sphere." The definition of the term "public" then becomes closer to that of John Dewey as having consequences of great importance to a large number of people. This meaning of the term "public" recognizes that matters of public concern take place in all three sectors. Just as the public nature of governmental organizations is extended in Van Til's conceptualization to become a more universal characteristic of organizations in general, so he extends the voluntarist nature of nonprofit organizations and the corporative character of business organizations. New theoretical questions emerge from this kind of characterization, questions that transcend the theoretical biases that have been evident in the study of nonprofit organizations to date. New questions include how much voluntary action and association occurs in government and in business, how businesslike nonprofits should be, and how public relations in all three sectors should be.

Moving from the most macro-level toward middle range, Kirsten Gronbjerg gives us a genuine new paradigm. Based on her recent empirical research in Chicago, Gronbjerg lays out four analytical patterns that define relations among the non-profit, for-profit, and governmental sectors: cooperation, accommodation, competition, and symbiosis. The patterns are formed, she shows us, through the dynamic interaction of two primary driving forces in society and in history: first, by the United States "public" welfare state and its dependency on nonprofits; and second, by the dominance of "private" proprietary institutions in American capitalism. Recognizing along with Hall the need to integrate historical analysis into the study of organizations, she uses historical data to demonstrate how and under what circumstances the four patterns arose in four distinct areas of activity: the cooperation pattern in child welfare; the accommodation pattern in health care; the competition pattern in education; and the symbiotic pattern in housing and community development. In a careful empirical demonstration of her categories, Gronjberg illuminates the nonprofit sector and its place in the United States welfare state and in American capitalism.

Pickvance continues in the middle range in what is the most empirical of the papers in this collection. Harkening Lester Salamon's call for new theories of the welfare state as well as new theories of the voluntary sector in order to fully understand the relationship between the two, Pickvance looks at the impact of dynamics between national and local government on voluntary sector activity. Pickvance's research challenges previous hypotheses about the relationship between centralization of state structures and voluntary action. His research in Great Britain shows that strong local government—local autonomy and a relatively decentralized national welfare state—is not necessarily conducive to voluntary action and to responsiveness to consumer need. He finds rather that actions by local government have represented not a concern for local consumer needs—a kind of action that might encourage voluntary participation—but is focused rather on the desire of professionals in local government for autonomy in decision-making. He attributes the lack of voluntary association defense of welfare state cuts to factors other than state decentralization. A major factor in inhibiting voluntary action is the absence of established participatory structures.

The final two papers in the collection move to a more micro-level analysis than the other three, closer to the day-to-day, face-to-face activity of people in the modern welfare state. The paper by Jacqueline DeLaat shows us how one activity often indentified with the nonprofit sector—volunteering—actually takes place in all three sectors. Concerned, as is Gronbjerg, with developing cooperative relations among the sectors, DeLaat shows how volunteering as an integrative, bridging activity can enhance cooperative lines among government, business, and nonprofits. Shifting our attention away from volunteering in the nonprofit or "voluntary" sector, she focuses on volunteering in government and in the business sector. She raises interesting issues for reconceptualizing volunteering including, for example, work done in the marketplace for which one is undercompensated as volunteer work. This effort reflects Van Til's view of voluntarism as a characteristic of activities in all organizations to a greater or lesser degree.

The final paper in this collection by Martin Bulmer reminds us that there are subjects whose lives are influenced by a reconceptualization of the boundaries of public and private sector relations. These subjects have an active role in play in how useful these reconceptualizations turn out to be. Specifically, Bulmer calls attention to the issue of personal privacy in efforts to link what is termed in Britain formal and informal care for groups such as the dependent elderly at home. He suggests that linking these types of care is more problematic than has been previously recognized, and that the nature and integrity of informal care networks (especially friends and neighbors) needs to be of more concern. In defining what makes a good neighbor, Bulmer notes the importance to subjects of "distance and privacy as much as friendliness or helpfulness." He suggests that these concerns must be taken into account as we discover the specific circumstances when informal care is appropriate, and how public and private care interact. Bulmer emphasizes the importance of seeing potential obstacles to linking public and private relations as we build new theory and of including ways to overcome them as part of our theoretical task.

Bulmer has begun what seems to be the next major agenda for scholars and practitioners in nonprofit sector relations: the spelling out of policy implications of the newly emerging theoretical directions such as those that make up this collection.

Abandoning the Rhetoric of Independence: Reflections on the Nonprofit Sector in the Post-Liberal Era

Peter Dobkin Hall

This paper argues that nonprofits scholarship before 1980 was premised on unexamined assumptions about the independence of the sector from government, business, and private wealth. These assumptions shaped the direction of empirical and theoretical research into nonprofits. They also underlay public policy towards nonprofits, particularly the 1969 Tax Reform Act. Only when the Reagan administration proposed massive cuts in federal spending did scholars begin to appreciate the dependence of the sector on government revenue. At the same time, they became aware of the importance of other kinds of dependency. The 1969 Tax Act had, in encouraging the professionalization of nonprofits management, created conflicts between professional managers and traditional financial, governance, and consumer constituencies, which in turn raised serious questions regarding organizational dependency. From within history and the social sciences came other theoretical and empirical insights that belied the sector's assertions of independence. The paper concludes by suggesting that the rhetoric of independence be replaced by an appreciation of the reality of dependency, by a concerted scholarly examination of organizational interdependence, and by an understanding of the range of dependency choices organizations confront according to the services they offer and the constituencies they serve.

Beginning in the mid-1970s, when one of the first major scholarly investigations of the private nonprofit sector was being framed out, the title of the project description was "Proposal for a Study of Independent Institutions." Its authors, all of whom possessed wide practical and theoretical knowledge of nonprofit organizations, did not question the independency of the third sector.[1] The investigation proposed by this 1976 document was to be focused not on the place of nonprofits in the total organizational universe (from which it was assumed to be largely independent) but, rather, on the efficiency and effectiveness of nonprofits in the various fields in which they operated.

Assumptions about the independence of the nonprofit sector were also fundamental premises of the work of the Filer Commission (The Commission on Private Philanthropy and Public Needs) as it launched its ambitious multivolume study of independent institutions in 1973: "Few aspects of American society are more characteristically, more famously American than the nation's array of voluntary organizations, and the support in both time and money that is given to them by its citizens"

Peter Dobkin Hall, Program on Nonprofit Organizations, Institution for Social and Policy Studies, Yale University, New Haven, CT.

(Commission, 1977: 9). This viewpoint permeated the Commission's research agenda which, while acknowledging the importance of government regulation and the tax code as environmental factors affecting the nonprofit sector, never seriously addressed the question of its independence. It assumed that "voluntary collaborative activities" were a fixed—if endangered—feature of American life.

It is only within the last five years that this view of the autonomy of private nonprofit organizations has begun to be seriously challenged. The challenge has come from scholars committed to the survival of the sector. Their approach was influenced by a set of overlapping crises in public policy, nonprofits management, and scholarly perception. This paper will examine these crises and their impact on the emerging revision of our understanding of the place of the nonprofit sector in American life. I will challenge conventional views of the independence of the nonprofit sector and argue that these views have, in many instances, worked against the best interests of nonprofit enterprise. The choice for nonprofits lie, I maintain, in the types and consequences of various types of dependency.

REAGANISM AND THE CRISIS OF THE NONPROFIT SECTOR

The election of Ronald Reagan in 1980 promised a fundamental reordering of institutions comparable only to the administrative revolutions mounted by Andrew Jackson and Franklin Delano Roosevelt. The Reagan revolution took two major forms. The first involved a strident rhetoric which characterized the federal government as a parasite usurper of the private sector: Reagan promised to return government to the states and localities, to deregulate the economy, and to reduce the federal social role. The second more concrete manifestation involved a series of proposed budget cuts that would impact with particular severity on federal programs concerned with social welfare, health, education, environment, and culture.

After six years, the Reagan revolution remains incomplete. Like other presidents who were swept into office promising radical changes, Ronald Reagan has discovered both the unwieldiness of representative government and the differences between the freedom of the office-seeker and the institutional constraints on the office-holder.

The real significance of the Reagan revolution may reside less in its success in translating campaign rhetoric into legislative reality than in its impact on certain institutions and interest groups in American society. In responding to the new administration's rhetoric and budgetary proposals, these institutions and groups have changed their own perceptions of their place in the polity. That is, I will suggest, particularly true of the nonprofit sector.

This paper will argue that the election of Ronald Reagan crystallized a set of disparate political, institutional, and intellectual concerns and moved them towards a common resolution. Specifically, I will argue that both the supporters and administrators of private nonprofit organizations and the scholars of American organizational life have been challenged by the implications of Reaganism to such a degree that a revolution in thought has occurred. This fundamental change in thinking may, in turn, lead to significant changes in American institutions.

The new administration initially believed that the nonprofits—in combination with an economic recovery that would reduce unemployment—could fill the gaps in services created by its proposed spending cutbacks. This viewpoint led to the creation in 1981 of the President's Task Force on Private Sector Initiatives. After months of well-publicized meetings, the task force failed to formulate a coherent program for the private sector. Although the administration increased the deductability of corporate charitable contributions from five to ten percent in its 1981 tax package, in the uncertain economic climate few corporations were willing at the time to commit themselves to even a two percent level of giving. Further, as Abramson and Salamon pointed out in their 1982 paper, *The Federal Budget and the Nonprofit Sector*, the administration had failed to appreciate the extent to which federal funds had become a crucial component in the revenues of the nonprofit sector and that, without such funds, the nonprofits were unlikely to maintain even their current levels of service. Finally, the administration failed to formulate a coherent overall policy on the role of nonprofits. One the one hand, it has continued to pare federal social and cultural expenditure and rhetorically support private voluntarism. On the other, it attempted to eliminate or reduce many of the tax incentives which ensured reasonable levels of private support for the sector. Similarly, its education policy, while appearing to favor private institutions through such devices as tuition tax credits, simultaneously advocated cuts in student loan programs, research support, and direct institutional aid, threatening to make the elite private institutions which historically have constituted the apex of the American educational system, accessible only to the wealthy.

It seems unlikely that the President set out to destroy or weaken the nonprofit sector. Rather, the administration's rhetorical emphasis on voluntarism suggests that its understanding of the place of the sector in the American institutional system was clouded by folkloric visions that had filled the vacuum created by the indifference of historians to this aspect of American life. The central irony of the impact of Reaganism on the nonprofit sector, as Lester Salamon has pointed out, is that its budget proposals "inadvertantly posed a serious threat to the viability of the . . . sector in pursuit of an effort to get government out of the sector's way" (Salamon, 1986: 3).

PROFESSIONALIZATION, ENTREPRENEURSHIP, AND THE CRISIS WITHIN THE THIRD SECTOR

Another important dimension of the crisis of public policy and the nonprofit sector was the political response of the sector as it reacted to the Reagan administration's initiatives. While nonprofits presented a remarkably united front in the face of efforts by the administration to remove the charitable deduction from the federal tax code, its apparent institutional unity obscured serious differences within the sector. These differences interfered with its ability to clearly formulate its own future role in the American polity.

The most important of these areas of dispute had to do with the professionalization of nonprofit organizations. While efforts to make both charitable giving and the delivery of welfare, health, education, and cultural services more disinterested and hence more effective date back to the nineteenth century, attempts to professionalize nonprofits management date only from the early 1970s.[2] The movement was both a specific response to the regulations contained in the 1969 Tax Reform Act and a general response to broad public criticism of the performance of private nonprofit organizations.[3] On the face of it, professionalization was a good thing. It increased the efficiency, accessibility, and accountability of nonprofits. In many instances, it dramatically improved the quality of services offered. But it was seen by some—and not without good reason—to be a sort of Trojan Horse.

Historically, managerial professionalization has tended to reduce the policy role of governing boards in favor of staff control. As staffs become more professionalized, institutional activities tend to reflect the priorities of their managers rather than their boards. Because professional managers tend to share common outlooks and to apply to the managerial task the same set of standards, their dominance in organizations promotes institutional homogenization. In any other organizational sector, this iso-morphism might be acceptable. In the nonprofit sector, which has been traditionally looked to as a fundamental source of citizen participation, of innovation, and of social and cultural diversity, it is problematic.

While the extent of conventionality in the nonprofit sector and the role of non-profits as a source of innovation remains to be assessed, the professionalization of the sector is likely to enhance conventionality and discourage innovation. There is good reason to believe that the rationalization of philanthropy has also threatened diversity. As the 1985 study of foundation careers by Terry Odendahl and her associates suggests, professionalization has in practical terms meant that an increas-ing number of foundation executives are being recruited from within the foundation world (p. 43ff). If, as Lindeman asserted, "fixed responsibilities of administration, especially administration of wealth, tends invariably to develop in executives habits of conservatism and conventionality" (p. 58)—and he was writing of trustees, most of whom were laymen—one would suppose that staff professionalization, whether in the form of sector inbreeding or academic training in nonprofit management, would only increase this tendency. Indeed, if the outcomes of professional business management criticized by Abernathy and Hayes (1982), Fallows (1986), and other commentators have any validity, the long-term consequence of philanthropic profes-sionalization will be a further narrowing of the outlook and activities of the sector.

It has also become apparent that professionalism carried with it a potential for politicization in a direction that conservatives found profoundly disturbing. By the 1970s, prominent businessmen like William E. Simon, David Packard, and Henry Ford II were warning corporations and foundations not to support institutions whose programs were detrimental to the interests of the free enterprise system. They sug-gested that the misdirection of philanthropy and its organizational beneficiaries was due to the power of professionalized staffers, whom Simon in 1980 identified with a "new class of reformers" who were seeking "to reshape the future along collectivist lines" (Simon, 1980: 8).

Even when political agendas are not the issue, managerial professionals may often reshape organizational policies in ways that run counter to the interests and desires of donors and trustees. Over the past five yeas, nonprofits management journals like *Museum News* have been full of articles on the stages of organizational development. Interestingly, the major factor in institutional transformation is identified as the introduction of professional managers and its impact on the board of directors (Bloch, 1984). Conflicts between professional managers and boards seldom involve politics. More often, they focus on the definition and implementation of organiza-tional goals, as well as adherence to standards of fiscal and curatorial responsibility. Nevertheless, their prevalence suggests a significant and largely unnoticed struggle for institutional control which, in terms of the debate over diversity in the nonprofit sector, may be of considerable significance.[4]

Even when not concerned with empowerment and social justice, these struggles between boards and managerial professions are in a certain sense political in nature. Traditionally, small nonprofits reflected the interests of members, donors, and charismatic amateurs capable of mobilizing the resources of communities of interest. To the extent that it was accountable to anyone, the nonprofessional management of these organizations was accountable only to the individuals who comprised them. The activities of the organization, whether of good, bad, or middling quality, were really of concern to no one else. The addition of professional management greatly increased the complexity of the organization. While technically subservient to the wishes of boards and members, professional managers defined their long-term career interests in terms of the profession. Thus, they would tend to shape their organizations' activities not only in terms of what would please the institutions that employed them, but also in terms of how those activities would be viewed by the profession.

Another factor in the professionalization of nonprofits management that has led to conflict between managers, boards, and donors is the freedom of the manager to cultivate and recruit new organizational constituencies. Whether taking the form of new funding sources, new members, or entrepreneurial strategies that enable the organization to be independent of board largesse, this freedom gives the professional manager substantial autonomy to fundamentally alter the direction of an institution, the composition of its board, and the nature of its membership.

Whatever benefits may accompany professionalization—and it is still too early to evaluate its impact—it may also bring with it serious problems. It may decrease incentives for large-scale charitable giving because, as nonprofits become more professionalized, the relationship between big givers and managers becomes increasingly impersonal. Historically, there has been a close relationship between large-scale giving and the likelihood that an organization would maintain the interests of donors, their families, their businesses and, in a more attenuated sense, their world view and their class interests. Traditionally nonprofits, especially in the fields of education and culture, have been inordinately dependent on small groups of large donors.[5] Managerial techniques which reshape the market for nonprofits, by identifying new donor and consumer constituencies, decrease the dependence of organizations on these small groups. As professionally managed nonprofits become more market-oriented, they may create disincentives for giving by large donors. This may make nonprofits more responsive to the desires of consumers of their services, making these organizations in a certain sense more democratic. But, as Paul DiMaggio has written, "where mass markets [for an art form] are sought, pluralism, innovation, and, from the standpoint of many artists and consumers, excellence suffer" (DiMaggio, 1983: 34-5).

The desirability of institutional democracy and rationality presents one of the most difficult policy choices about the future of private philanthropy. Because we are a democracy, we are necessarily uncomfortable with the idea of enormous accumulations of private wealth devoted in perpetuity to public purposes, but operating without public accountability. From the Walsh investigations of the Progressive years, through the writings of Coon (1938), Lundberg (1968), and Neilson (1972), critics of private philanthropy have scored the irrationality, self-serving tendencies, and undue public influence of such entities. At the same time, these features of private philanthropy are precisely the ones most productive of diversity, innovation, and pluralism—its most valuable contribution to the quality of American life. As Tocqueville noted with regard to the Ancien Regime, the very irrationality of its institutions "had the effect of maintaining in the minds of Frenchmen a spirit of independence and encouraging them to make a stand against abuses of authority" (Tocqueville, 1955: 110). In America, private nonprofit organizations came into being precisely for that purpose. But in the heydey of twentieth century liberalism, the power of private wealth was more feared than the professionally administered central state which, because its powers were untried, could still be regarded as the people's agent. The experience of the past two decades, however, has shown that the establishment of a healthy, well-ordered freedom may be a more complex matter than one of institutional rationality and professionalism. Though not without its hazards, institutional irrationality may also have its benefits. The rationalization of philanthropy was, therefore, a good idea—but one which was based on fundamental misconceptions about sectoral independence.

THE CRISIS IN NONPROFITS SCHOLARSHIP

The conception of the nonprofit sector as independent was appropriate to the years between 1945 and 1980, when the most obvious threats to the nonprofit sector appeared to be the rise of the welfare state and the "majoritarian" populisms of the right and left. These led both to increasing federal regulation and, with the rise of the Great Society, to the attachment of "strings" (such as affirmative action guidelines) to federal aid. No one imagined that the real threat to the sector consisted not of attacks on its independence, but on the fact that its independence was largely illusory.

As early as 1960, the illusory independence of the third sector began to be uncovered in the scholarly literature with the publication of Bernard Bailyn's historiographical essay, *Education in the Forming of American Society*. Bailyn points out that the problem in the relation between the history of education and mainstream historical scholarship was a failure to pursue historical research within a theoretical framework that demonstrated the relationship between education and other sectors of social, economic, political, and intellectual activity (Bailyn, 1960: 3-4). Bailyn locates the problem in the process of educational professionalization, in its isolation from scholarly and intellectual currents in historiography, in its focus on professional interests, and its ignoring of society and history (Bailyn, 1960: 9). Scholarship about nonprofits seems to be suffering from similar concerns.

It was only when the Reagan administration turned to the nonprofit sector to replace services of government—while at the same time promising to massively reduce public spending—that the issues brought forth by Bailyn in 1960 stressing the relationship between the various sectors in society began to be more generally perceived as significant. And this only happened because policy-oriented social scientists became aware, as they analyzed the likely effects of Reagan's bugetary measures, of the degree of the private nonprofit sector's dependence on federal revenues.

Certainly the most influential recognition of this fact came in 1982, when the Urban Institute published Lester Salamon and Alan Abramson's "The Federal Government and the Nonprofit Sector: Implications of the Reagan Budget Proposals." This work comprised detailed studies of federal spending in program areas of concern to nonprofits, the estimated impact of proposed federal budget cuts on nonprofit organizations, and the implications of those cuts for private giving and the future of the nonprofit sector. It projected an alarming scenario in which the administration's proposed spending cuts would fall hardest on education, social welfare, and the arts—areas of particular concern to the sector. These areas were, moreover, particularly dependent on public funding. The paper concluded with a grim assessment, based on past trends, of the likely inability of private giving to fill the revenue gap created by reductions in federal spending.

Although devoting little attention to the issue in the main text of the paper, Salamon and Abramson clearly recognized the interdependence of the public and nonprofit sectors. In their summary they referred to "the fact that nonprofit organizations have become active partners with the federal government" (Salamon and Abramson, 1982: ii). Salamon and Abramson evidently assumed initially that the public-private partnership they described was of fairly recent origin. But by 1985, Salamon had come to recognize that the relationship between government and the nonprofit sector was longstanding. In a forthcoming paper, Salamon begins by citing a 1914 commentary on the role of public funding in the realm of private charity (Fleisher, 1914). Salamon calls attention to:

> a point that current observers of American society have tended to ignore: that the "welfare state" has taken a peculiar form in the American context, a form that involves not simply the expansion of the state, but also an extensive pattern of government reliance on private, nonprofit groups to carry out public purposes. (Salamon, 1986: 1-2).

Salamon goes on to argue that the failure to scholars and policymakers to acknowledge the interpenetration of government and the private nonprofit sector is a product "not simply of an absence of research, but more fundamentally a weakness of theory" (Salamon, 1986: 6).

While Salamon's work has concentrated on the fiscal features of sectoral overlap, other research areas is suggesting further dimensions of government-nonprofit sector interpenetration. It appears, for example, that the career lines of policy makers have tended to occupy strategically important positions in all three sectors. Typical of such individuals were McGeorge Bundy, whose career path took him from the Council on Foreign Relations (1948-49), to professorships and deanships at Harvard (1949-61), to the White House as President Johnson's national security advisor (1961-66), to the presidency of the Ford Foundation (1966-1979), to an endowed professorship at New York University. Bundy's contemporary, Robert McNamara, moved from a professorship in the Harvard Business School (1940-43), to the Ford Motor Company (1943-61), to the Defense Department (1961-68), to the presidency of the World Bank (1968-82). He simultaneously served as a director of the Ford Foundation, the Brookings Institution, and the California Institute of Technology.

If the nonprofit sector is tied structurally to government and business as sources of revenue and personnel, it is also substantively connected. Few have noted that one of the greatest ironies of the expansion of the welfare state between 1933 and 1980 was its remarkable dependence of government on the private sector (particularly the private universities, foundations, and research institutes) as a source of policy formulation (Karl and Katz, 1982; Smith, forthcoming). There is hardly an area of federal activity (foreign affairs, race relations, economic policy) in which the primary intellectual paradigms and consensus-building activities have not originated in the private nonprofit sector. In the years leading up to American involvement in the Second World War, for example, the government, for obvious political reasons stemming from the strength of isolationist sentiment, was remarkably passive. The task of creating a bipartisan political consensus and shaping public attitudes in favor of American intervention fell entirely to a cluster of private voluntary organizations (Chadwin, 1968). They not only handled the immediate tasks of coordinating leadership and public information, but more importantly had, through the isolationist twenties and thirties, fostered the study of international affairs in the universities and served as conduits for academic work to the public. Similarly, the public policy approach to race relations originated in the close relationship between a handful of foundations (the Rosenwald Fund, the Laura Spelman Rockefeller Memorial Foundation, and the Carnegie Corporation), private universities, and, once the federal government became seriously concerned about the "Negro Problem" after the Second World War, the government bureaus whose task it was to translate privately generated research into workable legislation.

Some organizational theorists have come to acknowledge the interdependence of the sectors as a matter worthy of attention. Walter W. Powell and Paul J. DiMaggio (1982), for example, have discussed the phenomenon of organizational homogenization, that is, the tendency of organizations, whatever their purpose, to become more similar over time. This is contrary to conventions of organization theory which posit a "diverse and differentiated world of organizations" and explain institutional change in terms of rational responses to a variety of forces such as competition, innovation, public demand, and government policy. Powell and DiMaggio assert rather that the world of organizations is surprisingly homogeneous and that the sources of homegeneity have less to do with rational efforts to realize institutional goals than with nonrational efforts to attain stability and reduce unpredictability through the introduction of organizational routine (Powell and DiMaggio, 1982: 4). More significant than their focus on nonrational factors in organizational change is their suggestion that the unit of analysis for studying institutional isomorphism is the "organizational field." By this they mean

> those organizations in a population that, in the aggregate, are responsible for a definable area of institutional life. In an organizational field, we would include key suppliers, resource and product consumers, and regulatory agencies, as well as other organizations that produce a similar service or product. (Powell and DiMaggio, 1982: 10)

As Powell and DiMaggio recognized, their viewpoint represented a considerable departure from the conventions of the social sciences. Not only did it focus on nonrational factors, it also ignored the sectoral boundaries so central of most studies of institutional activity. Most interestingly, its central insights were derived not from the usual comparative and cross-sectional approach to organizations. Instead, like Salamon's recent work, it drew extensively on historical studies of institutional development.

This "new" nonprofits scholarship is still embryonic. Nevertheless, it appears to represent a powerful new direction of inquiry. This power stems from a number of sources. It draws on an intellectual discontent with unidisciplinary rationalism whose roots go back to the early 1950s (Cochran, 1954; Wright, 1958; Lazarsfeld, 1959; Bailyn, 1960; McClelland, 1961). This discontent was given added impetus in the 1970s, as it appeared that the economic and sociological models on which the policies of the welfare state had been based were wrong. The rise of massive social dislocation, political violence, and runaway inflation belied the confident promises of a half-century of social engineering (Gouldner, 1970; Johnson, 1983; Matusow, 1984). These two forces, one proceeding from intellectual inquiry, the other from public events, combined to give an urgency to efforts to look at the world in new ways. Within the field of history, a handful of scholars became aware that a focus on organizations could provide an integrated approach to the diversity of American life, tying together sectors as well as facilitating multidisciplinary approaches to complex developmental patterns (Galambos, 1970, 1982; Hawley, 1966, 1974; Weibe, 1967; Bledstein, 1976; Perkins, 1977; Hall, 1983). Within sociology, political science, and anthropology, small groups of scholars came to see both the importance of organizational studies as common disciplinary referent and the particular value of historical inquiry (Stinchcombe, 1965, Meyer and Rowan, 1977; Chandler, Ouchi, and Perrow, 1981; Coser, Powell, and Kadushin, 1982; Powell and DiMaggio, 1982).

But it was the Reagan revolution that brought about the final crystalization of the new approach to nonprofits. Its neofederalist rhetoric notwithstanding, Reaganism represented the naked raise of state power, purely politicized and uncloaked—as the liberal version had been—by a rhetoric of benevolence. Scholars who had been inclined to view the nonprofit sector somewhat cynically as part of the institutional system of corporate liberalism came to realize after 1980 not only that the sector was genuinely endangered, but also the possible consequences of its extinction. More important was the need to understand the conditions necessary for its survival.

To gain this understanding requires, as Salamon notes, not merely an increase in the quantity of scholarship, but major changes in the theoretical framework through which we view organizations. The interpenetration of sectors is an established fact. The epistemological problem is to devise methods which will enable us to grasp its extent and significance.

THEORY AND POLICY

If the patterns of sectoral hybridization described by Salamon, Galaskiewicz, Odendahl, Stanfield, and others are as important as they appear to be, it would appear that the pervasive characterization of the nonprofit sector as an independent one is not only misleading, but destructive. For at a time like the present, in which the fundamental public policies that will determine the future of the sector are under active consideration, brave but misled scholarship could—and, as this paper suggests, already has—work again the best interests of nonprofit enterprise.

The starting point for any serious consideration of the place of nonprofits in the American polity is to accept the policy implications of the scholarly recognition of sectoral interpenetration: that the nonprofit sector is a *dependent* sector, not an independent one. The choices that lie before it—and before the public as it seeks to redefine the role of government and its relation to the universe of private institutions—have primarily to do with the types and consequences of various kinds of dependency.

Dependency can be narrowly or broadly construed. Broadly, it involves fundamental positive conceptions of how states and societies should be organized: the boundaries between public and private spheres of action (sovereignty), the just distribution of resources and influence, and the accountability of corporate bodies public and private. Narrowly, dependency involves normative issues: sources of institutional revenue, governance mechanisms and constituencies, and the powers of regulatory agencies. The Tax Reform Act of 1969 focused on the normative issues of dependency. Its major provisions dealt with taxation on investment income and income from ownership of unrelated business, distribution of income requirements, self-dealing, excess business holdings, disclosure and reporting, and advocacy activities (Pattillo, et al., 1970). The positive issues, however, were left largely unexamined, primarily because both the congressional critics, led by Wright Patman, and "responsible" spokesmen from the foundation community fundamentally agreed that the nonprofit sector could and should be an independent one. To be sure, the foundation world was deeply troubled by the series of investigations leading up to the 1969 tax reform. Many viewed the act itself as an unwarranted intrusion of government into the private sector (Andrews, 1968). But differences over strategy and rhetoric aside, both Patman and the foundations shared the set of positive premises about the sector and sought to devise normative mechanisms that would assure its independence.

The 1969 Tax Reform Act promoted important and long needed reforms. But it also appears to have had distinctly negative effects on the nonprofit sector as a whole. Some of these effects did not become obvious until Salamon and Abramson's 1982 paper, which pointed out the dependency of the sector on government. Assessing the impact of the 1969 act on the relation between business, private wealth, and nonprofits is a more complex matter. Some critics of the Act argue that it has slowed the rate of foundation formation since 1970 (*Foundation Directory*, 1983: xv). Others assert that the result of the Act was an erosion of public support for charitable organizations (Pifer, 1984: 102). Whatever the final verdict on the 1969 Tax Reform Act, it is doubtful that anyone will conclude that it encouraged the growth, diversity, or innovativeness of the nonprofit sector. Whatever gains the sector may have made over the last decade and a half will have been in spite of rather than because of the Act.

The 1969 Tax Act was predicated on the false assumption that nonprofits were—or should be—an autonomous sector in which reforms could be instituted without regard to the social, political, and economic infrastructure on which they depended. The reality is that most nonprofits (churches aside) have depend for their survival on revenue supplied by private wealth, corporate and private. Thus, meaningful legislation affecting them necessarily has to take into account the variety of reciprocal and mutually beneficial relationships between donors and recipient institutions that constitute a major, though by no means the only, incentive for their support. A related misconception is the general assumption that tax avoidance has been a major incentive for individual and corporate philanthropy. While the federal tax code undoubtedly played a major role in influencing giving patterns, there is reason to believe that its importance has been vastly overstated (Smith, 1984). Not only is its importance belied by the long history of large-scale charitable giving that preceded the existence of a federal income tax, but also by the fact that once tax legislation containing incentives for giving was in place, giving levels seldom approached the maximum permitted by the code. The use of tax legislation to promote charitable giving in fact constituted a negative incentive: people were encouraged to give not because they believed in an institution, but because such giving was rewarded by a reduction in monies owed the government. The force of this negative incentive over time appears to have eroded the capacity of donors to formulate positive rationales for giving—with unfortunate effects on both the amount of imaginativeness of giving. The recent survey by Yankelovich, Skelly, and White (1982) of the attitudes of top business managers towards corporate philanthropy gives abundant testimony to limited conception of this activity that prevails today. Where once corporations made major investments in the welfare of their workers, in basic research and product development, and in their communities without any tax incentives for doing so, corporations today view giving programs primarily as tax avoidance and public relations devices—and support them accordingly. The need to encourage the development of positive rationales for individual and corporate giving constitutes one of the major challenges facing the nonprofit sector today. But, once again, it requires a frank appraisal of the relation between private wealth and public power and an understanding of the essential dependency of the nonprofit sector.

The health care issue raises in its clearest form the importance of moving the debate over nonprofits policy away from emotionally charged rhetoric and false definitions towards a more dispassionate conception of the institutional universe as it has actually developed. As it existed before World War II, the largely nonprofit health care system in the United States reflected primarily the interests of the medical professionals who ran it (Fox, 1984). Decentralized and dependent for its revenues on current charitable giving, endowment income, and fees, both the quality and accessibility of medical care varied enormously from place to place. Federal involvement in health care began after the war, with the underwriting of hospital construction and encouragement of the growth of private nonprofit medical insurance plans. Because of the political power of organized medicine, the equitable distribution of health services still remained a problem. Only with the creation of Medicare and Medicaid in the 1960s did quality health services become widely available. But the federal reimbursement system introduced serious fiscal distortions into the system, inflating health care costs, favoring certain medical specialties over others, and unjustly enriching dishonest practitioners. Finally, in the 1970s, fueled by the enormous federal and corporate outlays for health care costs and a rising tide of neoconservative political sentiment, hospitals began to reorganize themselves on a for-profit basis. The rapid growth of the proprietary sector in health care has, some have argued, distorted medical priorities, improving services to well-to-do consumers, while reducing them for the poor, emphasizing spectacular surgical feats in favor of preventative programs which serve greater numbers of people, and replacing medical judgements on courses of therapy with actuarial mandates. By early eighties, as federal spending on health diminished, medical treatment became unavailable in many places for the indigent and the uninsured.

The fundamental problem stemmed not from whether health care was organized on a for-profit, public, or nonprofit basis, but on the relation between the health care delivery agency and the organizational field of which it was a part. Each pattern of dependency brought with it definable sets of advantages and disadvantages. None represented a golden age of either fiscal or moral perfection. The real issue is not the relative advantages of for-profits over nonprofits, but the consequences of particular institutional configurations and, in particular, the relations between different institutional sectors.

HISTORY AND THEORY OF ORGANIZATIONS, PUBLIC POLICY, AND THE NEED FOR AN INTERMEDIATE SYNTHESIS

Certainly one of the most important lessons to be drawn from the tumultuous history of the modern world is that ideas matter. While the optimistic efforts of twentieth century social and economic planners to base public policy on the social sciences may have been premature, the impact of broad intellectual constructs about the possibilities and purposes of nations has been undeniable. And in times of social reconstruction, ideas and theories take on particular importance in shaping events.

The shortcomings of the social sciences have stemmed primarily from their ahistoricity and their tendency to fragment and thereby distort the continuum of collective action. The shortcomings of history have stemmed from its narrow preoccupation with politics and individual personalities, its resistance to the analysis of collective behavior and normative patterns, and its adherence to rationalistic models of explanation.

Over the last thirty years, the social sciences and history have been converging in both interests and methods. It is a convergence with particularly important policy implications. Contemporary social policy, if it is to work effectively, has to be based both on serious appraisals of the capacities and resources of groups of individuals and institutions and on an understanding of how they have behaved over time. The issue is no longer one of the superiority of facts over theory, but a recognition of the interaction between the two and their mutual grounding in the continuous nature of the social process.

Any really adequate reappraisal of the nonprofit sector, therefore, is inevitably tied to the broader effort to reconstruct the enterprise of social understanding and to tie it more usefully to the formulation of public policy. This effort, appropriately enough, has focused on the history and theory of organizations, since those are both the entities most immediately affected by policy and the aggregations of collective action most easily studied. It is not coincidental that the effort to reform ideas about society should focus to so large an extent on the institutions most centrally important to the generation and propagation of ideas. For, as the historical record shows, the process of social change often has more to do with changes in the institutional contexts in which activities are carried on than in the activities themselves.[6]

When *Education in the Forming of American Society* appeared twenty five years ago, Bernard Bailyn and other scholars in the avant garde of American history were concerned about the discipline's narrow preoccupation with political issues. Bailyn's booklet was an effort both to rescue the history of education from the educators, who had turned it into an exercise in self-justification, and to place at the center of scholarly awareness a concern with the crucial importance of infrastructure of cultural institutions in the unfolding of the historical process. Bailyn's essay focused only on education. The same set of concerns might have been expressed about any one of the institutional activities in the fields of charity, welfare, health care, and culture, none of which had received significant scholarly attention. Bailyn's *Education* was not idiosyncratic; it was symptomatic of a deeper concern within his field. And between 1960 and the present, some of the most interesting work in American history has been done by scholars who, in investigating the evolution of American society, have illuminated the development of cultural institutions—education, the professions, hospitals, museums, and foundations—as well as the philanthropic activities that made their growth possible. The burgeoning of these subfields has added immeasurably to the richness and variety of American historical scholarship. But, ironically, there has been little effort to synthesize this diversity.[7]

One of the most interesting dimensions of the movement in historiography towards a consideration of institutional universes is the accompanying recognition that, rather than borrowing from social theory, historians were making it.[8] A handful of scholars, however, have responded to the lure of theory and have directed their interests to exploring both the social context of organizational development (Allmendinger, 1975; Dawley, 1976; Haskell, 1977; Johnson, 1978; Story, 1980; Ryan, 1981) and the rise of organizational systems (Hawley, 1974; Galambos, 1970, 1982; Bledstein, 1976; Hall, 1982).

Intellectually, the bridge between these theoretically oriented historians and the social science of organizational behavior has been through economic history. Although the work of William Miller and others (1952) had suggested the importance of organizational and social structural issues in economic behavior, the issue did not receive major attention until 1977, when Alfred D. Chandler's monumental *Visible Hand* was published. Chandler's book demonstrated only the extent to which organizational and managerial issues had been overlooked by most historians, but also the theoretical impoverishment of organizational history even at its best. For although Chandler cast an impressively wide net, his delineation of the history of management was not only technologically deterministic and pervaded by a dubious economic rationality, it studiously ignored the interdependence of institutional sectors. Because *The Visible Hand* was published at a time in which both the overall direction of economic policy and the specific performance of American managers had become a matter of public debate, the responses to the book brought together historians with theoretical concerns and social scientists who had come to recognize the extent to which their theoretical concerns could be illuminated by historical research.

This set of concerns only began to intersect with the policy debate over the future of the private nonprofit sector with the beginning of the Reagan revolution in 1981. At this point, analyses of the consequences of the president's proposed budget cuts, his folkloric conceptions of the role of family, corporation, community, and private voluntarism in American life, and his challenge to the positive assumptions of twentieth century liberalism about the relation of public and private activity, fostered not only a convergence of scholarly concerns, but highlighted the policy implications of scholarship.

The consequences of crisis and convergence for nonprofits scholarship seem clear. First, political and economic realities constrain us to abandon the rhetoric of sectoral independence and philanthropy and to investigate those sensitive and often obscure regions of sectoral interdependence and interpenetration. To do this we must also abandon unidisciplinary approaches to organizational behavior. Such approaches invariably contain implicit premises about organizational and individual rationality that have little bearing on the realities of institutional life. These alterations in the normative dimensions of scholarship will necessarily have an impact on its positive content. For when scholars become conscious of the extent to which values are implicit in methods (and, consequently, the extent to which methods dictate outcomes), the importance of deliberate values choices is highlighted.

Viewed from this perspective, scholarship becomes an active exercise of the moral imagination rather than a passive, mechanical, positivistic venture in the gathering of facts. The implications of this may seem disturbing. But, as the current crisis in the nonprofit sector, in organizational scholarship, and in political life indicates, they present an unavoidable challenge.

NOTES

The research on which this paper is based has been funded by the Equitable Life Assurance Society of the United States, the Exxon Education Foundation, the AT&T Foundation, the Teagle Foundation, the American Council of Learned Societies, and the Program on Nonprofit Organizations, Institution for Social and Policy Studies, Yale University.

1. Like scripture and statistics, few literatures have been more conscientiously misconstrued than Alex De Tocqueville's pronouncements on the fundamental institutions of the United States in *Democracy in America* (1945). Defenders of the independency of the nonprofit sector, in particular, have delighted in citing Tocqueville's dicta on voluntary associations (1945, II: 115):

   Americans of all ages, all conditions, and all dispositions constantly form associations. . . . If it is proposed to inculcate some truth or to foster some feeling by the encouragement of a great example, they form a society. Wherever at the head of some new undertaking you see the government in France, or a man of rank in England, in the United States you will be sure to find and association.
   Tocqueville did not view private voluntarism as an amusing carnival midway of private intentions, but as a fundamental part of a national power system. At its core there was, as he observed, "a natural and perhaps a necessary connection" between civil associations and the political associations through which citizens combined to influence the state (II: 123).
2. By professionalization, I mean the deliniation of standards of behavior, the creation of a body of literature on nonprofits management, and the establishment of training programs for those wishing to work in the nonprofit sector.
3. While the 1969 Act was aimed specifically at foundations, its provisions affected the entire nonprofit sector both directly and indirectly. By enhancing the vigilence of the Internal Revenue Service in its oversight of foundations and other nonprofits, both in the granting of tax exempt status and in policing fiscal procedures, the act raised managerial standards. Compliance with the law increasingly required expertise rather than the "methodless enthusiasm" which once sufficed to keep small nonprofits going. Further, as the foundations were forced to comply with complex reporting requirements, tax and distribution regulations, and funding restrictions, it was to their advantage to bring in professional managers. But their doing so increased the formality and the complexity of the grantor-grantee relationship: applicant organizations had to be able to demonstrate degrees of financial responsibility and generate fiscal information of a kind that had been heretofore, beyond the ability of volunteer-operated entities. Finally, because the 1969 Act coincided with the economic crisis of the 70s—a catastrophic inflation that increased institutional costs and a downward trend in charitable giving—, nonprofits were forced to look beyond their traditional constituencies and to become enterpreneurial in order to survive.
4. In surveying *Museum News* over the past two decades, it is interesting to observe the shifting viewpoint on the relation between staff and board. In 1965, the journal published a symposium on museum organization and personnel policies. The participants, while acknowledging the importance of the staff's professional prerogatives, emphasized the preeminence of the board and viewed the most important attribute of the staff professional as his ability to be "sympathetic with its [the board's] policies and purposes" (Whitehill, 1965, p. 25). By the late 70s, the director's role had been dramatically recast and enhanced in importance. As a 1978 article on the duties of museum personnel noted (Museum Positions, 1978: 25):

   the director provides conceptual leadership through specialized knowledge of the discipline of the museum, and is responsible for policymaking and funding (with the governing board), planning, organizing, staffing, directing, and supervising/coordinating activities through the staff.
   The article went on to list thirteen other possible professional staff positions whose responsibilities required specialized training of a sort generally beyond the capabilities of the enthusiastic amateurs on whom small museums have traditionally depended. By the 1980s, articles like Milton J. Bloch's "Growing Pains: The Maturation of Museums" were focusing on the problems of young professionals "at the early stages of [their] administrative careers, eager and obviously frustrated" (p. 8). Bloch's article reverses Whitehill's 1965 formulation and views the good board as one which "never asks a director to compromise his position by pressing for favors or lobbying for a viewpoint at either the staff or board level" (p. 12). The shifting position of *Museum News* on the professional role is indicative of the extention of professionalism from large organizations to "small or possibly new museum with limited resources" (p. 8), organizations which had traditionally depended on amateurs rather than professional staffs.
5. The dependence of universities on large donors is remarkably constant over the past century and a half. Ronald Story's study of Harvard's financial history (1980: 26-27) shows that in the subscription drives of

the period 1805-1826, over half the funds subscribed came from between ten and twenty percent of the subscribers. Four percent (24) of the 597 subscribers to Yale's first endowment fund drive in 1832 contributed 40.3% of the total raised by the college. A century later, .3% (63) of 22,123 contributors to Yale's 1926-28 capital fund drive gave 53% of the $21 million total. Even small regional institutions like Reed College in Portland, Oregon remain dependent on large donors. The results of its on-going (1985-86) capital fund drive show that .3% (17) of 6,536 donors gave 67.1% of the $21.6 million raised. The level of participation in fund drives has unquestionably increased since the early nineteenth century: in Yale's 1832 drive, less than 20% of the college's living alumni contributed; over 60% supported the 1926-28 effort; Seymour Harris's study of Harvard's finances shows a steady growth in alumni participation twentieth century annual appeals, from 12.9% of living graduates in 1926 to 39.8% in 1967 (Harris, 1970: 302). In spite of these increases in the overall number of participants over the course of 150 years, the proportion given by small numbers of large givers has remained remarkably constant.

6. This is the central lesson to be learned from the work of the revisionist scholars David Rothman (1978) and Michael Katz (1976).

7. The burgeoning of these sub-fields has added immeasurably to the richness and variety of American historical scholarship. But, ironically, there has been little effort to synthesize this diversity. To be sure, some monographs made important linkages between the developing bodies of specialized knowledge: David Allmendinger's *Paupers and Scholars* (1975) connected the demographic crisis of nineteenth century New England to the growth of educational institutions; Thomas Haskell's *The Emergence of Professional Social Science* (1977) tied the evolution of the social sciences to the general crisis of authority in post-bellum America; and David F. Noble's *America by Design* (1977) firmly, though polemically, established the important relationships between business, the universities, and the natural sciences. But true efforts at synthesis have been few and far between. Louis Galambos, the dean of the historians of organization, has made an important effort to delineate an institutional universe encompassing both for-profit and non-profit entities (1982). And Burton Bledstein's *Culture and Professionalism* (1976) attempted a premature but nevertheless important overview of the relation between bureaucratic organizations and class development.

8. This awareness grew out of criticism of the ways in which some historians of the 1950s and 60s had misused sociological and psychoanalytic theory. The most devastating of these critics was political scientist Michael Paul Rogin, whose 1967 volume, *The Intellectuals and McCarthy*, took to task such pluralist historians as Richard Hofstadter. The main thrust of Hofstadter's work had been to use the theories of mass politics developed by the Frankfurt School as a basis for analyzing American political life. Rogin pointed out that Hofstader's dichotomizing of politics into an ideological tradition, which was based on the irrational impulses of status groups, and a pragmatic tradition, rational by virtue of its links to concrete class and market interests, was both inaccurate and self-serving. Robin's detailed political analysis showed that McCarthy's major electoral support came not from the projective rationalizations of old agrarian radicals, but from immigrant and other groups motivated by more tangible concerns. It also suggested that the pluralist analysis had distorted the facts of American political and institutional life in order to legitimate the political role of academic intellectuals.

REFERENCES

Abernathy, William J., and Hayes, Robert H.
     1980   "Managing Our Way to Economic Decline." *Harvard Business Review* 58: 4: 66-77.
Allmendinger, David F.
     1973   *Paupers and Scholars: The Transformation of Student Life in Nineteenth Century New England.*
                   New York: St. Martins Press.
Andrews, F. Emerson
     1967   "Introduction" in Marianna Lewis (ed.) *The Foundation Directory.* New York: The Foundation Center.
Bailyn, Bernard
     1960   *Education in the Forming of American Society.* Chapel Hill: University of North Carolina Press.
Bledstein, Burton, J.
     1976   *The Culture of Professionalism: The Middle Class and the Development of Higher Education in America.* New York: W.W. Norton & Company.
Bloch, Milton J.
     1984   "Growing Pains: The Maturation of Museums." *Museum News* (June), 8-14.
Chadwin, Mark L.
     1968   *The Warhawks: American Interventionists before Pearl Harbor.* New York: W.W. Norton & Company.

Chandler, Alfred D.
1977   *The Visible Hand: The Managerial Revolution in American Business.* Cambridge: Harvard
            University Press.
Chandler, Alfred D., Ouchi, William, and Perrow, Charles
1981   "Markets, Hierarchies, and Hegemony" in A.H. Van de Ven (ed.) *Perspectives on Organiza-
            tional Design and Behavior.* New York: Wiley & Sons.
Cochran, Thomas
1955   "The Role of the Entrepreneur in Capital Formation" in *Capital Accumulation and Economic
            Growth.* Princeton: National Bureau of Economic Research.
Commission on Private Philanthropy and Public Needs
1977   *Research Papers.* Washington, D.C.: Department of the Treasury.
Coon, Horace
1939   *Money to Burn: What the Great American Foundations Do with Their Money.* London: Long-
            mans, Green & Company.
Coser, Lewis, Kadushin, and Powell, Walter W.
1982   *Books: The Culture and Commerce of Book Publishing.* New York: Basic Books.
Dawley, Alan
1976   *Class and Community: The Industrial Revolution in Lynn.* Cambridge: Harvard University
            Press.
De Tocqueville, Alexis
1954   *Democracy in America.* New York: Alfred A. Knopf.
1955   *The Old Regime and the French Revolution.* New York: Doubleday & Company.
DiMaggio, Paul
1983   "Can Culture Survive the Marketplace?" *Arts Management Review* XIII: 1.
Fallows, James
1985   "The Case Against Credentialism." *American Monthly*
Foundation Directory: Tenth Edition
1985   New York: The Foundation Center.
Fox, Daniel M.
1985   "The Organization of National Policy in Medical Care, 1953-1980." A paper delivered to
            the Colloquium on Medical and Welfare Policy in the United States, 1860-1980 at the
            Shelby Collum Davis Center, Princeton University.
Galambos, Louis
1977   "The Emerging Organizational Synthesis in Modern American History" in Edwin J. Perkins
            (ed.), *Men and Organizations: The American Economy in the Twentieth Century.* New York:
            G.P. Putnam's Sons.
1983   "Technology, Political Economy, and Professionalization: Central Themes of the Organiza-
            tional Synthesis." *Business History Review* 57: 471-493.
Galaskiewicz, Joseph
1986   *Gifts, Givers, and Getters: The Study of a Corporate Grants Economy as a Social Institution.*
            New York: Oxford University Press.
Gouldner, Alvin W.
1970   *The Coming Crisis of Western Sociology.* New York: Basic Books.
Hall, Peter Dobkin
1982   *The Organization of American Culture, 1700-1900: Institutions, Elites, and the Origins of
            American Nationality.* New York: New York University Press.
1983   "Social Perception and Social Policy: Some Thoughts on the Task of Cultural History."
            Intellectual History Group Newsletter 5: 15-22.
Haskell, Thomas
1977   *The Emergence of Professional Social Science: The American Social Science Association and the
            Nineteenth Century Crisis of Authority.* Urbana: University of Illinois Press.
Hawley, Ellis W.
1974   "Herbert Hoover, the Commerce Secretariat and the Vision of an 'Associative State.'"
            Journal of American History 61: 131-148.
Johnson, Paul
1983   *Modern Times: The World from the Twenties to the Eighties.* New York: Harper & Row.
Johnson, Paul E.
1978   *A Shopkeeper's Millenium: Society and Revivals in Rochester, New York, 1815-1837.* New York:
            Hill & Wang.
Karl, Barry D. and Katz, Stanley N.
1982   "The American Private Philanthropic Foundation and the Public Sphere, 1890-1930."
            Minerva 19: 236-70 (1981).

Katz, Michael B.
1975   *Class, Bureaucracy, and the Schools: The Illusion of Educational Change in America.* New York: Praeger Publishers.

Lazarsfeld, P.F.
1959   "Reflections on Business: Consumers and Managers." unpublished paper.

Lindemann, Eduard C.
1936   *Wealth and Culture: A Study of One Hundred Foundations and Community Trusts and Their Operations during the Decade 1921-1930.* New York: Harcourt, Brace and Company.

Lundberg, Ferdinand
1968   *The Rich and the Super-Rich.* New York: Lyle Stuart.

Matusow, Allen J.
1984   *The Unraveling of America: A History of Liberalism in the 1960s.* New York: Harper & Row.

McClelland, David C.
1961   *The Achieving Society.* New York: D. Van Nostrand Company, Inc.

Meyer, John W. and Rowan, Brian
1977   "Institutionalized Organizations: Formal Structure as Myth and Ceremony." *American Journal of Sociology* 83 (July): 340-63.

Miller, William, ed.
1952   *Men in Business: Essays in Entrepreneurial History* Cambridge: Harvard University Press.

Neilson, Waldemar
1972   *The Big Foundations.* New York: Columbia University Press.
1979   *The Endangered Sector.* New York: Columbia University Press.

Noble, David F.
1977   *America by Design: Science, Technology, and the Rise of Corporate Capitalism.* New York: Oxford University Press.

Odendahl, Teresa, Boris, Elizabeth, and Daniels, Arlene
1985   *Working in Foundations: Career Patterns of Women and Men.* New York: The Foundation Center.

Pattillo, Manning M., et al.
1970   *Foundations and the Tax Reform Act of 1969.* New York: The Foundation Center.

Perkins, Dennis N.T., Nieva, Veronica F., and Lawler, Edward E.
1983   *Managing Creation: The Challenge of Building a New Organization.* New York: John Wiley & Sons.

Pifer, Alan J.
1984   *Philanthropy in an Age of Transition: The Essays of Alan Pifer.* New York: The Foundation Center.

Powell, Walter W. and DiMaggio, Paul J.
1982   "The Iron Cage Revisited: Conformity and Diversity in Organizational Fields." New Haven: Program on Nonprofit Organizations.

"Proposal for a Study of Independent Institutions"
1976   Unpublished grant proposal, Institution for Social and Policy Studies, Yale University.

Rogin, Michael Paul
1967   *The Intellectuals and McCarthy: The Radical Specter.* Cambridge: MIT Press.

Rothman, David J., et al.
1978   *Doing Good: The Limits of Benevolence.* New York: Pantheon Books.

Ryan, Mary P.
1981   *Cradle of the Middle Class: The Family in Oneida County, New York, 1790-1865.* New York: Cambridge University Press.

Salamon, Lester M. and Abramson, Alan J.
1981   *The Federal Budget and the Non-Profit Sector.* Washington, D.C.: The Urban Institute Press.

Salamon, Lester
1986   "Partners in Public Service: Government and the Nonprofit Sector in Theory and Practice," in Walter W. Powell (ed.) *Handbook of Nonprofit Organizations.* New Haven: Yale University Press.

Simon, William E.
1980   "Reaping the Whirlwind." *Philanthropy Monthly* 13: 1: 5-8.

Smith, Hayden
1984   "Corporate Contributions Research since the Filer Commission." Unpublished paper: Council for Financial Aid to Education.

Smith, James
forth-   *Private Policy Organizations in the United States.*
coming

Stanfield, John S.
  1984   *Philanthropy and Jim Crow in American Social Science.* Westport, Connecticut: Greenwood Press.
Story, Ronald
  1980   *The Forging of an Aristocracy: Harvard and Boston's Upper Class, 1800-1870.* Middletown: Wesleyan University Press.
White, Arthur, and Bartolomeo, John
  1982   *Corporate Giving: The Views of Chief Executive Officers of Major American Corporations.* Washington, D.C.: Council on Foundations.
Whitehill, Walter M.
  1965   "Professional Staff Relationship." *Museum News* (September 1965): 24-26.
Wiebe, Robert
  1967   *The Search for Order.* New York: Hill and Wang.
Wright, C.W.
  1949   *Economic History of the United States.* New York: McGraw-Hill.

Of Market Failure, Voluntary Failure, and Third-Party Government: Toward a Theory of Government-Nonprofit Relations in the Modern Welfare State

Lester M. Salamon

Despite the fact that government in the United States relies more heavily on nonprofit organizations than on its own instrumentalities to deliver government-funded human services, and that nonprofits receive more of their income from government than from any other single source, the phenomenon of government-nonprofit partnership has been largely overlooked both in analyses of the welfare state and in research on the voluntary sector. This article argues that this neglect of government-nonprofit ties is less the product of a lack of research than of important weaknesses in theory. Both the theory of the welfare state and the theory of the voluntary sector, moreover, are deficient. To overcome these weaknesses, the article advances an alternative theoretical formulation that replaces the prevailing conception of the welfare state with the concept of "third-party government," and replaces the current "market failure-government failure" theory of the voluntary sector with a theory built around the concept of "voluntary failure" instead. Viewed through these alternative conceptual lenses, the phenomenon of government-nonprofit partnership comes into far better view and becomes far more understandable. Against the backdrop of this alternative theory, the article then identifies a number of principles that should guide government-nonprofit relations in the years ahead.

Few facets of the American welfare state have been so thoroughly overlooked or so commonly misunderstood as the role of the nonprofit sector and the relationships between nonprofit organizations and government. Yet few facets also are as important.

According to widespread beliefs, the social welfare programs of the New Deal and Great Society effectively displaced voluntary agencies in the United States and led inevitably to their decline. In fact, however, the voluntary sector has retained a vital, indeed growing, role in the American welfare state. It has done so, moreover, not in spite of government but, to an important degree, because of it. This is so because government has turned extensively to private, nonprofit organizations to deliver publicly financed services. In some cases, government has even created new nonprofit organizations where none existed. In others, nonprofit organizations have benefitted from government payments to individuals for the purchase of services that nonprofits provide (e.g., higher education, hospital care).

Through these and other channels an elaborate network of partnership arrangements has come into existence linking government and the nonprofit sector. So extensive are these arrangements, in fact, that in a number of human service fields—

Lester M. Salamon, director of the Institute for Policy Studies, Johns Hopkins University, Baltimore, Maryland 21218.

such as health and social services—nonprofit organizations actually deliver a larger share of the services government finances than do government agencies themselves. (Salamon, 1987) (See Table 1 below).

Not only is the resulting partnership important for government, however. It is also important for the nonprofit sector. In fact, government has emerged as the single most important source of nonprofit sector income. This is apparent in Table 2, which draws on a survey of nonprofit, public-benefit service organizations—exclusive of hospitals and schools—across the country (Salamon, 1984). As this table shows, as of 1981 nonprofit organizations received 40 percent of their income from government. By contrast, they received only 20 percent of their income from all types of private giving—corporate, foundation, and individual. In short, cooperation between government and the voluntary sector has become the backbone of this country's human-service delivery system, and the central financial fact-of-life of the country's private nonprofit sector.[1]

Despite its scale and importance, however, this partnership between government and the voluntary sector has attracted surprisingly little attention. Even the basic scope of the partnership has been unknown until recently, while serious analyses of its strengths and weaknesses have been virtually nonexistent. Like the broader question of the scope and character of the voluntary sector, the phenomenon of government-nonprofit interaction has been largely ignored in both public debate and scholarly inquiry, as attention has focused instead on the evolution of government policy.

This neglect has continued in more recent years as well despite a revival of interest

TABLE 1
Share of Government-Funded Human Services Delivered by Nonprofit, For-Profit, and Government Agencies in Sixteen Communities, 1982 (Weighted Average)[a]

| Field | Proportion of Services Delivered by | | | |
	Nonprofits	For Profits	Gov't.	Total
Social services	56%	4	40	100%
Employment/training	48	8	43	100
Housing/comm. devel.	5	7	88	100
Health	44	23	33	100
Arts/culture	51	*	49	100
Total	42%	19%	39%	100%

SOURCE: The Urban Institute Nonprofit Sector Project

*Less than 0.5 percent

[a]Figures are weighted by the scale of government spending in the sites. Percentages shown represent the share of all spending in all sites taken together that fall in the respective categories.

TABLE 2
Sources of Support of Nonprofit Human Service Agencies, 1981

Sources	Share of total Income
Government	41
Private Giving	20
Fees	28
Other[a]	10
TOTAL	99

Source: The Urban Institute Nonprofit Sector Project Survey

[a]Includes special fundraisers, sale of products and endowment income.

in the voluntary sector prompted by disenchantment with the costs and effectiveness of government. A major three-year study of "mediating structures" conducted by the American Enterprise Institute in the mid-1970s, for example, made the creation of a partnership between government and the nonprofit sector its major policy recommendation without ever acknowledging the extent to which existing government action already embodied this approach. (Berger and Neuhaus, 1977). What attention government-nonprofit cooperation has attracted, moreover, has tended to be critical, emphasizing the threat that governmental support poses to the nonprofit sector's ideals of independence and voluntarism. What has so far been lacking, however, is a coherent analysis of the role this partnership has played or the reasons for its evolution.

How can we explain this paradox? Why has so important a feature of modern American social policy remained so obscure for so long? Why has so little attention been paid to this partnership arrangement between government and the nonprofit sector, despite the dominant role that this partnership plays in our system of human service delivery?

A Long-Standing Pattern

One possible explanation is that the phenomenon of widespread government-nonprofit cooperation is simply too new to have attracted much attention. In fact, however, this explanation is hard to support. To the contrary, extensive government-nonprofit cooperation has substantial roots deep in American history. Well before the American Revolution, for example, colonial governments had established a tradition of assistance to private educational institutions, and this tradition persisted into the nineteenth century. In colonial Massachusetts, for example, the Commonwealth government not only enacted a special tax for support of Harvard College, but also paid part of the salary of the President until 1781 and elected the College's Board of Overseers until after the Civil War. The State of Connecticut had an equally intimate relationship with Yale, and the state's Governor, Lieutenant Governor, and six state senators sat on the Yale Corporation from the founding of the school until the 1870s.

The prevailing sentiment was that education served a public purpose regardless of whether it was provided in publicly or privately run institutions and that it therefore deserved public support (see Whitehead, 1973, 3-16).

A similar pattern was also evident in the hospital field. A survey of seventeen major private hospitals in 1889, for example, revealed that 12-13 percent of their income came from government (Stevens 1982). So widespread was the appropriation of public funds for the support of private, voluntary hospitals, in fact, that an American Hospital Association report referred to it in 1909 as "the distinctively American practice" (Stevens 1982; Rosner 1980).

In the social welfare field, government support of nonprofit organizations has long long been even more extensive. State and local governments turned extensively to private, voluntary organizations to help relieve the suffering occasioned by rapid urbanization and industrializations in the mid-nineteenth century. In New York City, for example, the amount the city paid to private benevolent institutions for the care of prisoners and paupers grew massively, from 2 percent of total city expenditures on the poor in 1850 to 57 percent in 1898. (Fetter 1901/2, p. 376). Indeed, reflecting this, a study of 200 private organizations for orphan children and the friendless in New York state in the late 1880s showed that twice as much of their support came from the taxpayers as from legacies, donations, and private contributions (Warner, 1894, p. 337). Similarly, in the District of Columbia, about half of the public funds allocated for aid to the poor went to private charities as of 1892. More generally, a 1901 survey of government subsidization of private charities found that: "Except possibly two territories and four western states, there is probably not a state in the union where some aid [to private charitie.] is not given either by the state or by counties and cities" (Fetter 1901, p. 360).

The Argument: The Need for Theory

If the widespread neglect of the partnership between government and the voluntary sector cannot be attributed to the newness of this partnership, to what can it be attributed? It is the argument here that the real answer to this question lies in the realm of theory: The partnership between government and the nonprofit sector has been overlooked, in my view, not because of its novelty or because of a lack of research but because of a weakness in theory. It is the role of theory, after all, to direct attention to the facts that are most relevant to a particular process. As Thomas Kuhn put it in his classic book, *The Structure of Scientific Revolutions*, "In the absence of a paradigm [or theory] . . . all of the facts that could possibly pertain to the development of a given science are likely to seem equally relevant" (Kuhn, 1962, p. 15). Lacking a valid theory, crucial facts can therefore be overlooked or misperceived. "Facts do not speak for themselves," Stephen Jay Gould has observed, "they are read in the light of theory" (Gould, 1977). It is for this reason that Karl Deutsch has argued that "progress in the effectiveness of symbols and symbol systems [i.e. theory] is . . . basic progress in the technology of thinking and in the development of human powers of insight and action" (Deutsch, 1963 p. 10).

It is the argument here that such "basic progress in the technology of thinking" is very much needed in the analysis of the voluntary sector and its relationships with government. Our failure to perceive the reality of extensive government-nonprofit ties is, I believe, in substantial part a product of the limitations of the conceptual

nership, the existing theories of the voluntary sector likewise leave little room to expect effective cooperation between nonprofit organizations and the state. In fact, it was to get away from such blurring of the boundaries between the public and private sectors that the concept of the private nonprofit sector was invented in the latter nineteenth century. Prior to this time, charitable organizations were considered part of the public sector because they served public objectives. As business interests sought to free themselves from government involvement in economic affairs in the latter 1800s, however, it became important to draw a sharper distinction between public and private action, and the notion of a separate private, nonprofit sector took shape as one of the consequences (Hartz, 1948; Stevens, 1982).

If the concept of the nonprofit sector thus had its origins in a broader effort to distinguish the private sector from government, this division has since been further elaborated in the more formal economic theories of the voluntary sector that have surfaced in recent years. Broadly speaking, two such theories have been advanced to explain the existence of the voluntary sector, and neither provides much reason to expect extensive government-nonprofit cooperation.

The Market Failure/Government Failure Theory. The first of these theories views the existence of the voluntary sector as the combined product of what economists term "market failure" and "government failure"; i.e., of inherent limitations in both the private market and government as providers of "collective goods" (Weisbrod 1978). "Collective goods" are products or services like national defense or clean air that, once produced, are enjoyed by everyone whether or not they have paid for them. Providing such goods exclusively through the market will virtually ensure that they are in short supply since few consumers will volunteer to pay for products they could enjoy without having to pay. With market demand low, producers will produce less of these goods or services than the public really needs and wants. This phenomenon is commonly referred to as the "free rider" problem, and it serves in traditional economic theory as the major rationale for government. Since government can tax people to produce "collective goods" it can overcome this "market failure."

But government too has certain inherent limitations as a producer of collective goods. Most importantly, in a democratic society it will produce only that range and quantity of collective goods that can command majority support. Inevitably, this will leave some unsatisfied demand on the part of segments of the political community that feel a need for a range of collective goods but cannot convince a majority of the community to go along.

It is to meet such "unsatisfied demand" for collective goods, the argument goes, that a private, voluntary sector is needed. Private, nonprofit organizations thus exist, according to the market failure/government failure theory, to supply a range of "collective goods" desired by one segment of a community but not by a majority. From this it follows that the more diverse the community, the more extensive the nonprofit sector it is likely to have. Because the nonprofit sector is viewed as a substitute for government, providing goods and services that the full political community has not endorsed, however, government support to nonprofit organizations has little theoretical rationale. To the contrary, under this theory, to the extent that nonprofits deliver services that government underwrites, they violate their theoretical *raison d'etre*, which is to supply the goods government is not providing. The market failure/government failure theory would thus predict that little government-nonprofit cooperation would occur, and that what little of it exists cannot be easily justified.[3]

The "Contract Failure" Theory. The second broad theory of the voluntary sector attributes the existence of voluntary organizations to a different kind of market failure, what one theorist terms "contract failure" (Hansmann 1981). The central notion here is that for some goods and services, such as care for the aged, the purchaser is not the same as the consumer. In these circumstances, the normal mechanisms of the market, which involve consumer choice on the basis of adequate information, do not obtain. Consequently, some proxy has to be created to offer the purchaser a degree of assurance that the goods or services being purchased meet adequate standards of quality and quantity. The nonprofit form, in this theory, provides that proxy. Unlike for-profit businesses, which are motivated by profit and therefore might be tempted to betray the trust of a purchaser who is not the recipient of what he buys, nonprofit firms are in business for more charitable purposes and may therefore be more worthy of trust.

Since most government programs involve a substantial amount of regulation, however, this theory provides little rationale for government reliance on nonprofits, or for government regulation of nonprofits (Rose-Ackerman 1985). In fact, since government agencies might be expected to have even less reason to betray trust than nonprofit ones, this theory might lead one to expect more reliance on government agencies than nonprofit ones.

THIRD-PARTY GOVERNMENT AND VOLUNTARY FAILURE: TOWARD A NEW THEORY OF GOVERNMENT-NONPROFIT RELATIONS

Given the prevailing perceptions of the American welfare state and the prevailing theories of the voluntary sector, it should thus come as no surprise to find little awareness of the continued vitality of the nonprofit sector or of the immense importance of government-nonprofit cooperation. In neither set of theories is there much hint that the nonprofit sector should play as substantial a role as it does in the provision of government-financed services. How, then, are we to account for this phenomenon? Are the continued vigor of the nonprofit sector and the extensive pattern of government-nonprofit cooperation accidents, or is there some theoretical rationale that can better help us come to terms with these phenomena?

It is the argument here that the answer to these questions lies in certain shortcomings in the prevailing theories. Both the theory of the welfare state and the theory of the voluntary sector, moreover, are deficient, though for different reasons. To bring the prevailing reality into better focus, therefore, both sets of theories need to be reworked.

Third Party Government: A New Theory of the American Welfare State

The central problem with the theory of the welfare state as it has applied to the American context is its failure to differentiate between government's role as a provider of funds and direction, and government's role as a deliverer of services. In point of fact, it is largely in the former capacity that government—certainly the national government—has grown in the United States. When it comes to the actual delivery of services, by contrast, the national government has turned extensively to other institutions—states, cities, counties, universities, hospitals, banks, industrial corporations, and others. Far from the bureaucratic monolith pictured in conventional theories, the welfare state in the American context makes use of a wide variety of third parties to carry out governmental functions. The result is an elaborate system of "third-party government" (Salamon 1981), in which government shares a substantial degree of its discretion over the spending of public funds and the exercise of public authority with third-party implementers.

This pattern of government action is evident in a wide assortment of domestic program areas and involves a diverse array of actors. Under the more than 900 grant-in-aid programs, for example, the federal government makes financial assistance available to states and local governments for purposes ranging from aid to families with dependent children to the construction of interstate highways. Under the federal government's "loan guarantee" programs, close to $150 billion in loan money is lent by private banks to individuals and corporations, with federal backing, for everything from home mortgages to college education.

In each of these programs the federal government performs a managerial function but leaves a substantial degree of discretion to its nongovernmental, or nonfederal, partner. In the Aid to Families with Dependent Children program, for example, the federal government reimburses states for a portion of their payments to mothers with dependent children, but leaves to the states the decision about whether to have such a program, what the income eligibility cut-offs will be, and even what the benefits will be.

This form of government action reflects America's federal constitutional structure, with its sharing of governmental functions between federal and state governments (Grodzins 1966; Elazar 1972). But "third-party government" extends well beyond the domain of relations among the different levels of government. It also applies to relationships between government and a host of private institutions. As such, it reflects as well the conflict that has long existed in American political thinking between a desire for public services and hostility to the governmental apparatus that provides them. Third-party government has emerged as a way to reconcile these competing perspectives, to increase the role of government in promoting the general welfare without unduly enlarging the state's administrative apparatus. Where existing institutions are available to carry out a function—whether it be extending loans, providing health care, or delivering social services—they therefore have a presumptive claim on a meaningful role in whatever public program might be established.

This pattern of government action is also encouraged by the country's pluralistic political structure. To secure needed support for a program of government action, it is frequently necessary to ensure at least the acquiscence, if not the whole-hearted support, of key interests with a stake in the area. One way to do this is to give them a "piece of the action" by building them into the operation of the government program. Thus, private banks are involved in running the government's mortgage guarantee programs, private health insurers and hospitals in the operation of the Medicare and Medicaid programs, states and private social service agencies in the provision of federally funded social services.

Finally, this pattern of government action is motivated in part by concerns about flexibility and economy. Where existing institutions are already performing a function, government can frequently carry out its purposes more simply and with less cost by enlisting these other institutions in the government program, thereby avoiding the need to create wholly new organizational structures or specialized staffs. This is particularly true where programs are experimental. This way of organizing government services also makes it easier to adapt program operations to local circumstances or individual needs and thus to avoid some of the drawbacks of large-scale governmental bureaucracy and some of the limitations of the civil service. Finally, some argue that the use of outside contractors lowers costs by stimulating competition and promoting economies of scale, though the evidence here is far from conclusive (Fitch 1974; Savas 1984).

Private, nonprofit organizations are among the most natural candidates to take part in this system of third-party government. Far more than private businesses, these organizations have objectives that are akin to those of government. Indeed, as noted earlier, they were regularly considered part of the "public sector" until the late nineteenth century because they served essentially "public" purposes. In addition, in a wide range of fields, nonprofit organizations were on the scene before government arrived. It was therefore frequently less costly in the short run to subsidize and upgrade the existing private agencies than to create wholly new governmental ones.

In short, the extensive pattern of government support of nonprofit institutions can be viewed as just one manifestation of a much broader pattern of third-party government that reflects deep-seated American traditions of governance as well as more recent concerns about service costs and quality. Instead of the hierarchic, bureaucratic apparatus pictured in conventional images, the concept of third-party government emphasizes the extensive sharing of responsibilities among public and private institutions and the pervasive blending of public and private roles that is characteristic of the American welfare state. Because a number of different institutions must act together to achieve a given program goal, this pattern of government action seriously complicates the task of public management and involves real problems of accountability and control (Salamon 1981; Smith 1975; Staats 1975). But it also has much to recommend it. It makes it possible to set priorities for the expenditure of societal resources through a democratic political process while leaving the actual operation of the resulting public programs to smaller-scale organizations closer to the problems being addressed. It thus creates a public presence without creating a monstrous public bureaucracy. And it permits a degree of diversity and competition in the provision of publicly funded services that can improve efficiency and reduce costs.

So long as the image of the welfare state in America remains tied to its conventional European model, the phenomenon of extensive government support to voluntary organizations has no apparent place and therefore tends to be overlooked. But once we adjust our conceptual lenses to take account of the reality of third-party government, it becomes clear why nonprofits play so important a role. These organizations predated government in many fields and operate in ways that are congenial to public objectives. Given a welfare state that is characterized by an extensive pattern of third-party government, the persistence of a voluntary sector and widespread government-nonprofit cooperation are not a mystery at all: they are perfectly understandable phenomena that are fully consistent with theoretical expectations.

Voluntary Failure: A New Theory of the Voluntary Sector

If the failure to acknowledge the reality of third-party government in the conventional image of the American welfare state explains part of the neglect of government-nonprofit relationships in recent decades, shortcomings in the existing theories of the voluntary sector explain the rest. Essentially, as we have seen, those theories explain the existence of the voluntary sector in terms of failures of the market system and of government. The voluntary sector is thus seen as derivative and secondary, filling in where those other systems fall short.

It may be more meaningful, however, to turn this theory on its head, to reject the view that government is the typical response to market failure and to see voluntary organizations as the primary response mechanism instead. Rather than treating voluntary organizations as derivative institutions filling in for "government failure," for inherent limitations of government as a mechanism for providing collective goods, such a theory would turn the argument around and view *government* as the derivative institution responding to "voluntary failure," to inherent limitations of the voluntary or nonprofit sector.

The central argument for this reformulation is that the "transaction costs" involved in mobilizing governmental responses to shortages of collective goods tend to be much higher than the costs of mobilizing voluntary action. For government to act, substantial segments of the public must be aroused, public officials must be informed, laws must be written, majorities must be assembled, and programs must be put into operation. By contrast, to generate a voluntary-sector response, a handful of individuals acting on their own or with outside contributed support can suffice. It is reasonable to expect, therefore, that the private, nonprofit sector will typically provide the first line of response to perceived "market failures," and that government will be called on only as the voluntary response proves insufficient. So conceived, it becomes clear that government involvement is less a substitute for, than a supplement to, private nonprofit action. What is more, this reformulation of the market failure theory does a far better job of making sense of the fundamental reality of extensive government-nonprofit ties. And it suggests a theoretical rationale for these ties that fits into a broader, and more positive, conception of the voluntary sector, thus rescuing this fundamental fact of voluntary-sector life from the limbo to which it has been consigned by existing theories.[4]

But what are the "voluntary failures" that have necessitated government action and that justify government support to the voluntary sector. Broadly speaking, there are four: first, philanthropic insufficiency; second, philanthropic particularism; third, philanthropic paternalism; and fourth, philanthropic amateurism.

Philanthropic Insufficiency. The central failing of the voluntary system as a provider of collective goods has been its inability to generate resources on a scale that is both adequate enough and reliable enough to cope with the human-service problems of an advanced industrial society. In part, this is a reflection of the "free rider" problem inherent in the production of collective goods. Since everybody benefits from a society in which those in need are cared for whether or not they have contributed to the cost of the care, there is an incentive for each person to let his neighbor bear most of the cost. So long as sole reliance is placed on a system of voluntary contributions, therefore, it is likely that the resources made available will be less than those society considers optimal. Only when contributions are made involuntary, as they are through taxation, are they therefore likely to be sufficient and consistent. As one early student of American charity put it:

The law is primarily an agency for bringing up the laggards in the march of progress, and when the community on the average wants benevolent work done, this is the method of pushing forward those who hang back. . . . The stingy man is not allowed to thrive at the expense of his benevolent neighbor (Warner 1894, p. 306).

Since the range of "benevolent work" that is thought necessary has expanded considerably over the years, moreover, this problem has grown increasingly important over time.

Beyond this "free rider" problem, however, philanthropic insufficiency also results from the twists and turns of economic fortune. The economic fluctuations that have accompanied the growing complexity of economic life mean that benevolent individuals may find themselves least able to help others when those others are most in need of help, as happened with disastrous results during the Great Depression. Similarly, the voluntary system often leaves serious gaps in geographic coverage, since the resources are frequently not available where the problems are most severe. In short, the voluntary system, despite its advantages in terms of reducing transaction costs and creating a meaningful sense of social obligation and legitimacy, nevertheless has serious drawbacks as a generator of a reliable stream of resources to respond adequately to community needs.

Philanthropic Particularism. If resource inadequacy is one source of voluntary-sector weakness, the "particularism" of the voluntary sector constitutes another. Particularism, the tendency of voluntary organizations and their benefactors to focus on particular subgroups of the population, is, of course, one of the purported strengths of the voluntary sector. Voluntary organizations provide the vehicle through which such subgroups—ethnic, religious, neighborhood, interest, or other—can join together for common purposes. Indeed, in some theories, as we have seen, it is precisely this particularism that provides the theoretical rationale for the existence of the nonprofit sector.

But particularism also has its drawbacks as the basis for organizing a community's response to human needs. For one thing, there is the possibility that some subgroups of the community may not be adequately represented in the structure of voluntary organizations. Even voluntary organizations require resources, after all, and it is quite possible that those in command of the needed resources—financial as well as organizational—may not favor all segments of the community equally. As a result, serious gaps can occur in the coverage of subgroups by the existing voluntary organizations. Close observers of the nonprofit scene in New York City, for example, have observed that up through the early 1960s, the lion's share of the child-welfare services were provided through essentially Catholic and Jewish agencies. Since most of the poor blacks who migrated to the city in the post-World War II era were Protestants, they did not immediately find a "home" in the established agency structure (Beck 1971, p. 271). Other groups—gays, the disabled, Hispanics, women—have found similar difficulties establishing a niche in the voluntary system and locating a source of support for their activities. More generally, the private nonprofit sector has long had a tendency to treat the more "deserving" of the poor, leaving the most difficult cases to public institutions. Indeed, the survey we conducted of 3,400 human service organizations revealed that the poor comprised the majority of the clients of only about 30 percent of the agencies, and that for half of the agencies, the poor constituted less than 10 percent of the clientele (Salamon, 1984b).

Not only can particularism, and the favoritism that inevitably accompanies it, leave serious gaps in coverage, but also it can contribute to wasteful duplication of services. Voluntary organizations and charitable activity are motivated not alone by considerations of social need, but also by considerations of communal or individual pride. Each group wants its own agencies, and appeals to donors are frequently made along religious, ethnic, or sectarian lines. The upshot is that the number of agencies can increase well beyond what economies of scale might suggest, reducing the overall efficiency of the system and increasing its costs. This was a great concern of early students of American social welfare policy, who viewed the duplication of facilities and the resulting waste of resources as one of the great drawbacks of the private, voluntary system (Fetter 1901/02, p. 380; Fleisher 1914, p. 111). As Amos Warner (1894, p. 359) put it in his classic treatise on American charity in the 1890s:

> The charities of a given locality, which should for useful result be systematically directed to the accomplishment of their common purposes, are usually a chaos, a patchwork of survivals, or products of contending political, religious, and medical factions, a curious compound, in which a strong ingredient is ignorance perpetuated by heedlessness.

Left to their own devices, therefore, voluntary organizations may leave significant elements of the community without care and make wasteful use of what resources are available.

Philanthropic Paternalism. A third class of problems with the voluntary system of responding to community problems results from the fact that this approach inevitably vests most of the influence over the definition of community needs in the hands of those in command of the greatest resources. This is so despite the importance of volunteer effort in this sector. For one thing, voluntarism itself requires resources of time and knowledge. But in addition, the growing need for professional approaches to social problems has made it necessary to go beyond voluntary effort. So long as private charity is the only support for the voluntary sector, those in control of the charitable resources can determine what the sector does and whom it serves. The nature of the sector thus comes to be shaped by the preferences not of the community as a whole, but of its wealthy members. As a consequence, some services favored by the wealthy, such as the arts, may be promoted, while others desired by the poor are held back. Since these private contributions are tax-deductible, moreover, they have the effect not only of allocating private expenditures, but also of allocating foregone public revenues as well, though without the benefit of any public decision process.

Not only is this situation undemocratic, but also it can create a self-defeating sense of dependency on the part of the poor since it gives them no say over the resources that are spent on their behalf. Aid is provided as a matter of charity, not of right. And in the past it was often accompanied by various moral preachments of the sort that George Bernard Shaw immortalized in his play *Major Barbara*. A central premise of much early philanthropic activity, in fact, was that the poor were responsible for their own destitution and needed to be uplifted religiously and morally through the work of sectarian agencies. Even in more recent times, close students of social policy have criticized the funnelling of funds "into the hands of upper-class and middle-class people to spend on behalf of the less privileged people" as "the most pernicious effect" of the private, charitable system because of the dependency relationship it creates (Beck, 1971 p. 218). In short, for all its strengths and value, private, charitable support cannot easily escape its "Lady Bountiful" heritage and establish a claim to assistance as a right.

Philanthropic Amateurism. One final problem with the voluntary system has been its association with amateur approaches to coping with human problems. In part, this has been a reflection of the paternalism of the sector noted above: for a considerable period of time, the problems of poverty and want were attributed to the moral turpitude of the poor. Care of the poor, the insane, the unwed mother was therefore appropriately entrusted to well-meaning amateurs and those whose principal calling was moral suasion and religious instruction, not medical aid or job training.

As sociological and psychological theory advanced, however, these approaches lost favor and emphasis turned to more professional treatment modes involving trained social workers and counsellors. Agencies stressing volunteer effort and limited by dependence on contributions from providing adequate wages were in a poor position to attract such professional personnel. It was partly for this reason that social-welfare advocates of the late-nineteenth and early-twentieth centuries opposed public support for private charitable institutions, fearing this would siphon off resources needed to build an adequate system of professional, public care. As one of these advocates put it in 1914: "No appropriations should be made to charities under private management until the reasonable needs of the charities managed and supported by the state have been fully met and an adequate system of state institutions developed" (Fleisher 1914, p. 112).

Summary: A Theory of Government-Nonprofit Partnership

In short, for all its strengths, the voluntary sector has a number of inherent weaknesses as a mechanism for responding to the human-service needs of an advanced industrial society. It is limited in its ability to generate an adequate level of resources, is vulnerable to particularism and the favoritism of the wealthy, is prone to self-defeating paternalism, and has at times been associated with amateur, as opposed to professional, forms of care.

Significantly, however, the voluntary sector's weaknesses correspond well with government's strengths, and vice versa. Potentially, at least, government is in a position to generate a more reliable stream of resources, to set priorities on the basis of a democratic political process instead of the wishes of the wealthy, to offset part of the paternalism of the charitable system by making access to care a right instead of a privilege, and to improve the quality of care by instituting quality-control standards. By the same token, however, voluntary organizations are in a better position than government to personalize the provision of services, to operate on a smaller scale, to adjust care to the needs of clients rather than to the structure of government agencies, and to permit a degree of competition among service providers. Under these circumstances, neither the replacement of the voluntary sector by government, nor the replacement of government by the voluntary sector, makes as much sense as collaboration between the two. In short, viewed from a theoretical perspective that acknowledges the widespread pattern of third-party government in the American version of the modern welfare state, and that posits the voluntary sector as the principal mechanism for providing collective goods, but one that has certain inherent limitations or "failures," extensive collaboration between government and the nonprofit sector emerges not as an unwarranted aberration, but as a logical and theoretically sensible compromise. The "voluntary failure" theory of the voluntary sector and the "third-party government" theory of the American welfare state outlined here thus allow us to come to terms with the reality of government-nonprofit relationships far more effectively than the alternative concepts now in use. Given the fundamental importance of these relationships, this is reason enough to lend these theories some credence.

IMPLICATIONS

To say that a strong theoretical rationale exists for government-nonprofit cooperation is not, of course, to say that this cooperation has worked out in practice the way the theory would suggest. To the contrary, any relationship as complex as this one is likely to encounter immense strains and difficulties, especially given the somewhat different perspectives of the two sides. Government officials, for example, worry about the problems of exercising management supervision, ensuring a degree of accountability, and encouraging coordination when decision-making authority is widely dispersed and vested in institutions with their own independent sources of authority and support. Within the philanthropic community, the issues raised by the prevailing pattern of government support of nonprofit organizations are of a far different sort. Of central concern here are three other potential dangers: first, the potential loss of autonomy or independence that some fear can result from heavy reliance on government support; second, "vendorism," or the distortion of agency missions in pursuit of available government funding; and third, the danger of bureaucratization or over-professionalization resulting from government program and accounting requirements.

In the absence of a firm theoretical basis for government-nonprofit relations, it has been difficult to sort through these issues effectively. Indeed, the existence of strains has been taken in some quarters as evidence that the partnership between government and the nonprofit sector cannot work and should be dismantled. Against the backdrop of the theoretical notions developed above, therefore, it may be useful to revisit these issues and explore the implications that flow for the future of government-nonprofit relations and for the roles and responsibilities of the respective partners. Four such implications in particular seem most important.

Retention and Strengthening of "Nonprofit Federalism"

Perhaps the central conclusion that emerges from the preceding discussion is that the partnership that has been forged in this country between government and the nonprofit sector is worth preserving and strengthening. In all likelihood, had we not invented this mechanism for delivering needed services already, we would be thinking about inventing it now, rather than subjecting it to serious strain.

What "nonprofit federalism" offers is the opportunity to combine the service-delivery advantages of voluntary organizations with the revenue-generating and democratic priority-setting advantages of government. In many cases, moreover, this mechanism makes it possible to match publicly generated funds with privately generated ones to provide a better service than either could provide on its own. This is not to say that all services should be distributed through this mechanism since there are disadvantages as well. But a strong case can be made for promoting this approach as one important element of the nation's service delivery system.

Accommodation by Government of the Organizational Needs of Nonprofit Organizations

"Nonprofit federalism" has advantages as a form of service delivery in large part because of certain distinctive characteristics of nonprofit agencies. These characteristics reflect the role that private, nonprofit organizations have traditionally played not so much as contributors to efficiency as mechanisms for promoting other important social values, such as group and individual freedom, diversity, a sense of community, civic activism and charity. These features have long made it in the national interest to protect and nurture the voluntary sector even if there were costs involved.

The nonprofit sector also offers a number of more practical advantages as well in the delivery of human services, however. Among these advantages are the following:

- A significant degree of flexibility resulting from the relative ease with which agencies can form and disband and the closeness of governing boards to the field of action.
- Existing institutional structures in a number of program areas resulting from the fact that voluntary agencies frequently begin work in particular areas prior to the development of government programs in these areas.
- A generally smaller scale of operation, providing greater opportunity for tailoring services to client needs.
- A degree of diversity both in the content of services and in the institutional framework within which they are provided.
- A greater capacity to avoid fragmented approaches and to concentrate on the full range of needs that families or individuals face, to treat the person or the family instead of the isolated problem.
- Greater access to private charitable resources and volunteer labor, which can enhance the quality of service provided and "leverage" public dollars.

Whether intentionally or not, involvement in government programs can threaten some of these inherent advantages of nonprofit agencies. For example, such involvement often creates a tension for nonprofit agencies between their service role and their advocacy role, between their role as deliverers of government-funded services and their role as critics of government and private policies. Such involvement can also put a strain on other importance features of the organizations, such as their reliance on volunteers, their sense of independence, their frequently informal and nonbureaucratic character, and their direction by private citizens along lines that these citizens think appropriate. Since many of these features are the ones that recommend nonprofit organizations as service providers in the first place, it would be ironic if government programs seriously compromised these features. What this suggests is the need for some forbearance on the part of government with respect to some aspects of the relationship between the two sectors, and for structural features that help to strengthen rather than weaken the distinctive elements of the nonprofit sector. Among other things this might include:

- Payment schedules on grants and contracts that avoid costly cash-flow problems for nonprofit organizations.
- Avoidance of undue interference with the nonservice functions of the organizations.
- The use of challenge grants or other funding devices that reward agencies for the use of volunteers or the generation of private-sector funds to supplement public resources.

- Continued encouragement of private giving, which is crucial for the preservation of an element of independence and flexibility for nonprofit agencies.

Recognition of the Need for Government Involvement and of the Legitimate Accountability Requirements of Government

If the partnership between government and the nonprofit sector gains strength from the involvement of the nonprofit partner, it also gains strength from the involvement of the governmental partner. Indeed, the whole thrust of the "voluntary failure" theory outlined above is that the voluntary sector, for all its advantages, has certain limitations that make sole reliance on it unwise. In particular, four major considerations make government involvement desirable even when voluntary associations are involved.

Financial: While private giving and voluntary activity remain vitally important, it seems unreasonable to expect that these sources can be counted on to generate the levels of support needed to sustain the kinds of services, including human services, that our advanced industrial society has come to require in order to make the most effective use of human resources. This was a lesson taught at considerable cost through the late nineteenth and early twentieth centuries in most of the advanced industrial societies of the world, including our own, and that remains relevant today.

Equity: Not only is government in a better position to finance needed services, it is also in a better position to ensure the equitable distribution of those resources among parts of the country and segments of the population. Private charitable resources may or may not be available where the need for them is greatest. In the absence of some mechanism like government, it is extremely difficult to channel the available resources reliably to the areas and populations that need them the most. In addition, sufficient nonprofit agencies with the experience and capability to provide certain services may not be available in particular locales, making it necessary to rely on direct public provision instead.

Diversity: While the nonprofit sector has a number of advantages as a service provider, it also has a number of disadvantages. For example, private voluntary agencies have been known to intrude more than some people might like into personal religious or moral preferences. Similarly, established agencies can sometimes monopolize the flow of private philanthropic dollars, limiting the resources available to newer or smaller groups. Finally, there are purposes for which existing institutions are considered inappropriate or are unreliable, and for which public stimulation of the creation of new institutions is in the public interest. For all of these reasons, there is an argument for a government role to ensure a sufficient degree of diversity in the service delivery system, including the funding of for-profit providers.

Public Priority-Setting: A central tenet of a democratic society is that the public should be able to set priorities through a democratic political process and then muster the resources to make sure those priorities are addressed. Complete reliance on private sector initiative and action robs the public of that opportunity and leaves the setting of priorities in the hands of those with the most control over private resources.

The fact that government has a crucial role to play in the government-nonprofit partnership means, of course, that government has certain legitimate expectations to place on nonprofit organizations. At a minimum, these include requirements for basic financial accountability in the expenditure of public funds and adherence to the purposes for which the funds are authorized. Beyond this, involvement in government programs also appropriately carries with it an obligation to be non-discriminatory. The key, however, is to find a balance that protects the legitimate public interest in accountability without undermining the characteristics that make nonprofits effective partners of government.

The Need for Improvement in the Management of the Partnership

Although a substantial financial "partnership" has emerged in the human services area between government and philanthropic institutions, this partnership remains, in many senses, one in name only. For the most part, the resource allocation processes in these two sectors proceed independently, and often in ignorance, of each other. Public sector organizations have little clear idea of the uses to which private philanthropic dollars are being put, and the charitable sector frequently has only imperfect knowledge of, and limited influence over, the allocation of public funds. Even basic information about the scope and structure of the private, nonprofit delivery system is unavailable in most locales, making coherent policymaking difficult.

While this diversity and lack of coherence is one of the strengths of the current pluralistic delivery system, it also has significant costs in terms of the effective use of limited resources. As governmental resources become even tighter and corporate and other philanthropic institutions begin to play a larger role, it may be appropriate to consider ways to achieve a greater degree of dialogue on questions of resource allocation, division of responsibilities for meeting community needs, and joint public-private ventures. At a minimum, this will require developing a more complete picture of the extent and character of the private, nonprofit delivery system and its interaction with the public sector. Beyond this, it will likely require the establishment of some more formal communication and decision-making apparatus to systematize the flow of information between these two sectors and among the component parts of each. The myth of separation that now characterizes public and private thinking on these issues needs to broken down and more explicit recognition made of the mixed economy that actually exists. This is not to suggest that a single, comprehensive public-private planning and decision-making apparatus should be created to set priorities and make decisions on all local funds. Such a development would be resisted by all parties, and rightly so. But between this "red herring" and the chaotic situation that now exists in most locales lies ample room for a middle course of cooperation and information-sharing that could improve the use of resources and possibly contribute to some fruitful cooperative ventures.

CONCLUSION

The partnership that has emerged between government and the nonprofit sector in the delivery of human services is one of the more significant, though hardly unique, American contributions to the evolution of the modern welfare state. It is therefore ironic that this partnership has been so thoroughly overlooked in both public debate and scholarly research. It has been the argument here that this neglect reflects a number of shortcomings in the prevailing theories used to portray both the welfare state and the voluntary sector. By adjusting these theories to take account of the phenomenon of third-party government and to recognize the primacy of the voluntary sector as a provider of collective goods and the presence of crucial "voluntary failures" that limit the sector's ability to perform this role, the existing partnership comes into far clearer focus and its rationale becomes much easier to understand.

The discussion here just begins to scratch the surface of the theoretical exploration that is needed on these issues, however, and barely hints at the empirical work that is still required to bring this partnership into clearer view.[5] Hopefully, however, enough has been said to make clear what an important and fruitful area of inquiry this is, and to stimulate the additional work that is needed.

NOTES

This article draws on a longer exploration of the relationship between government and the nonprofit sector in Salamon, 1987, and in a paper presented at the 1985 Annual Meeting of the Society for the Study of Social Problems.

1. For further detail, see Salamon, 1987.
2. For a more complete statement of the criteria for choosing among theories or models of different social or physical processes, see Salamon, 1970.
3. Burton Weisbrod, the principal architect of this theory, does acknowledge the possibility of government subsidization of voluntary organizations, but this is treated as an exception, not as the core of our human-service system. (Weisbrod, 1978:66).
4. This reformulation is also more consistent with American traditions of freedom and individualism, which suggest that the creation of a sense of "social obligation" of the sort that is required to support collective action is best done on a voluntary basis and at the local or group level, where individuals can participate with their neighbors without sacrificing their freedom of choice (Schambra, 1982). The more the fostering of a sense of social obligation moves away from this level, therefore, the more tenuous it becomes. Treating government, particularly the national government, as the first line of defense for the provision of needed collective goods, as is done in economic theory, is therefore to create a far less secure basis for the provision of these goods than voluntary action can provide. Only when voluntary action proves incapable, then, should government be called into action. Viewed from this perspective, government support to voluntary organizations, and government-nonprofit partnerships, emerge as the ideologically most palatable form that the government response to "voluntary failure" can take.
5. For a fuller statement of what is known about the partnership between government and the voluntary sector, see Salamon, 1987.

REFERENCES

American Association of Fund-Raising Counsel, Inc.
    1981   *Giving USA: 1981 Annual Report* (New York: American Association of Fund-Raising Counsel).

Beck, Bertram M.
    1971   "Governmental Contracts with Non-profit Social Welfare Corporations." Pp. 213-228 in Bruce L.R. Smith and D.C. Hague, eds. *The Dilemma of Accountability in Modern Government.* New York: St. Martin's Press.

Berger, Peter and John Neuhaus
    1977   *To Empower People: The Role of Mediating Structures in Public Policy.* Washington, D.C.: The American Enterprise Institute.

Bolling, Landrum R.
    1982   *Private Foreign Aid: U.S. Philanthropy for Relief and Development.* Boulder, CO: Westview Press.

Deutsch, Karl
    1963   *The Nerves of Government: Models of Political Communication and Control.* New York: Free Press.

Dripps, Robert D.
    1915   "The Policy of State Aid to Private Charities." *Proceedings of the 42nd National Conference of Charities and Corrections.* Chicago: Hildman Printing.

Elazar, Daniel
    1972   *American Federalism: The View from the States.* New York: Thomas Y. Crowell.
Fetter, Frank
    1901/02   "The Subsidizing of Private Charities," *American Journal of Sociology*, VII: 359-385.
Fitch, L.C.
    1974   "Increasing the Role of the Private Sector in Providing Public Services." Pp. 264-306 in
                W.D. Hawley and D. Rogers, eds., *Improving the Quality of Urban Management.* Beverly
                Hills: Sage Publications, pp. 264-306.
Fleisher, A.
    1914   "State Money and Privately Managed Charities," *The Survey* 33:110-112.
Gould, Stephen J.
    1977   *Ever Since Darwin: Reflections in Natural History.* New York: W.W. Norton.
Grodzins, Morton
    1966   *The American System.* Chicago: Rand-McNally.
Hansmann, Henry
    1981   "The Role of Nonprofit Enterprise." *Yale Law Journal*, 89, (5): pp. 1-15.
Hargrove, Erwin
    1975   *The Missing Link.* Washington, D.C.: The Urban Institute Press.
Hartogs, Nelly and Joseph Weber
    1978   *Impact of Government Funding on the Management of Voluntary Agencies.* New York: The
                Greater New York Fund.
Hartz, Louis
    1948   *Economic Policy and Democratic Thought: Pennsylvania, 1776-1860.* Cambridge: Harvard
                University Press.
Kerrine, Theodore M. and Richard John Neuhaus
    1979   "Mediating Structures: A Paradigm for Democratic Pluralism," *The Annals of the American
                Academy of Political and Social Sciences*, 446: 10-18.
Kramer, Ralph
    1980   *Voluntary Agencies in the Welfare State.* Berkeley: University of California Press.
Kuhn, Thomas S.
    1962   *The Structure of Scientific Revolutions.* Chicago: University of Chicago Press.
Nielson, Waldemar
    1980   *The Endangered Sector.* New York: Columbia University Press.
Nisbet, Robert
    1962   *Community and Power.* New York: Oxford University Press [c 1953].
Rose-Ackerman, Susan
    1985   "Nonprofit Firms: Are Government Grants Desirable?" Mimeo.
Rosner, David
    1980   "Gaining Control: Reform, Reimbursement and Politics in New York's Community Hospi-
                tals, 1890-1915." *American Journal of Public Health*, 70(5): 533-542.
Salamon, Lester M.
    1970   "Comparative History and the Theory of Modernization," *World Politics*, XXIII, (1): 88-103.
Salamon, Lester M.
    1981   "Rethinking Public Management: Third-Party Government and the Changing Forms of
                Public Action." *Public Policy* 29:255-275.
Salamon, Lester M.
    1984a   "Nonprofit Organizations: The Lost Opportunity." Pp. 261-286 in John Palmer and Isabel
                Sawhill, eds., *The Reagan Record.* Cambridge: Ballinger.
Salamon, Lester M.
    1984b   "Nonprofits: The Results are Coming In," *Foundation News.* 25(4): 16-23.
Salamon, Lester M.
    1987   "Partners in Public Service: The Scope and Theory of Government-Nonprofit Relations."
                Pp. 99-117 in Walter Powell, ed., *The Nonprofit Sector.* New Haven: Yale University Press.
Salamon, Lester M. and Alan J. Abramson
    1982   *The Federal Budget and the Nonprofit Sector.* Washington, D.C.: The Urban Institute Press.
Savas, E.S.
    1984   *Privatizing the Public Sector: How to Shrink Government.* Chatham, N.J.: Chatham House.
Schambra, William
    1982   "From Self-Interest to Social Obligation: Local Communities vs. the National Community."
                Pp. 34-42 in Jack Meyer, ed., *Meeting Human Needs: Toward a New Public Philosophy,*
                Washington, D.C.: American Enterprise Institute.
Smith, Bruce
    1975   "The Public Use of the Private Sector." Pp. 1-45 in Bruce L.R. Smith, ed., *The New Political
                Economy: The Public Use of the Private Sector.* London: The MacMillan Press, Ltd.

Staats, Elmer
    1975   "New Problems of Accountability for Federal Programs." Pp. 46-67 in *The New Political Economy: The Public Use of the Private Sector*, edited by Bruce L.R. Smith, London: The MacMillan Press, Ltd.
Stevens, Rosemary
    1982   "A Poor Sort of Memory: Voluntary Hospitals and Government Before the Depression," *Milbank Fund Quarterly/Health and Society*, 60(4): 551-584.
Warner, Amos
    1894   *American Charities: A Study in Philanthropy and Economics*. New York: Thomas Y. Crowell.
Weisbrod, Burton
    1978   *The Voluntary Nonprofit Sector*. Lexington: Lexington Books.
Whitehead, John S.
    1973   *The Separation of College and State: Columbia, Dartmouth, Harvard, and Yale, 1776-1876*. New Haven: Yale University Press.

The Three Sectors: Voluntarism in a Changing Political Economy

Jon Van Til

The structure of the third, or independent sector, is analyzed in this paper from the perspective of its place in an integrated political economy. Using the method of John Dewey to distinguish acts that are public from those that are private, a set of propositions are developed regarding the close links between voluntarism and the acts of corporate and governmental institutions. This interrelated social reality is examined in terms of major approaches of social scientists. Functionalist approaches are found to predominate over interpretive, radical structuralist, and radical humanist paradigms in the area of voluntary action research. Drawing on recent British experience, it is suggested that approaches to research might benefit from the development of a full-blown theory of mediating institutions. The paper concludes with a brief examination of policy issues in contemporary voluntarism, and points to the importance of what Meister has called the role of voluntary associations in contributing to self-management in a postindustrial society.

We have created in our complex society three separate institutional worlds. We define them as different from each other. We create separate places in which to learn about them. We prepare for careers within them by learning what seem to be very different skills.[1]

Business, the largest of these three sectors, commands 80% of the United States company (Hodgkinson and Weitzman, 1984). Often viewed as the "business of America" (to use Calvin Coolidge's phrase), this sector occupies most of the attention of the field of economics and is the focus of a very large applied academic focus, "business studies." Government, the sector second in size, weighs in at about 14% of the economy. Its importance is subject to cyclical forces, sometimes reduced to providing for domestic and international security, and other times invested with a wide reach in the provision of human betterment. Government is studied by the political science and is the focus of the applied academic disciplines of "public policy" and "public administration." The third sector, called "voluntary" or "independent" or "nonprofit," amounts in size to the remaining 6% of the national economy. It accounts for 9% of total national employment. Commonly defined as residual, this sector extends into many corners of society. No single academic discipline currently exists for its study, although many sociologists make it the focus of their scholarly work. No applied discipline has yet emerged for the preparation for careers in the voluntary sector.

This paper explores the interrelations of the three sectors in an era of fundamental

Jon Van Til, Department of Urban Studies and Community Development, Rutgers University, Camden College, Camden, NJ 08102.

institutional change. I argue for a view of the three sectors as separate but related components of a single political economy in society. This view makes visible important functions of the voluntary sector that are obscured if the sector is studied separately from the other two. This paper is presented as a set of notes which may be considered to be pretheoretical. In the course of this paper, I review perspectives on the relations between voluntary institutions and the major structures of governmental and business life, deriving propositions regarding their connections. I suggest that the third sector both articulates and mediates the crucial boundary between the state and the economy in contemporary Western industrial society. I examine claims that voluntarism contributes uniquely to the sustenance of such societies. I also review major theoretical perspectives in social science and begin to apply them to voluntary sector research, laying out some implications for research and policy.

Robert Bellah and William Sullivan (1981:46) provide a point of departure for the view being developed here. They assert that:

> To view economic institutions as "private" made sense when most Americans spent their lives on family farms or in family firms. But today, when most American men and a rapidly increasing proportion of American women spend much of their lives in large economic structures that are for most purposes "public" except that the profits they make go to an impersonal collection of institutional and individual "private" stockholders, it becomes imperative to bring the forms of citizenship and of civic association more centrally into the economic sphere.

This assertion links three concepts that are central to my argument here: the public, the private, and mediating institutions. The contention that mediating structures are important in the business corporation and the state as well as the voluntary sector requires a consideration of the role of the voluntary sector in a broad political economy.

The view advanced here that the voluntary sector has a key role to play in modern societies—in the political economy—is not reflected in conventional scholarship. Typically, the "third sector" receives relatively little attention and is often confused with the other "private institutions" of the business world, or dismissed as the locus of mere "do-gooding." This conventional view is reflected in the residual terms with which the third sector is commonly defined. For example, Theodore Levitt, editor of the *Harvard Business Review*, considers that "conventional taxonomy divides society into two sectors—private and public. Private is business. Public is presumed to be 'all else.'"[2] Considering "all else" too inclusive, Levitt makes room for an "enormous residuum," which he calls "the third sector." This third sector is "to do things business and government are either not doing, not doing well, or not doing often enough" (1973: 49).[3]

This paper seeks to develop an alternative view that this "third sector" is more central to society than previously recognized, that it is much more than simply residual or derivative. Of all the terms commonly used to described this sector, only "voluntary" and "independent" are not essentially derivative, though even they are not wholly free of derogatory implications. The "independent" sector implies a freedom from something and leads one to ask: independent of what? What of the implication of dependence? The term "voluntary" is clouded by diverse uses of the term. For example, in philosophy it means "freely willed," and in physiology it means "under conscious control."[4] The characterization of the sector as "voluntary" and "independent," though overstated, does provide a beginning point for exploring its relations to the other two sectors.

HOW INDEPENDENT IS THE THIRD SECTOR?: RELATIONS TO THE OTHER SECTORS AND THE SEARCH FOR INTELLECTUAL AUTHORITY

Focusing on the "voluntary" or "independent" aspects of the third, "private," or nonprofit sector, we ask: Just how does this sector relate to the other major institutions? In what ways is it independent? In what ways dependent? How does this accord with normative judgments of what ought to be? A solid theoretical base, an intellectual authority, is required to answer such questions. With some arbitrariness (inevitable, I would argue), I turn to the authority of John Dewey, who in 1927 addressed the question of institutional interrelations in his fruitful book, *The Public and Its Problems*.

In this work, Dewey sought to make as clearly as he could the distinction between what is "public" and what is "private." He began by describing a conversation between two individuals, a transaction apparently private rather than public. But the distinction depends upon the consequences of the conversation, Dewey notes: "If it is found that the consequences of the conversation extend beyond the two directly concerned, that they affect the welfare of many others, the act acquires a public capacity, whether the conversation be carried on by a king and his prime minister . . . or by merchants planning to monopolize a market" (1927:13). The distinction between public and private, Dewey (1927:15) concludes, not the same as that between the individual and the social. What makes an act public is that it has consequences "which are so important as to need control, whether by inhibition or by promotion."

Dewey's approach to the problem is in contrast to the more conventional approach presented by Levitt. If we follow Dewey, we may conclude that while it is acceptable to speak of corporations or voluntary associations as "private" (i.e., not governmentally owned), it would be misleading to conclude that all acts of such private bodies are themselves private in their consequences. Private sector activity may involve, as William Goldsmith and Harvey Jacobs have noted, such questions as: "What shall be produced, and where? What shall be invested, and where? How shall work places be organized? How much shall workers be paid? Who shall get to work?" (1982: 64). These questions have become public issues in this age of economic anxiety. Presidential campaigns are run on them; they are the stuff of our daily headlines; and they are left by almost no political grouping to the untrammeled workings of what economists formerly called, with a certain quaintness, "the private marketplace."

Relations between governmental, corporate, and voluntary structures come to take a lively and dynamic appearance if the Deweyan view is accepted. Most importantly for the view being developed here, we begin to look at the public consequences of economic behavior and the social context of economic and political organization.

Bruce Smith has referred to this welter of interrelations as the "new political economy." It is from this point that the central contention of this paper derives. By this concept, Smith intends to "convey the meaning of the large, and growing, share of the public's business that is conducted outside of the regular departments and ministries of government" (1975: ix). "So great is the interpenetration between the 'public' and 'private' sector," Smith contends "that this basic distinction—on which the political rhetoric and dialogue of modern times has rested—has ceased to be an operational way of understanding reality."

Further spelling out interrelations in this "new political economy," economists Charles Wilber and Kenneth Jameson (1981: 28) apply the concept of "mediating institutions" (developed by a study group at the American Enterprise Institute, cf. Berger and Neuhaus, 1977). By this concept is meant the linking of individuals to larger institutional structures by groups and associations, the mediating structures that facilitate both individual influence upward and the downward transmission of institutional response. The concept is central to the view being developed here of the key role of the voluntary sector in modern societies, since it is in this sector that mediating structures are most prominent. Wilber and Jameson see these structures challenging all existing modes of political thought: Our modern political philosophies—liberalism, conservatism, socialism—have failed precisely because they have not understood the importance of mediating institutions. Liberalism has constantly turned to the state for solutions to social problems while conservatism sought the same in the corporate sector. Neither recognized the destructiveness to the social fabric caused by reliance on mega-institutions. Socialism suffers from this same myopia. Even though it places its faith in renewed community, it fails to see that socialist mega-institutions are just as destructive as capitalist ones.

This view enables Wilber and Jameson to develop a central proposition regarding societal change and the importance of mediating institutions in it: "Choices made at the national level cannot be relied upon as the most effective manner of working toward revitalization of the U.S. economy. They will (only) create more mega-institutions" (1981: 28).

There are several important implications of the Dewey-Wilber-Jameson position. First, the distinction between the public and the private sectors become far more complex than it initially seems. As the line between public and private blurs, the voluntary sector takes on startlingly new roles and responsibilities. Viewed as the locus of mediating structures, the voluntary expands to the very heart of governmental and corporate system, to the core of the political economy. No longer simply the residual sector, voluntary action as mediating structure is a central focus in the life of society. The sector is no longer defined simply as residual, in negatives such as nongovernmental or not-for-profit. Hearkening to the call of Bellah and Sullivan, the development of mediating structures within state and corporation (as well as in voluntary organizations) is seen as crucial to the development of modern society.

VOLUNTARY ASSOCIATIONS IN THE POLITICAL ECONOMY

A group of distinguished political theorists, writing in the NOMOS XI yearbook of the American Society for Political and Legal Philosophy (Pennock and Chapman, 1969), directly address how voluntary associations relate to other institutional structures in the contemporary political economy. From this work, I have identified seven major propositions that are useful in developing the perspective of voluntary sector relations as spanning and mediating all three major institutional sectors in modern society:

(1) *All associations are in part voluntary in aim and principle.* This point is clearly established by Robert MacIver in his classic work, *Society*, with its consideration of governments and corporations as associations. More recently, Fuller has argued that

nearly all human associations contain within themselves two polar principles—that of "shared commitment" and that of "legal principle" (1969: 12). It is the idea of shared commitment, freely given, that is central to the concept of voluntarism. And it is Fuller's point that such commitment is often found to some degree in both governmental and business activity, and not just in its most prevalent locus, the voluntary sector.

(2) *Voluntary associations (those in which the principle of shared commitment predominates) may be either productive or destructive of democratic values and societal stability.* Rousseau warned of the dangers of "party, faction, and cabal" (quoted in Goldschmidt, 1969: 122). Madison wrote of the "dangerous vice" of "faction"; the U.S. Constitution "contains no explicit guarantee of the right to form associations" (Fuller, 1969: 12-13). Jouvenal argues (in Chapman's words (1969: 102) that "voluntary associations are not only agencies of defense and integration but also, and perhaps more importantly, demolition teams wreaking revolutionary reorganizations."

(3) *Associational development involves a process of change, typically in the direction of* Michels' "iron law of oligarchy." As Fuller (1969: 12,13) puts it: "When an association is first brought into being the principle of shared commitment will tend to be explicit and dominant. . . . In the normal course of its development an association tends to move toward dominance by the legal principle." Thus is seen a trend toward formalization and bureaucratization.

(4) *Evaluation of voluntary associations is importantly affected by methodological proclivities, particularly the selection of either an individualistic or a holistic orientation.* McBride (1969:229) argues that the most fundamental reason to regard "voluntary association as so worthwhile . . . depends on a view of the individual as the focalpoint of social values." And Boonin urges a middle position, which he calls "persons-in-relation" as best suited to the values of voluntarism (1969: 82).

(5) *The roles of voluntary associations become complex and labyrinthine as a society moves toward a "managed" or "managerial" form.* Lakoff (1969) and McBride note the increasing prevalence of executive domination in political and executive life. McBride (1969:226) "sees on many sides a growing advocacy of the principles of elitism and bureaucracy, together with growing resignation, willingly abetted by the elites, to this tendency on the part of large segments of the population."

(6) *Careful attention needs to be paid to the role of the corporation as it related to voluntary action.* As Miller notes (1969: 234-238), not only did the corporation historically emerge defined as a voluntary association, but it still retains the constitutional status of a voluntary association (or "social group"). Miller's reasoning bears careful attention (1969: 241,258):

> There is no such thing as *the* corporation or *the* voluntary association. The convenient fiction of calling corporations persons in law should not be taken to hide the reality that they are collectives, federations of interests grouped together under a concept of cooperation, albeit often antagonistic cooperation.

> The corporation (is) perhaps the most important of the "voluntary," "private" associations within the American polity. That they are neither voluntary nor private is a second conclusion that emerges from this preliminary excursion into the constitutional position of the corporation.[5]

(7) *U.S. society is well on its way to a corporative form.* As Miller puts it: "The

corporate state, American style, is in process of being created. Best seen in those corporations that make up the 'military-industrial-scientific complex' (the power of which worried President Eisenhower) but also exemplified in the other super-corporations within the government-business partnership, this is a new form of social order that demands systematic and comprehensive analysis. It has the most portentous (*and* actual) consequences for Americans and the nature of American constitutionalism" (1969: 258).

These propositions are far-reaching. They suggest a close interpenetration of the voluntary sector with both government and corporations—that is, they portend a view of the voluntary sector as existing in the political economy of society. They challenge practitioners of voluntary action to accept a "proactive" rather than a residual societal role. And they suggest that the building of effective interinstitutional partnerships will not be a simple or painless task.

The propositions are also controversial. Not everyone would agree with either the statements or the uses to which they might be put. The failure of consensus, or to put it more positively, the presence of pluralism, suggests that we need to pursue vigorously the search for theoretical positions from which to analyze and evaluate the role of the third sector in society. The next section considers the range of social science approaches to the study of voluntary action available in existing social theory.

SOCIAL THEORY AND VOLUNTARY ACTION

Social scientists do not share a single paradigm for their studies. Neo-Marxism is perhaps the most dramatic example of an alternative theoretical perspective. The neoconservatism of the 1980s is another perspective outside the mainstream. To try to argue that a single paradigm prevails is to find oneself embroiled in argument with colleagues whose sense of what is known, and how and why, is radically different.

These paradigms are, however, asserted with varying presence in the different subfields of the social sciences. In the area of voluntary action research, for example, it is nearly impossible to find a systematic Marxian or neo-Marxist presentation. Such theory as exists in the field overwhelmingly reflects pluralist or neocorporatist perspectives (cf. Van Til, 1981).

Social scientists are increasingly recognizing the existence of these widely different paradigms in their research and writing. Such diversity is becoming an ineluctable part of the social science, as well as the policy world. In a major recent statement, Alford and Friedland (1985) have argued that three major perspectives (pluralist, managerial, and class) inform almost all political sociology and political science, and that these perspectives approach mutual exclusivity as commonly employed. Slowly, it seems to dawn upon self-styled "empiricists" and "Marxists" and "phenomenologists" and "humanists" alike that they do not share common assumptions about the bases of their knowledge and their craft. Gradually, they begin to see that however they seek to impose in the name of "science" or their discipline an orthodoxy of theory or method, they are engaged in the political process of changing someone else's mind, rather than the scientific process of testing for the presence of truth.

Burrell and Morgan (1979) have demonstrated the existence of four archetypical modes of defining the field of organizational theory, a scholarly field notable for the efforts of its practitioners to assume and enforce a single methodological and theoretical orthodoxy. Drawing broadly on the philosophical traditions underlying social and political theory, Burrell and Morgan argue that social scientists differ profoundly among themselves on both the nature of their task (social science) and on the nature of their field of study (society itself).

Some social scientists define their task as essentially "subjectivist." That is, they adopt an *ontology* of nominalism (focusing on concepts and labels) rather than realism. They assume an *epistemology* of antipositivism (relating what is known to the knower, rather than searching for universal laws) as against a positivistic belief. They hold to a view of *human nature* as voluntaristic (free-willed) rather than determined. They take on a *methodology* of ideography (focusing on first-hand experience) rather than a nomothetic one.

Other social scientists adopt the opposite position. They may be seen as "objectivists." Their beliefs are those of *realism* (a hard, knowable, certain social world exists), *positivism* (laws can be discovered), *determinism* (by the environment rather than by free-willed behavior), and *nomothetic method* (using systematic research techniques).

Not only do social scientists differ among themselves on these fundamental questions of how to know about society, Burrell and Morgan argue that they also differ on their assumptions about the nature of society itself. Some adopt a position which emphasizes values of order or integration: societal stability, integration, functional coordination, and consensus. Others approach society from a conflict perspective, seeing change, conflict, disintegration, and coercion as basic social processes.

Combining the subjectivist and objectivist dimensions, Burrell and Morgan derive four resulting paradigms: 1) the functionalist (objective in methodology, oriented to the sociology of regulation); 2) the interpretive (subjective in methodology, oriented to the sociology of regulation; 3) the radical structuralist (objective in methodology, oriented to the sociology of radical change); and 4) the radical humanist (subjective in methodology, oriented to the sociology of radical change).

Applying the Burrell-Morgan typology to the study of voluntary associations and nonprofit corporations, I have developed the following five propositions:

(1) *The study of voluntary action and nonprofit organizations may be approached from each of the major paradigms of social science study.* This point seems true *ceteris paribus.* If social scientists choose one of these four paradigms for their intellectual home, then that subgroup of social scientists who study voluntary action will by necessity face the same choice. Thus Alperovitz and Faux (1984) and Kramer (1981) develop typologies that highlight the range of voluntary responses to political economy, ranging from change (social democracy, nationalization) to regulation (neocorporatism, reprivatization). Gamwell (1984) has developed a philosophical justification for focusing on the "public-regarding" subsector of the nonprofit sphere as "teleologically prior," using a subjective methodology that ranges between the interpretive and radical humanist approaches identified by Burrell and Morgan.

(2) *Both regulation and radical social change paradigms raise central themes of voluntary action and nonprofit organizational behavior.* Thus, a review of Smith's influential listing of voluntary sector impacts (1973) reveals the regulatory themes of social integration, play (need satisfaction), value preservation (status quo), economic networking (social order), and latent goal-attainment (consensus). Smith's list also includes a number of radical change impacts: nurturing challenging ideologies,

embodying mystery and the sacred (potentiality), and liberating individual expression (emancipation). Two other impacts combine themes from both societal views: developing societal innovations and providing feedback for system change and correction. Both of these impacts may be seen, from the perspective of open systems theory, as involving either regulation or radical change.[6]

(3) *Studies of voluntary action tend to focus most centrally on the use of the functionalist paradigm.* This proposition is more clearly subject to empirical test than the first two. And to test it, a preliminary analysis was conducted of all articles published during an eight-year period in the *Journal of Voluntary Action Research.* The analysis, which must be considered "interpretive" in light of the fact that the author currently edits the journal, and has published in it (this is his third "interpretive" article), shows that 78% of the articles published in JVAR took the functionalist approach to social science, while 21% approached their task from the interpretive perspective. During this period, only two articles employed a radical social change perspective (both "structuralist," rather than "humanist").

(4) *When studies of voluntary action address change organizations from the functionalist paradigm, a "mobilization of bias" may be discovered such that some organizations are considered "dangerous and deviant" while others are "acceptable and appropriate."* By the term "mobilization of bias," political scientists have indicated the tendency of organizations to create assumptions that things are always and properly done the way they are presently being done within that organization.[7]

David Horton Smith argues that this position may prove short-sighted: the voluntary sector often provides "the social risk capital of human society," and can play the role of "gadfly, dreamer, and moral leader in society" (1973: 388-389). Those who seek to apply the label of "deviance" or "un-American" to an organization, then, run the risk of foreclosing a future option for society that may prove invaluable to its development.

(5) *The development of trans-paradigmatic theories (such as open systems theory, "transformational" theory) may be useful in creating an appropriately catholic, broadly based science of voluntary action.* Open systems theory may bridge the gap between theories of regulation and those of radical change. A similar hope is held by many students of societal transformation.[8] The persuasive development of such transcendent paradigms, however, awaits future development.

A number of research questions are suggested for exploration, linking these macro-level concerns with the daily realities of institutional life. These questions focus on the elaboration of our understanding of the role of mediating structures in western industrial-urban society. Among these questions are the following:

First, how does the presence of voluntary sector mediation actually serve to restrain the excesses of untrammeled state and corporate action?

Second, does each form of voluntary association serve equally in this restraint? If not all, which tend to play what particular roles? Which associations serve more directly as part of the "transmission belts" of the state and corporation? Which serve more directly as most autonomous, citizenship-enhancing, and countervailing in their powers?

Third, how precisely do voluntary structures "mediate"? Conventionally, mediation involves the presence of an accessible organization between the individual and a mega-structure, an organization that provides for some form of linkage and (presumably) two-way communication between the individual and the over-arching institution. Such mediation has typically been posited as crucial to the development of large-scale democracy. If indeed this mediation is seen as appropriate to the corporation as well, then we shall need to study in these terms such structural reforms as worker-ownership, consumer participation, and quality of work-life changes.

The study of these questions has perhaps been most sophisticated and detailed in recent years in Britain. There a lively debate has been joined on the question of "welfare pluralism," or the proper mix of public, voluntary, informal, and proprietary provision of social services. Theoretical studies by Stephen Hatch and Roger Hadley (Hatch, 1980; Hadley and Hatch, 1981) advocated a more prominent role for voluntarism in the welfare mix, celebrating the values of decentralization and local control while criticizing the bureaucratic sterility of the contemporary welfare state. Governmental reforms in social service provision were introduced pursuant to these ideas in the form of the "patch" model, involving "the deconcentration of local authority social services from their large area offices to smaller administrative areas and even neighborhoods" (Brenton, 1985: 119). Later studies by Hadley, Hatch, and associates (cf., for example, Hadley and McGrath, 1984) examined a number of these patch reforms in detail, as did the more critical research of Beresford and Croft (1986).

Together with these forays into policy discussion and the evaluation of innovations in service delivery involving voluntary sector organizations, recent British social researchers have paid careful attention to the role of informal social activity and care-provision [cf. the work of Abrams cited by Bulmer in his essay in the present issue; the ongoing work on domestic care provision by Claire Ungerson of the University of Kent; and the detailed research on community care by Davies and Challis (1986)]. A recent and careful summary of much of this experience is provided by Brenton (1985: 220), who concludes that the most productive voluntary sector role is a dual one, involving on the one hand the provision of services complementary to those of the state (mutual aid, self-help, community and neighborhood action, information services) and on the other the "mounting of a watchdog role over the main-line provisions of the welfare state." Brenton is dubious of "partnership" arrangements that are undertaken in times of welfare-state retrenchment. As Beresford and Croft (1986: 149) put it from their action-research perspective:

> The irony is that while patch and welfare pluralist philosophies are framed in terms of giving a greater role to voluntary organisations and informal effort in place of statutory provision, it is the *state* which is seeking to mobilise such non-statutory and unpaid caring. Thus they can be seen as concerned not so much with a reduced role for the state, as a different kind of intervention. Instead of primarily providing services to meet our needs, the state will be involved in organising, supervising, extending and even reinterpreting our own self-help.

By late 1986, a personal visit to Britain convinced this author that the welfare pluralism question had reached an impasse as political philosophy, as Donnison (1983) had earlier suggested. Many British social administration researchers who specialize in the study of voluntarism have begun to articulate support for limited sectoral autonomy and a clearer distinction from governmental control, while others observe a softening of the "ideological edge" of the debate and a blurring of institutional lines between organizations in the three sectors.

Yet to develop in Britain (and the United States as well), though much needed, is a fully articulated theory of voluntary associations as mediating structures possessed of their own distinctive goals and processes. The development of such a theory would have enormous implications for the reshaping of not only the governing structures of government, but also the governing structures of businesses and corporations.[9] If it no longer suffices to claim that what goes on outside of government and politics is by definition private, then it must be recognized that the public interest is greatly affected by many actions and decisions taken within corporations or voluntary organizations. There is no shirking the responsibility of acts of public consequence, particularly in an era in which voluntarism has itself become an issue of public policy concern.

VOLUNTARISM AS AN EMERGENT POLICY ARENA

There is no indication at present that the interdependence between government, corporations, and voluntary organizations that is central to the perspective being developed here will recede in the years ahead. Voluntarism has emerged in recent years as a full-blown policy arena, and it is likely that future will be replete with proposals for new and expansive forms of "public-private partnerships." Among the reasons for this development are the following forces, roughly drawn from a larger literature on voluntary futures (cf. Rydberg and Peterson, 1980; Van Til, 1982):

1. A long-term process of governmental fiscal exigency, occasioned by unprecedented levels of federal fiscal imbalance.
2. A secular drift toward private business enterprise as both a vocation and a valued way of life in contemporary society.
3. A rapid increase in attention to the professionalization and importance of the third sector.

As these powerful trends develop, new understandings and interrelationships come to prevail between those who work within the confines of each major institution. Shifting institutional boundaries give rise to changing forms of structures, and to conflicts regarding these patterns.

The prominence of the voluntary sector in the contemporary United States may be indicated, at least in part, by the attention it has received from recent presidents. President Carter, a committed volunteer, sought to revitalize the governmental commitment to neighborhood and community volunteerism during his term in office. President Reagan has attributed an even more central role to voluntarism in his statements on national redirection, and established a blue-ribbon Task Force on Private Sector Initiatives. No less a policy research body than the Urban Institute gives voluntarism one full chapter (out of ten) in its recent study of *The Reagan Record* (Palmer and Sawhill, 1984).

Despite this Presidential attention, the voluntary sector in the U.S. has experienced a dual attack on its resources in recent years. Federal dollars, which amount to some 40% of the income of nonprofit organizations, have been greatly cut since 1982. Charitable contributions have stayed below 2% of total income as a series of tax changes have reduced philanthropic incentives, particularly for persons in the highest income brackets.

Elsewhere (Van Til, 1985), I have identified six major policy issues that require address regarding the role of the voluntary sector in the contemporary political economy: 1) How business-like should the voluntary/nonprofit sector be in its structure? 2) How much emphasis should be placed on increasing the professionalism of the sector? 3) What should the weighting of emphasis be between the themes of leadership vs. management? 4) How best should we address the problem of partnering? 5) What principles should guide the selection of clientele? and, 6) Just how important, in comparative analysis, is voluntary action?

My responses to these questions involve balancing forces of efficacy and responsiveness, always recalling the potential of effective voluntarism to create a mediating and clarifying force. For example, in the area of creating effective partnerships between institutions in the three sectors, we may wish to reconsider the utility of railing against the unproductivity of government or the sterility of corporations, along with guarding against inflating our claims of the contributions of voluntarism. It may be that we need all our major institutions—churches, corporations, national government, voluntary social service organizations, schools, small businesses, universities, local governments, neighborhood organizations, colleges and universities, labor unions, citizen cooperatives, and on and on—working in concert, to meet our pressing societal needs. It may prove more productive to regroup and reinspire forces rather than to fantasize that one set of institutions will surely lead the way to the future we desire.

Dennis Young (1983: 99), in his essay on the role of entrepreneurialism in nonprofit activity, identifies the exceptionalism of the sector in terms of the kinds of leaders it attracts: "believers," "conservers," "poets," "searchers," and "professionals," in particular. These individuals, whose orientations fit them better to success in nonprofit action than in business or government, have much that is valuable to offer to the development of a free and humane society.

The late Swiss-French sociologist, Albert Meister, drew a useful distinction between voluntary association leaders who were "militants" (or agents of change) and those who are "animators" (or group facilitators who serve the interests of elites in calming mass unrest). As we enter the rigors of postindustrial society, Meister contended, we must recognize that it can easily become an "age of the animator." Our best hope in preserving a truly democratic society under such conditions, he wrote, lies in the development of institutions that provide both access to power and information: "What remains is nothing less than the fundamental problem of self-management" (Meister, 1984: 241).[10]

The task of self-management requires not only the consistent meshing of the gears of the three sectors in interaction, but also the development of the particular contributions voluntarism can provide in the political economies of modern societies. It also requires the further development of a theoretical perspective that sees voluntary action in a broad societal context, as an integral and key component in the national political economy, infusing both business and governmental activity.

NOTES

I am grateful to Susan Ostrander and William Van Til for their helpful comments on an earlier draft of this paper.

1. British research, in particular, reminds us of the presence of a fourth sector, that of informal social action, which includes such actions as neighboring and such institutions as the household, the kinship system, and the neighborhood (Cf. Bulmer's paper in this issue). I shall hold to the "three sectors"

concept in this paper, but do recognize that this perspective limits attention to institutional sectors that are, at least in part, mega-institutional.

2. Levitt deviates from conventional usage in studies of the third sector by placing voluntary action and governmental action under the rubric "public." More conventional is Sumariwalla's identification of "for-profit" and "non-profit" entities as the two chief inhabitants of the "private sector." Levitt's concept receives support, however, from an American Management Associations publication, where government is also considered a "nonprofit corporation" (Borst and Montana, 1975: 1).

3. Pifer (1975: 72-75) has specified these contributions, to wit: 1) to provide participation in the provision of services; 2) to safeguard academic, professional, and artistic freedom; 3) to "bring to our national life vital elements of diversity, free choice, and heterodoxy"; and 4) to serve as an important contributor to an open and pluralist society.

4. Bruce Smith (1975: 3) lists other related terms in common usage: quasi non-governmental organization, modern public sector, managed economy, contract state, and pluralist state.

5. For highly useful discussions of the role of the corporation in the modern political economy, see Herman (1981) and Lindblom (1977).

6. For a further discussion on open systems theory as a potential synthesis of regulation and radical change theory, see Burrell and Morgan (1979: 160).

7. On the concept of "mobilization of bias," see E.E. Schattschneider's *The Semi-Sovereign People* (New York: Holt, Rinehart and Winston, 1960) and Peter Bachrach's *Theory of Democratic Elitism* (Boston: Little Brown, 1967).

8. Among the clearest and most influential presenters of the theory of societal transformation are such authors as Willis Harman, Alvin Toffler, Marilyn Ferguson, and John Naisbitt.

9. I am examining in greater detail the effort to develop such theories in my ongoing research, in a volume tentatively titled as the present paper.

10. Meister's vision of voluntarism is pursued in contemporary France by the organization "Fonda" (fondation pour la vie associative), which represents the interests of the associational sector as a whole in France much as the organization "Independent Sector" does in the U.S. Fonda's "lettre d'information no. 39" presents several statements on the role of associations in a modern "social economy." Particularly notable therein is Guy Raffi's statement, "Enjeux associatifs, enjeux de societe" (Associational stakes, societal stakes).

REFERENCES

Alford, Robert R. and Roger Friedland
　　1985　　*Powers of Theory: Capitalism, The State, and Democracy.* Cambridge University Press,.
Bellah, Robert N. and William M. Sullivan
　　1981　　"Democratic Culture or Authoritarian Capitalism." *Society* 18 September/October:41-50.
Bellah, Robert N., et al.
　　1985　　*Habits of the Heart.* Berkeley: University of California Press.
Beresford, Peter, and Suzy Croft
　　1986　　*Whose Welfare: Private Care or Public Services.* Brighton, East Sussex: The Lewis Cohen Urban Studies Centre of Brighton Polytechnic.
Berger, Peter L., and Richard John Neuhaus
　　1977　　"To Empower People: The Role of Mediating Structures in Public Policy." Washington, D.C.: American Enterprise Institute for Public Policy Research.
Boonin, Leonard G.
　　1969　　"Man and Society: An Examination of Three Models." Pp. 69-84 in Pennock and Chapman, eds.
Borst, Diane, and Patrick J. Montana, eds.
　　1975　　*Managing Nonprofit Organizations.* New York: AMACOM.
Brenton, Maria
　　1985　　*The Voluntary Sector in British Social Services.* London and New York: Longman.
Burrell, Gibson, and Gareth Morgan
　　1979　　*Sociological Paradigms and Organizational Analysis.* London: Heinemann.
Butler, Stuart
　　1983　　"Research into the Impediments to Voluntarism." Pp. 369-382 in Independent Sector.
Chapman, John
　　1969　　"Voluntary Association and the Political Theory of Pluralism." Pp. 87-118 in Pennock and Chapman, eds.
Davies, Bleddyn, and David Challis
　　1986　　*Matching Resources to Needs in Community Care.* Brookfield, VT: Gower Publishing Company.

Dewey, John
    1927   *The Public and Its Problems.* Denver: Alan Swallow.
Dolbeare, Kenneth and Mary
    1976   *American Ideologies.* Chicago: Rand McNally.
Donnison, David
    1983   "The Progressive Potential of Privatisation," pp. 45-57 in Julian Le Grand and Ray Robin-
                son, eds., *Privatisation and the Welfare State,* London: George Allen and Unwin.
Fuller, Lon L.
    1969   "Two Principles of Human Association." Pp. 3-23, in Pennock and Chapman, eds.
Gamwell, Franklin I.
    1984   *Beyond Preference: Liberal Theories of Independent Association.* Chicago: University of Chi-
                cago Press.
Goldschmidt, Maure L.
    1969   "Rousseau on Intermediate Associations." Pp. 119-137 in Pennock and Chapman, eds.
Hadley, Roger, and Stephen Hatch
    1981   *Social Welfare and the Failure of the State: Centralized Social Services and Participatory Alter-
                natives.* London: Allen & Unwin.
Hadley, Roger, and M. McGrath
    1984   *When Social Services are Local: The Normanton Experience.* London: George Allen and
                Unwin (National Institute Social Services Library No. 48).
Hatch, Stephen
    1981   *Outside the State: Voluntary Organisations in Three English Towns.* London: Croom-Helm.
Herman, Edward S.
    1981   *Corporate Control, Corporate Power.* Cambridge: Cambridge U. Press.
Hodgkinson, Virginia Ann, and Murray S. Weitzman
    1984   *Dimensions of the Independent Sector: A Statistical Profile.* Washington D.C.: Independent
                Sector,.
Independent Sector
    1983   *Working Papers for Spring Research Forum: Since the Filer Commission . . .* Washington, D.C.
Koster, Marvin
    1983   "Government Regulation, Non-Commercial Activities and the Public Interest." Pp.
                403-416 in Independent Sector.
Lakoff, Sanford A.
    1969   "Private Government in the Managed Society." Pp. 170-201 in Pennock and Chapman,
                eds.
Levitt, Theodore
    1973   *The Third Sector: New Tactics for a Responsive Society.* New York: AMACOM.
Lindblom, Charles E.
    1977   *Politics and Markets.* New York: Basic Books.
McBride, William Leon
    1969   "Voluntary Association: The Basis of an Ideal Model, and the 'Democratic' Failure." Pp.
                202-232 in Pennock and Chapman, eds.
McConnell, Grant
    1969   "The Public Values of the Private Association." Pp. 147-160 in Pennock and Chapman, eds.
Meister, Albert
    1984   *Participation, Associations, Development, and Change.* Ed. and Trans. by Jack C. Ross. New
                Brunswick: Transaction Press.
Miller, Arthur Selwyn
    1969   "The Constitution and the Voluntary Association: Some Notes Toward a Theory." Pp.
                233-262 in Pennock and Chapman, eds.
Nielsen, Waldemar
    1979   *The Endangered Sector.* New York: Columbia University Press.
Pennock, J. Roland
    1979   *Democratic Political Theory.* Princeton: Princeton University Press.
Pennock, J. Roland, and John W. Chapman, eds.
    1969   *Voluntary Associations.* New York: Atherton.
Peterson, Mark
    1985   "Ideology and Community Development: Friend or Foe?" Presentation to the annual
                conference of the Community Development Society, Logan, Utah.
Pifer, Alan
    1975   "The Jeopardy of Private Institutions." Pp. 68-82 in Bruce L.R. Smith, ed.
Rydberg, Wayne, and Linda Peterson, eds.
    1980   *Volunteerism in the Eighties.* Appleton WI: Aid Association for Lutherans.

Smith, Bruce L.R., ed.
1975   *The New Political Economy: The Public Use of the Private Sector.* New York: Wiley.
Smith, David Horton
1973   "The Impact of the Voluntary Sector on Society." Pp. 387-399 in David Horton Smith, ed., *Voluntary Action Research: 1973.* Lexington, MA: Lexington Books.
Sumariwalla, Russy D.
1983   "Preliminary Observations on Scope, Size, and Classification of the Sector." Pp. 181-228 in Independent Sector.
Van Til, Jon
1985   "Voluntarism and Social Policy." Social Policy 15: 28-31.
Van Til, Jon
1982   *Living With Energy Shortfall: A Future for American Towns and Cities.* Boulder: Westview Press.
Van Til, Jon
1981   "Volunteering and Democratic Theory." Pp. 199-220 in John D. Harman, ed., *Volunteerism in the Eighties.* Washington, D.C.: University Press of America.
Wilber, Charles K., and Kenneth P. Jameson
1981   "Hedonism and Quietism." *Society* 19 (1): 24-28.
Young, Dennis R.
1983   *If Not for Profit, for What?* Lexington, MA: Lexington Books.

Patterns of Institutional Relations in the Welfare State: Public Mandates and the Nonprofit Sector

Kirsten A. Gronbjerg

Patterns of institutional relations in the American welfare state are shaped by two major driving forces in American society: (1) the execution of public mandates with its dependency on nonprofit and other nongovernmental service providers, and (2) by the intrusion and dominance of the American capitalist system. These two driving forces combine to produce four patterns of nonprofit-public interactions: Cooperation, characterized by public sector dependence on the nonprofit sector and the absence of a strong proprietary sector; Accommodation, characterized by public sector dependence on the nonprofit sector and the presence of a strong proprietary sector; Competition, characterized by the absence of a strong proprietary sector and the absence of public sector dependence on nonprofit service providers; and Symbiosis, characterized by absence of public sector dependence on nonprofit service providers and the presence of strong proprietary actors. The theoretical model is derived from an examination of public-nonprofit interactions in several different service sectors in Chicago. The paper traces the historical emergence of these four patterns in Chicago, using child care, health, education, and the housing and community development areas to demonstrate the patterns and the processes by which they developed.

The American welfare state continues to be characterized by extensive public mandates in spite of a recent decline in governmental services.[1] Mandated public services are provided, however, through a delivery system which relies heavily on nongovernmental service providers. These include nonprofit organizations and private businesses.[2] The linkages between these major institutional actors in the American welfare state are not well understood, particularly between the public and nonprofit sectors. This paper seeks to identify major dimensions which characterize those institutional relations.

No single pattern adequately describes the range of relationships that exists between the public sector and nonprofit organizations.[3] I develop and describe here four analytical patterns of relationships and two driving forces that form them, and then demonstrate how each pattern characterizes particular service fields. My perspective is historical; that is, I see current nonprofit-public relations as resulting from historical events and developments in public policy and in nonprofit activities.

My examples are drawn from Chicago and from the following service areas: child welfare, health, housing and community development, and education. The extent to

Kirsten A. Gronbjerg, Department of Sociology-Anthropology, Loyola University of Chicago, 6525 North Sheridan Rd., Chicago, IL 60626.

which the four analytic patterns of relations exist in other cities remains to be explored, and I make no claim as to whether or how other types of services than those considered here fit the particular patterns presented. To the extent that Chicago has shared in larger national developments, similar relationships should have emerged elsewhere.

PATTERNS OF NONPROFIT-PUBLIC INTERACTIONS

In principle, the public and nonprofit sectors share certain basic goals and structures,[4] and some degree of coordination between the two should be expected. But the degree and type of coordination is significantly influenced by two major driving forces in American society: first, by the tendency for American public welfare mandates to be executed with the aid of nonpublic service providers, and second, by the dominance of proprietary institutions because of the general strength of the American capitalist system.

For historical and political reasons the public sector has made use of nonprofit organizations to provide publicly mandated services in several service areas. While shared goals facilitate this mutual dependency, there are also circumstances that exist which impede such close relations. These circumstances include the constitutional separation of church and state and highly politicized service fields where contractual arrangements are highly visible and closely watched. Under these conditions, the interactions between the public and nonprofit sectors may not develop the ease and frequency of communication needed to resolve conflicts and develop mutual dependency. Dependency by the public sector on nonprofit service providers is thus compelling but at times so problematic that it may not develop.

Dominance of proprietary organizations in particular service sectors also modifies or "cools" the relationship between the public and nonprofit sectors. The entrance of a third party affects an otherwise dyadic relationship, especially when the third party operates on a fundamentally different basis, namely the profit motive. The overall strength of the American capitalist system is such that where the proprietary sector is active, it tends to dominate and provide the model for interactions.

Such "coolness" occurs particularly where the volume of transactions is high and important to public budget officials who must closely watch their expenditures, or where a large number of organizations are involved, making it difficult to maintain close communication. The proprietary sector is attracted by the former (high volume) and creates the latter (large number of service providers). Thus, a market system of transaction will be adopted and the presumption of shared goals and clientele by the nonprofit and public sectors can no longer be easily maintained.

Where the public sector does not rely heavily on nonprofit organizations to provide publicly mandated services, the entrance and dominance of the proprietary sector also significantly modifies the relationship between the public and nonprofit sectors. In this case, the nonprofit sector shifts from being a more or less equal competitor with the public sector, to playing an intervening role in what become the overwhelmingly political interactions of the public and proprietary sectors. The last two may attempt to enlist the nonprofit sector on their side, just as nonprofit organizations may attempt to negotiate alliances with either.

The result is four patterns of nonprofit-public interactions which arise out of the interplay of the two driving forces. They are diagrammatically represented in Figure

FIGURE 1
Patterns of Institutional Relations Between the Nonprofit and Public Service Sectors

		Dominance of Proprietary Service Sector	
		NO	YES
Public Sector Dependency on Nonprofit Sector	YES	COOPERATION	ACCOMMODATION
	NO	COMPETITION	SYMBIOSIS

1. These four analytic patterns and their paradigmatic relations emerged inductively out of my attempts to examine and understand how nonprofit organizations were being affected by changing public policies in different service fields.[5] I define them here at the outset and explain their interactive relationships for conceptual clarity, to provide the reader a framework for the subsequent discussion. These patterns, however, and the theory behind them, were derived from the analysis to follow.

In the pattern of *cooperation* (see Figure 1) between the public and nonprofit sectors, there are insufficient incentives for the proprietary sector to enter the field, because of the types of clients involved. In this case, the service arena has been left to the public and nonprofit sectors. Their shared purposes and the limited public resources devoted to the field encourage early public dependence on the more developed nonprofit sector for execution of public mandates. The result is cooperation between the two sectors, although the balance of influence may shift between them.

In the pattern of *accommodation* the public and nonprofit sectors are also mutually dependent on one another, but in addition, the proprietary sector has clear interests in the service fields. The nonprofit sector has little alternative but to attempt accommodation with both the public and proprietary sectors.

An alternative pattern, that of *competition*, occurs where sufficient public resources are devoted to developing a strong, but highly specialized public sector. A proprietary sector does not come into existence, nor is the public sector dependent on the nonprofit sector. The absence of a strong proprietary sector reflects the extensive assumption of public responsibilities. The result is that the public and nonprofit sectors operate under an implicit division of labor, but one which easily deteriorates into direct competition, especially under conditions of scarcity.

Finally, the pattern I have called *symbiosis* occurs where the proprietary sector has strong, even primary, interests in the service fields. Public investments are also extensive. By symbiosis, I mean coexisting to mutual advantage, sometimes to the point of mutual exploitation. Under these conditions, the role of the nonprofit sector becomes a highly specialized one. The sector cannot compete with the other two in delivering direct services, but can mediate or accentuate the decision-making process of the two other sectors.

In the rest of this paper I use particular services to demonstrate each of these four patterns: child welfare services to demonstrate the cooperation pattern, health care the accommodation pattern, education the competition pattern, and the housing and community development area the symbiosis pattern of interaction between the public and nonprofit sectors.

Cooperation

The child welfare field in Chicago provides a prime example of close cooperation.[6] There is a presence of mutual dependency between nonprofit service providers and public authorities and an absence of proprietary services in this field. Close personal contacts exist between nonprofit managers and program directors and their counterparts in public agencies: they work together on special task forces, join in coalitions, cooperate on public hearings, express their respect for the quality of work being done on the other side, and recommend one another as experts with special knowledge and understanding of the field.

Consistent with Figure 1, government depends heavily on nonprofit service providers to execute its mandate in this field. In 1982, about 43 percent of all public expenditures for youth and other child services in Cook County were used to purchase such services from nonprofit agencies. There are no significant proprietary service providers in this field and virtually none of the public spending for youth and other child welfare services goes to such providers.[7] A large part of the explanation for this particular pattern of interaction can be traced to the historical development of child welfare in Illinois and Cook County.

In the earliest period (1827), the state of Illinois charged county governments with the responsibility to care for paupers unable to care for themselves. Cook County quickly found itself unable to handle a rapidly growing population of newly arrived migrants and immigrants.[8] Many of the new residents were poor. Combined with a series of cholera epidemics, the result was a large number of orphans and other paupers. The county's attempts to deal with these problems were continuously inadequate, and the gap became partially filled by charitable groups (Brown, 1941). The first efforts of these groups were to care for orphans. The ethnic and religious heterogeneity of Chicago meant that there was a fairly large number of such child care institutions, since most major ethnic and religious groups established their own agencies (Johnson, 1931). As a result, nonprofit child care institutions were among the earliest and most institutionalized of Chicago's nonprofit organizations.

These child care institutions were also soon closely linked to county and city government. Several appointed the mayor of the city of Chicago as guardian for those of their children who would otherwise have been state wards; some obtained county funds in return for accepting children from the poorhouse; and some received a wide range of informal public support, including use of city property for storage or designation of special taxes for their support (Brown, 1941; Johnson, 1931).

The relationship between the child care institutions and county government became fully institutionalized after 1879, when the state authorized the county to provide per capita subsidies for girls placed in "training schools" (extended to boys in 1882). This was an important development, because the state constitution of 1870 prohibited the use of public funds for sectarian purposes and also outlawed special grants and privileges to charitable organizations. These two developments effectively limited the institutionalization of public-nonprofit relationships to those involving child care (Johnson, 1931; Werner, 1961). The establishment of the Juvenile Court in Cook County in 1898 extended county per capita payments to child welfare organizations caring for children under the jurisdiction of the court.[9]

The state did not accept direct responsibility for child care: it had limited its role to establishing the public mandate for county government and attempts at regulating charitable organizations. By doing so, the state created a no-win situation for Cook County: it had to provide for the care of paupers and orphans, but the state did not provide it with any resources to do so. The subsidies made possible by the Training School Acts represented the state's attempt to make the resources of charitable institutions available to the counties, in spite of the limitations imposed by the 1870 Constitution. The only child care institution operated by the state was a small one, limited to the care of children of veterans. The state even found it difficult to execute its own mandate to regulate charities and, in 1925, began to use several Cook County nonprofit organizations to investigate foster homes operating under their auspices.

The development of such a highly institutionalized relationship between nonprofit child welfare organizations and state and county governments served important purposes for both parties. For the nonprofit organizations, the system provided them with considerable financial resources to care for "their" children—by 1927 as much as 63 percent of the operating income of some "training schools" came from county subsidies (Johnson, 1931). The result was also that these nonprofit organizations became the *only* institutions to specialize in child care: it was difficult to argue for the establishment of public child care institutions, when so many charitable ones existed.

In effect, the county was relieved from providing directly for a number of children that otherwise would have been its responsibility under state law. It was much cheaper for the county to pay relatively low subsidies than to operate its own facilities. Moreover, the county poor house was under continuous and considerable criticism for its deplorable conditions. Had the county had to care for these additional children, the uproar would have been considerably louder. Consequently, the county quickly became dependent on private child care institutions, especially as the Juvenile Court came into operation and mandated placement of its wards as well. By 1927 almost 25 percent of total county expenditures of $2.1 million for child care went to 23 industrial schools and 4 child-placing organizations.

The system was not without its serious problems. Most prominent of these were the "left out" children, those for whom the county had legal responsibility under the Juvenile Court, but which the established child care institutions refused to take. Most of these were Protestant and black. It created a source of continuous tension between the charitable institutions and county government.

Nevertheless, this system of cooperation and mutual dependency in the child care field persisted until the 1960s and is still evident (Gronbjerg, Musselwhite, and Salamon, 1984). This long and highly institutionalized relationship between nonprofit organizations and county government contrasts with relationships in other social service areas where the interactions are more recent and less developed.

Beginning in the 1950s Chicago child care agencies increasingly turned their attention to the state, which in 1943 began to reimburse counties for up to 50 percent of the cost of child care. That policy was implemented with the strong support of nonprofit organizations and county governments. The role of the state in child welfare was further strengthened by the extension of AFDC payments for foster care in 1961, but most particularly with the establishment of the state's Department of Children and Family Services in 1964. Most observers consider this a critical step, because it opened the door for direct public services and full state fiscal responsibility for child, youth, and family services. A number of subsequent developments (merger of the DCFS with the Cook County Department of Public Aid; limitation on the jurisdiction of the Juvenile Court; and the beginning of Title XX federal reimbursements to the state) completed the transfer of public responsibility for child welfare from county governments to the state.

For the nonprofit child care providers, the implications of these public policy changes were several. They were intimately involved in shaping several of the changes in significant ways. The increased state role and the availability of federal funds to the state meant more funds available to the nonprofit organizations. The changes also simplified the public private partnership for large nonprofit organizations, who now only had to deal with one level of government. And the new division of labor allowed nonprofit child care agencies to emphasize their professional treatment and innovation, and request higher rates of reimbursements. On the other hand, the emphasis on foster care, deinstitutionalization, and growth of a variety of social services under Title XX meant that child care institutional services, and thus many child care organizations, became relatively less important.

The result has been a more even balance between the child care institutions and public agencies. However, the remnants of the previous dependencies are still there. The child care institutions remain important to public service providers, and have broadened their services to include foster care, adoption services, child abuse, and even day care. They continue to emphasize the importance of professional, high quality services, and adequate state reimbursement policies. In turn, they remain among the organizations called upon to help formulate or comment upon public policies.

The child welfare field illustrates how the public sector becomes dependent upon a nonprofit service delivery system and how cooperation between the two emerges. Extensive mechanisms for continued and close communication and the absence of a strong proprietary sector involved in child care and child welfare services allowed the two sectors to maintain an image of shared goals.[10] However, this close cooperation and mutual dependency does not extent to all nonprofit-public interactions. It seems to be limited to those fields in which public authorities early made the decision to use, or were forced to accepted the extensive or exclusive use of, nonprofit service providers to meet public mandates.

In the health care field, by contrast, Chicago area public agencies followed a very different pattern of development and made early deliberate choices to provide all or most publicly mandated services directly themselves. As a result, when federal funding for expanded health services became available in the mid-1960s (Medicare and Medicaid), the basis for nonprofit public interaction was considerably different.

Accommodation

The pattern of interaction between nonprofit service providers and public agencies that appears to exist in the health area is best characterized by the term "accommodation." As suggested in Figure 1, the health care field is one where there is considerable public dependence on nonprofit service providers, as well as a sizeable proprietary service sector. More than half of all public expenditures for health in the Cook County area are used to purchase services from nonprofit health providers. An additional 22 percent are used to purchase services from for profit providers (Gronbjerg, Musselwhite and Salamon, 1984, Ch. 3). Moreover, the 22 percent public reliance on proprietary health providers underestimates the importance of these providers: there are hundreds of proprietary health professionals, laboratories, nursing homes and home health agencies, that provide the bulk of health care outside of hospitals.

The public and nonprofit health sectors are of considerable importance to one another, but the character of the interaction appears more limited and contractual in nature than in the child welfare fields. There is even some informal indication of mutual distrust and doubt. Thus, recent years have seen several court cases by health service coalitions against the major public agencies involved in health financing.

Although a large number of health coalitions exist in Chicago, most of these seem to be limited to nonpublic health providers, often including both nonprofit and proprietary service providers (such as Illinois Hospital Association and several associations of nursing homes). This illustrates the extent to which nonprofit organizations are oriented towards the proprietary sector at least as much as towards the public sector. Although there are some coalitions that involve public as well as nonprofit organizations, most of these extend into the social services field, such as one focussing on infant mortality.

The reasons for this more limited pattern of interaction are several and reflect the way in which the early public mandates in the health areas were established and executed; early patterns of separation between the public and nonprofit subsectors; high degree of institutionalization of the nonprofit sector; and the existence of an extensive for profit health service sector alongside the nonprofit one.

On the surface, early public mandates in the health field appear to be quite similar to those in the social services area: the state early made counties responsible for providing free medical care and burial services to nonresidents and paupers (1827); there were close relations between the county and some nonprofit health providers, particularly dispensaries and hospitals; and the rapid population growth meant that public resources were constantly inadequate to meet even the limited public mandates.

However, some aspects of the health field were significantly different from the child care field. Thus, the public mandate was not as clearly located at the county level: the state assumed responsibility for disability and to some extent mental health care; the city was charged with problems surrounding public health and contagious diseases; and the county was left with direct medical care, and especially hospital care. This division of labor meant that borderline problems could be ignored, that coordination between the various types of public services was problematic (Brown, 1941), and that debates about the extension of public mandates for health services could be easily derailed.

In contrast to the need for social services, everyone in Chicago, not just paupers, were likely to find themselves in need of health care. As a result, an extensive private health care system quickly came into existence. The field was not limited to public or charitable providers as was the case in the child care field. In fact, most health care was provided directly by private physicians in the patient's own home. These physicians also provided most of the "charitable" health care in the city, either individually with a sliding fee system or under contract with the county.

Although hospitals were not recognized as genuine treatment centers until around the turn of the century, a number of nonprofit dispensaries and hospitals came into existence in Chicago in the latter part of the nineteenth century. These hospitals were established for reasons very similar to the development of nonprofit child care agencies: rapid population growth placed inordinate strains on public services, mainly provided under terrible conditions in the almshouse, and various ethnic and religious groups were eager to provide alternative care for their "own" people.

Once the city had established its TB and cholera hospitals in 1843, its public health department in 1837, and the county its own public hospital (Cook County Hospital in 1862), there was resistance to further expansion of public medical services to the poor, or the development of contractual relationships with nonprofit organizations. The only exception was a long-standing, but controversial, contract between Cook County Hospital and the nonprofit Illinois Training School for Nurses to staff the hospital.

Also in contrast to the child care field, there were only a few instances of formal appropriations by the county or city for direct support of nonprofit health institutions, although such appropriations were made possible by state law in 1889 and 1913 (Johnson, 1931). Not only did local governments in Cook County make less use of this provision than elsewhere in the state, but this limited support rarely amounted to more than 5 percent of the revenues of the receiving institutions.

Contributing to the limited public nonprofit relationship were two additional factors. First, Cook County hospital was dominated by private physicians who served as volunteer staffs (as late as 1950 the hospital had no more than half a dozen full-time physicians). The hospital staff, and some of its key administrators, saw the hospital's role as a residual one: doing only what private medical care and hospitals could not or would not provide. Second, Chicago is the home of the American Hospital Association, the American Medical Association, and Blue Cross/Blue Shield, all of which have acted to protect the interests of private medicine locally as well as nationally.

In contrast to the child welfare field, the state did not become extensively involved in health care[11] until the mid-1960s, and then opted mainly to reimburse costs. Nor had the state a prior set of health care mandates that were as extensive as in the social services field, which local governments had been unable to meet without state support. Also in contrast to child care services, a substantial portion of public expenditures for health care services are direct federal expenditures (Medicare), entirely separate from state and local governments. These federal expenditures are in the form of payments for services delivered, not in the form of purchase of service agreements or contracts with particular providers as is the case in social services. The dominant payment system is one which does not distinguish between nonprofit and proprietary service providers, but is modelled on the existing proprietary health insurance system.

Even if an extensive system of nonprofit-public institutional relations at the state and local level had existed prior to 1965, the adoption of such a proprietary model and the dominance of direct federal programs virtually guaranteed a much different pattern of public-nonprofit interactions in health than in the child care field. As it was, the Medicare and Medicaid programs greatly expanded the health care service fields and had considerable impact on nonprofit health care providers in Chicago. However, the result was not a pattern of close cooperation between the public and nonprofit sectors, but one more along the lines of commercial transactions.

It is important to keep in mind, however, that from a purely *financial* point of view, the mutual dependency between the nonprofit and public sectors is greater in the health field than in child welfare. Not only are overall public expenditures for health significantly greater than for child welfare,[12] but nonprofit service providers receive a greater proportion of public expenditures for health (54 percent) than is the case for social services (45 percent) (Gronbjerg, Musselwhite and Salamon, 1984: Ch. 3).[13] It is obvious that public authorities would be unable to assume the full and direct responsibility for providing publicly mandated health care in Chicago without substantial capital investments and greatly expanded operational expenses. A similar hierarchical pattern exists in the extent to which nonprofit organizations depend on public sources of revenue for their operations.[14]

Historically, the relationship between the public, proprietary, and nonprofit health sectors in Chicago was one of limited interaction. The recent, but extensive, financial dependency between nonprofit and public institutions in the health field has forced the two sectors to accommodate one another, in large part because they must adjust to the large proprietary sector as well. Even the current pattern of institutional accommodation is under increasing strains, characterized by intense lobbying by health care providers, court cases, and several aggressively negotiated settlements between the three sectors over the state's medical care reimbursement system.

In both of the two patterns of institutional relations discussed so far, the current situation is one in which there is considerable fiscal interactions between the nonprofit and public sectors. To that extent, the two sectors are important to one another: for the nonprofit sectors to survive, and for the public sectors to perform their mandates. As I will show next, this is not the case for the two remaining patterns of interaction: direct competition and symbiosis.

Competition

In education, as well as in and housing and community development, the amount of public funding going to nonprofit organizations is quite small, especially compared to the volume of public spending in these fields. Thus, the public sectors do not "need" the nonprofit service providers' infrastructure in order to meet their own legal mandates, although the nonprofit service providers indirectly help alleviate the pressure on public agencies for services. Hence both of these fields are characterized by low public dependence on the nonprofit sector.

As in the health area, both of these services are in demand by wide segments of the population, not just the poor. But only in education are the public and nonprofit sectors are of comparable size, infrastructure and degree of institutionalization. Also, there is no sizeable proprietary service sector in the education field to modify the public-nonprofit pattern of interaction as there is in the health or housing and community development areas.

The relatively equal strength of the two sectors, absence of mechanisms of integration, and the relative sophistication of clients (Khandwalla, 1984) explain why the pattern of interaction in the education field is best characterized by competition. At both the elementary and higher levels of education, public and nonprofit institutions compete for students and philanthropic support. State support for public education, especially elementary education, is closely tied to student enrollment and is a sizeable component of total public education expenditures. The competition for students thus has a direct effect not only on the revenues of the nonprofit institutions, but on the funds available for public education as well.

There have been attempts to develop closer cooperation between the two sectors, such as several attempts at establishing a system of state subsidies for nonprofit educational institutions. But only in the area of higher education has such a system come into existence, and primarily in the form of state scholarship programs.[15] It is noteworthy that these funds are distributed in a manner similar to that in the health area: funds are administered by a public agency (State Scholarship Committee) which does not itself provide services in the field; and the individual service recipient chooses the service provider. However, in contrast to the health area, there is here a well established set of public institutions, but very few proprietary ones, that compete for the cash-bearing client.

As in the health area, the current pattern of institutional relations in the education area emerged in full force only during the last 20 years, and mainly as the result of federal initiatives. Particularly important was the Elementary and Secondary Education Act of 1965, but increased federal support for research, specialized training and construction, and the earlier GI Bill also had major impact.

The early history of public education in Chicago was significantly different from what developed in health or child care services, although in all three fields there were early and specific mandates for public services. But the public mandate in education was entirely local in origin and character: while the state made provisions for local governments to operate schools, it did not require them to do so until 1855, as it had required these levels of government to provide health and social services in the 1820s.

In education, local governments in Cook County were beset with the same problems of rapid population growth and inadequate public facilities as in health and child care. In all three fields, the inadequate public resources gave rise to the development of nonprofit counterparts. For example, between 1850 and 1870 thousands of students were turned away by the public schools and 21 Catholic elementary and secondary schools were established. By 1870, 20 percent of students were attending nonpublic schools (Herrick, 1971). However, there was a considerable investment in public infrastructures in education, which did not occur in health and child care and by 1880, close to 60,000 students were enrolled in public schools.

The education field differed in other ways from health and child care: a genuine division of labor developed between the public and nonprofit sectors. Public schools focussed almost entirely on elementary education, leaving high school, college and university training to the nonprofit sector. The first public high school was not established until 1855 or 1856, and only about 2,800 students attended public high schools in Chicago as late as 1890, when the city's population had topped 1 million (Herrick, 1971). Similarly, there was only one public institution of higher education, the Chicago Normal School established in 1867 to train teachers, while there were 16 nonprofit colleges and universities by 1870.

Finally, the state constitutional prohibition against the use of public funds to benefit sectarian organizations could not be overcome in the field of education, as it was in child welfare and in health. There were two reasons for this. First, most nonprofit elementary schools were Catholic parochial schools, established to prevent the "Protestantization" of Catholic children in public schools and to preserve the ethnic identity of Catholic parishioners.[16] Any attempt to provide public support for nonpublic schools would involve de facto favoritism for Catholics. Second, because the primary purpose of the nonpublic schools was so closely linked to their sectarian character, any attempt to use public funds in ways that could be construed as supporting them was quickly opposed as violating the principle of separation of church and state.[17]

The predominant pattern of public-nonprofit interaction in primary education remained one of no direct fiscal relations and very little other contact as well until the late 1960s. The state did not even attempt to regulate or license nonpublic elementary and secondary schools, and it still operates with only a voluntary registration system. In fact, only the local truant officer has authority to evaluate a nonpublic school, and then only to the point of saying that students attending such a school fail to meet the state's mandatory attendance requirement. Since the state accepts home instruction as meeting those requirements, the threat to nonpublic schools has remained virtually nonexistent.

The reasons for this hands-off attitude by public authorities were several. Most schools were part of the Catholic parochial system, a very powerful force in Chicago politics. They were also highly institutionalized and looked and acted like schools. Further, the public school system was constantly faced with rapidly growing enrollments as Chicago's population continued to increase until the early 1950s and as the baby boom expanded the child population into the 1960s. The local public education systems also continued to experience significant increases in state support until the early 1970s and did not see nonpublic schools as threats until then.

In higher education, the growth of public colleges and universities coincided with the maturation of the baby boom generation and the explosion in college attendance that occurred in the 1960s. The nonprofit colleges and universities, already highly institutionalized and well established, continued to grow during this period, although not as rapidly as the public institutions.

By the mid-1970s the two sectors had arrived at a more direct level of competition at both levels of education, but for different reasons. In higher education, nonprofit colleges and universities saw a drop in their share of student enrollment from about fifty percent in 1960 to about 26 percent in 1982. At the same time, the end of the baby boom meant a smaller graduating high school class during the 1980s and into the 1990s.

In primary and elementary education, public schools experienced an absolute and relative loss of students, especially in Chicago, whose population stagnated. When local and state fiscal conditions deteriorated in the late 1970s, funding for public education became endangered and public school officials concerned about their ability to maintain a viable school system. They pointed to the nonpublic schools as a threat to public education: creaming off the best students, depriving public schools of state per capita student support, and contributing directly or indirectly to a segregated education system.

The competition that now exists between the public and nonprofit sectors of education is closely linked to scarce resources. The institutional separation of the two sectors historically has meant that they have not developed mechanisms for cooperation and adaptation. Moreover, the emergence of a vast public bureaucracy and related infrastructure has created a set of vested interests, able to counteract those of the nonprofit sector. The public sector could provide the services now provided by nonprofit schools.[18] That is not the case in the health or child care fields. The absence of a viable proprietary educational sector, with the possible exception of trade schools, has meant that the primary institutional interactions in education have been those between the nonprofit and the public sector.

The three service areas described so far thus illustrate the extent to which public dependence on nonprofit service providers result from, and in turn shape, patterns of collaboration and coordination. Where no proprietary sector exists these patterns often develop into one of close coordination. Where a proprietary market system of transaction comes into existence, reflecting the existence and dominance of a proprietary sector, the coordination remains one of accommodation. Alternatively, where collaboration between highly institutionalized public and nonprofit sectors has been restricted, either because of an effective division of labor, or because of formal restrictions, the two sectors move towards direct competition.

Symbiosis

The final pattern of institutional relations between the public and nonprofit sectors is that of symbiosis, coexistence for mutual advantage at times bordering on mutual exploitation. It is found where the following two conditions exist: a public sector which operates quite independently of the nonprofit sector, but which occasionally finds use for some of the special capacities of nonprofit organizations; and the dominance of a strong private sector economy that is seen as the primary service provider in the field. The pattern is found particularly in the fields of housing, environmental protection, conservation, and community development.

With the exception of community development, extensive mandates for direct public services in these fields are recent, and still somewhat limited.[19] Until recently, the private marketplace has been seen as the primary solution and service provider: realty and construction firms providing housing; manufacturers and businesses handling environmental and conservation problems associated with their own activities. Public agencies were primarily involved in developing and maintaining public infrastructures, such as streets, bridges, sidewalks, etc.

The expansion of these public mandates to housing, conservation, and environmental protection came in the late 1930s and then at the federal level, mainly to provide public and private employment. That is still seen as one of the major benefits of public expenditures in these areas. Most public funding for these fields has continued to be federal in origin, although often administered by state and local governments. They involve considerable investment in new infrastructure and are capital intensive. Since the public sector has usually relied on the expertise of the private economy to accomplish its mandates, these fields are an important source of public funding for the proprietary sector and highly politicized.

The combination of high capital investments and the dominance of the private economy relegates the nonprofit sector to a highly specialized role. It does not have the capacity or resources to enter these fields directly as service providers. Only relatively few nonprofit organizations have been actively involved in providing housing, community development, conservation, or environmental protection services themselves, primarily in the late 1960s and early 1970s, and almost always with the support of public funding. Instead, the role of the nonprofit sector has been limited to: (1) identifying the needs or gaps in services, and related to that, the promotion of or resistance to proposed public services or private sector actions; and (2) limited partnerships with the public or private sectors, especially in the planning phases of housing and community development projects.[20]

While the nonprofit sector has not very been important as a direct service provider in these fields, it has nevertheless played an active role. Because of the importance of "brick and mortar" services and projects, the focus tends to be geographical in nature. That makes community organization and involvement in politics with a capital "P" a much more effective tool for nonprofit organizations than is the case in other fields. Their activities then tend to focus on active community organization efforts, direct attempts at stimulating economic development, and intensive lobbying and organizing efforts aimed at the public sector and at private business and industry, rather than direct services to a client population. Obviously, such activities may have important consequences for the agendas of both public and private industry sectors.

Similarly, public policies and decisions in the private economy are critical to the nonprofit organizations: these actions provide the nonprofit organizations with their major reasons for existence and with their agenda for action. Without public policy decisions and private economy actions, there would be little occasion for these organizations to do what they do best: mobilize and educate the general public to become involved in the decision-making process. Clearly, the nonprofit sector needs the public sector for its continued operation, in a way that is not the case in the other service fields discussed above.

Because "brick and mortar" projects either are proposed and die, or come into existence and are no longer optional, nonprofit activities in these fields tend to be volatile and weakly institutionalized. They come into existence when special needs arise and often disappear when some resolution has been reached. Expectably, nonprofit organizations involved in community organizing are among the smallest and youngest of the nonprofit organizations in Chicago (Gronbjerg, Kimmich and Salamon, 1985: Ch. 2).

Nonprofit activities in these fields have been promoted by a series of historical factors in Chicago. Prominent among these are a series of demographic and political factors which created particular community problems on the one hand, and strengthened the sense of community on the other. Rapid population growth until the late 1940s meant that housing was of critical concern to large portions of the city's population, especially low-income and some racial and ethnic groups. Urban renewal, demolitions, and condominium conversions have continued the housing pressure for those groups. Changes in the city's industrial mix and its economic decline in recent years have kept community development and environmental issues high on the agenda as well.

On the other hand, the development and continued existence of ethnic and racial residential areas in the city facilitated the establishment of local organizational infrastructures. Racial and ethnic residential succession and urban renewal efforts have contributed to the development of "defended neighborhoods" that are easily mobilized by existing nonprofit organizations (Suttles, 1972). Similarly, the existence of the political machine and its emphasis on neighborhood services and voter mobilization also serves as a focal point for many of Chicago's nonprofit community organizations.

Chicago, then, has seen the development of several models of local communities and plans for their mobilization. The Settlement House movement, the Chicago School of Sociology, the Industrial Areas movement of the post-1930s have provided perspectives on the local communities and motivated public and nonprofit leaders to focus on their organizations. These local nonprofit organizations are important organizational resources for public agencies and private business and industry. Often difficult to control, they still represent political mobilization that the other sectors have to contend with. More commonly, each sector attempts to utilize the other for its own purposes and agenda. It is because of this limited, but potentially mutually exploitative, role that nonprofit organizations play for the public sector that I have termed this pattern of institutional relations between the sector for symbiosis.

The breakdown of the Chicago political machine, along with the "council wars," has intensified the political role of Chicago's nonprofit community organizations in recent years. They have formed the basis for new political constituencies and alliances.

CONCLUSION

The four patterns of institutional relations between the nonprofit and public sectors that I have described here reflect current interactions but are the product of more or less distant historical circumstances. Most reflect national developments. I have suggested a number of conditions that underlie these patterns: the extent of public-nonprofit financial interaction and how dependent the public sector is on nonprofit service providers; the presence of strong proprietary service sectors; the early patterns of nonprofit-public relations and dependencies that developed in Chicago; and the extent of institutionalization of the two sectors. Two of these dimensions are in my judgment particularly important and I have defined those as the two driving forces that create the four patterns that are central to my argument: first, whether the public sector depends on the nonprofit sector for the execution of its own mandate; and second, the presence or absence of a strong proprietary or private sector economy.

The first driving force that defines the four patterns of institutional relations, public sector dependence on the nonprofit sector, separates the child care and health sectors from the education and housing, community development, and environmental protection sectors. In the former cases, the public sector simply does not have the institutional capacity or infrastructure to deliver its mandated services directly. In the latter cases, the public sector does, or could do it, with the help of the proprietary sector.

It is important to point out that I am talking here about government's current dependency on the nonprofit sector, not how dependent the nonprofit sector is on government. To some extent this reflects the dominance of the welfare state: these patterns are driven by characteristics of the state, not of the nonprofit sector. This dependency may have come about as a result of different historical paths, reflecting at times, as in health and child care, the early strength of nonprofit organizations (McCarthy, 1982) to protect their turf vis-a-vis weak public sectors. Although strong charitable institutions also developed in the field of education, ideological arguments about the separation of church and state and the primacy of public education prevented these organizations from dominating the public sectors.

The peculiar nature of the American welfare state, its late development, the reluctance with which public mandates have been assumed, and the tendency to allow nonpublic service providers an important role in executing public mandates are fully revealed in these patterns of institutional relations. They show, indirectly, the extent to which the nature of the American welfare state and the manner in which it performs its services, are shaped by the nonprofit sector. In the final analysis, however, the nonprofit sector is more dominated by public sector developments than vice versa, and has been for some time.

The second driving force I have identified is the presence or absence of a strong proprietary or private economy sector that interacts extensively and intensively with the public sector, often in competition with the nonprofit sector. This dimension separates the child care and education fields from those of health, housing, environmental protection, and community development. The presence of this third sector fundamentally changes the relations between the nonprofit and public sector. Relations appear to become somewhat more antagonistic and opportunistic. It appears that this third sector, when present and prominent, tends to set the major tone of interaction, which nonprofit organizations may then join, as in the case of health, or react to, as in the case of community organizations. It should perhaps not be surprising that capitalist institutions dominate in a capitalist society, when given the opportunity to do so.

Recent Chicago developments appear to be in the direction of less government reliance on nonprofit organizations (Gronbjerg, Musselwhite and Salamon, 1985: Ch. 5); the emergence of for profit service companies in fields previously dominated by nonprofit organizations (day care, home health); and the movement of nonprofit organizations in the direction of for-profit operations. The latter is implied by nonprofit organizations' greater reliance on fees and service charges (Gronbjerg, Kimmich and Salamon, 1985: Ch. 4), the development of proprietary subsidiaries by such organizations, and the adoption of proprietary management styles (especially by hospitals).

If these changes continue, they would seem to suggest a movement away from the pattern of cooperation towards the other three patterns of institutional relations between the nonprofit and public sectors: accommodation, competition, and symbiosis. The result would be a smaller, more limited and specialized role for the nonprofit sector—a transition that might not easily be made by all nonprofit organizations.

NOTES

1. This is a revised version of a paper presented at the Annual Meetings of the Society for the Study of Social Problems, Washington, D.C., August 23-26, 1985. Some of the interpretations presented in this paper were developed while I was a Field Associate for the Urban Institute on its Nonprofit Sector Project ("The Nonprofit Sector in an Era of Governmental Retrenchment"). As part of that project I prepared a draft report on "Historical Perspectives on Chicago Nonprofit Sectors" (August 1983) from which most of the examples used in this paper are drawn. I want to acknowledge the research assistance provided by Denise O'Brien, David Sheagley, and Steven Varnis at various stages of my attempt to come to grips with the Chicago history of nonprofit development. I am indebted to Gerald Suttles, Joseph Galaskiewicz, Mayer Zald, David Fasenfast, and Susan Ostrander for their very helpful comments and suggestions. I also want to thank by colleagues and the graduate students in the Department of Sociology and Anthropology at Loyola University of Chicago for their comments. However, the interpretations presented in this paper are mine entirely and do not necessarily reflect the position of the Urban Institute, the sponsors of the Nonprofit Sector Project, or members of the Chicago Area Advisory Committee for the Urban Institute's Nonprofit Sector Project.
2. Findings from the Urban Institute's Nonprofit Sector Project give some indication of the extent of the relationship between the three sectors. Thus almost half of the $4.1 billion in public expenditures for five major service fields, (social services, health, employment and training, housing and community development, and arts and culture) in Cook County in 1982 went to nonprofit organizations which in fact provided the actual services. An additional 18 percent of these public expenditures went to for profit service providers (Gronbjerg, Musselwhite and Salamon, 1984, Ch. 3).

3. I will use the term "nonprofit" throughout this paper to describe the charitable, voluntary organizations that provide services of general public interest. Excluded from consideration are those voluntary membership associations which operate primarily to benefit their own members. The "nonprofit sector" is also sometimes referred to as the "voluntary," "charitable," "independent" or "third" sector.

4. Both are "public benefit" types of organizations, existing for the explicit purpose of providing services to particular clients or the general community. These similarities are formally acknowledged in the special tax privileges granted to nonprofit organizations. Moreover, neither type of institution is "owned," in the formal sense, by particular individuals or specific groups, nor can profit be accumulated and distributed to specific individuals.

5. These particular interaction patterns are of course not entirely of my own invention. They were among those identified by Park and Burgess (1969) as characterizing human ecology. More recently, these concepts have been used by those examining interorganizational systems (see f. ex., Phillips, 1962 and Khandwalla, 1984).

6. The child welfare field includes institutional care, foster care, adoption services and child abuse services.

7. Even in the day care field, where there are substantial proprietary sector involvement, more than half of public expenditures in Cook County went to nonprofit organizations, only 8 percent to for profit service providers.

8. Chicago grew from a village of about 40 people in 1830 to a town of over 30,000 by 1850, the population tripled during each of the next two decades and reached more than 1 million in 1890 (Brown, 1941; Hillman, 1940).

9. Not surprisingly, there were numerous court challenges to the Training School Acts, claiming that the subsidies violated the state constitutional prohibitions against special privileges for charitable organizations and use of public funds for support of sectarian purposes—many of the "training schools" were affiliated with particular denominations. However, none of these challenges succeeded against the argument that the subsidies paid less than the actual cost of providing the child care.

10. For somewhat different reasons, relations among the public and nonprofit sectors in the arts area also belong in this category of close cooperation. In this case, mostly small, new, endangered public programs provide sporadic support for a large number of arts organizations, including some extremely prestigious ones. The public agencies exist specifically to support such nonprofit groups and hence have both the opportunity and motivation to maintain close contacts with them.

11. Excluding mental health, where the state early had taken extensive responsibilities.

12. In Cook County, total public expenditures for health care amounted to $3,194.9 million in 1982, compared to $331.7 million for all of social services (see Gronbjerg, Musselwhite and Salamon, 1984: Ch. 1).

13. Public reliance on nonprofit health providers is unusually high in Chicago, reflecting primarily the overwhelming dominance of nonprofit hospitals in the area.

14. Close to 50 percent of hospital revenues in the Chicago SMSA come from public sources, compared to 38 percent for nonprofit social service agencies (see Gronbjerg, Kimmich and Salamon, 1985: Ch. 3). Any significant reduction in public funding for health care services has immediate and considerable impact on the area's nonprofit health providers.

15. About $94 million in state scholarship funds were distributed to Illinois students in 1982. Sixty percent of the funds were used by students to attend private universities and colleges in the state, although these institutions had only about 26 percent of all students enrolled in colleges and universities (Federation of Independent Colleges and Universities, 1982).

16. Even as recent as 1968-69, 98 percent of all nonpublic school students in Illinois were enrolled in religiously affiliated schools, 91 percent in Catholic schools (Rader, 1974).

17. This argument still held force in 1970 when the state adopted its new Constitution and failed to eliminate the prohibition against use of public funds for the benefit of sectarian organizations.

18. The nonprofit education sector also is not nearly as dependent on public funding for their revenue bases as is the case in health or social services. Although almost all nonprofit colleges and universities receive considerable public funds, these constitute only about 14 percent of total revenues for Chicago area institutions (Gronbjerg, Kimmish and Salamon, 1985: Ch. 3). The proportion of revenues coming from public sources is likely to be even smaller for nonprofit primary and elementary schools, although most receive some public funding. Thus Gertler (1974) reported that 92 percent of nonpublic primary and elementary schools in Chicago (93 percent statewide) received some public funds in 1970-71. This was mostly from school lunch programs, text book support, and other federal programs.

19. That, of course, is not the case for sanitation, closely linked to environmental protection. Most American cities began extensive sanitation projects in the late 19th century. However, the primary purpose of these projects was to promote public health, not environmental protection.

20. The nonprofit sector occasionally administers some of these services after the original infrastructure has been constructed with public funding, using private contractors. Thus some public housing projects and subsidized housing developments have been administered by nonprofit organizations.

REFERENCES

Brown, James
    1941   *The History of Public Assistance in Chicago: 1833 to 1893*. Chicago: University of Chicago
                Press.
Federation of Independent Colleges and Universities of Illinois
    1982   Pamphlet.
Gertler, Diane B.
    1974   *Nonpublic Schools in Large Cities*: 1970-71 Edit. National Center for Education Statistics.
                Washington, D.C.: U.S. Government Printing Office.
Gronbjerg, Kirsten A.
    1983   Historical Perspectives on Chicago Nonprofit Sectors. Draft Report for the Urban Institute's
                Nonprofit Sector Project.
Gronbjerg, Kirsten A., James C. Musselwhite Jr., and Lester M. Salamon
    1984   *Government Spending and the Nonprofit Sector in Cook County/Chicago*. Washington, D.C.:
                The Urban Institute Press.
Gronbjerg, Kirsten A., Madeleine Kimmich, and Lester M. Salamon
    1985   *The Chicago Nonprofit Sector in a Time of Governmental Retrenchment*. Washington, D.C.:
                The Urban Institute Press.
Herrick, Mary J.
    1971   *Chicago Schools: A Social and Political History*. Beverly Hills: Sage Publishers.
Hillman, William Arthur
    1940   Urbanization and the Organization of Welfare Activities in the Metropolitan Community
                of Chicago. Unpublished Ph.D. Dissertation, The University of Chicago.
Johnson, Arlien
    1931   *Public Policies and Private Charities: A Study of Legislation in the United States and of Admin-
                istration in Illinois*. Chicago: The University of Chicago Press.
Khandwalla, Pradip
    1984   "Properties of Competing Organizations." Pp. 409-432 in *Handbook of Organizational De-
                sign*. Vol. 1. *Adapting Organizations to Their Environments*. Ed. by Paul C. Nystrom and
                William Starbuch. Oxford: Oxford University Press.
McCarthy, Kathleen D.
    1982   *Noblesse Oblige: Charity and Cultural Philanthropy in Chicago, 1849-1929*. Chicago: The
                University of Chicago Press.
Park, Robert E. and Burgess, Ernest W,
    1969   *Introduction to the Science of Sociology*. With an Introduction by Morris Janowitz. Chicago:
                The University of Chicago Press.
Phillips, Almarin
    1962   *Market Structure, Organization, and Performance*. Cambridge, MA: Harvard University
                Press.
Rader, Herschel
    1974   The Politics of State Aid to Nonpublic Schools in Illinois, 1969-1970. Unpublished Ph.D.
                Dissertation, The University of Chicago.
Suttles, Gerald D.
    1972   *The Social Construction of Communities*. Chicago: University of Chicago Press.
Werner, Ruth
    1961   *Public Financing of Voluntary Agency Foster Care*. New York: Child Welfare League of
                America.

Central Government, Local Government, Voluntary Associations and the Welfare State: Some Reflections on Opposition to Recent Public Spending Cuts in Britain

Christopher G. Pickvance

The relation between the state and voluntary associations is explored by a study of voluntary organization responses to deep funding cuts of local governmental expenditures in Britain. Why have voluntary associations not been at the forefront in opposing these cuts, which impact so deeply on their viability? The main opposition to these funding cuts by central government has come from the local councils themselves. The basis for the restoration of cuts has been cast in terms of preserving local government's autonomy, rather than in terms of preserving an endangered welfare state. The relative weakness of the voluntary association response is accounted for in large part by the perceived (rather than the actual) degree of centralization of government in contemporary Britain.

The focal question of this paper concerns one aspect of the relation between the state and voluntary associations in Britain. What theories about the relationship between the state and voluntary consumer action groups can explain why, when local level public spending is cut, are voluntary associations not at the forefront of opposition? Why is the lead taken by local government itself? Is local government defending the interests of consumers of local public services—in which case the lack of voluntary action by consumers themselves might be less important—or is it pursuing its own interests distinct from those of consumers?

Three areas of theoretical debate are relevant to these questions: 1) the rise of the welfare state, and the security of its base—is it economically indispensable, or is it conditional on a politically fragile coalition of interests? 2) the structure of the state—are centralized states more effective in initiating and sustaining welfare state spending, but also more able to reduce such spending in the face of economic crisis and? 3) the role of voluntary consumer action groups—are they actively or passively involved as service consumers, and likely or unlikely to respond to service cuts?

Until the mid-1970s, the rise of the welfare state was treated as an ineluctable process, an unavoidable concomitant of economic growth. It scarcely needed explanation, but if explanations were sought these were found in the realm of values such as the triumph of collectivism over individualism; technology and its imperatives; pressure groups, such as political parties and enlightened government officials; or

Christopher G. Pickvance, Urban and Regional Studies Unit, University of Kent at Canterbury, Canterbury, Kent CT2 7NF Great Britain.

class conflict, where the welfare state was part of the "postwar settlement" with the working class (Gough, 1979; Pickvance, 1982). Left critiques argued that the welfare state was funded by the working-class itself and was accompanied by an even larger system of transfers to the rich and to companies via tax reliefs and direct subsidies. They argued further that the form in which certain benefits (e.g., social security, council housing) were provided was highly stigmatizing (LEWRG, 1979; Le Grand, 1982). This critique was taken to extremes in the functionalist argument that the welfare state had come about because it was ultimately in the collective interest of capitalists. All benefits to individuals were seen simply as ways of aiding the reproduction of their labor power (Ginsburg, 1980). It was left to critics on the right to question the economic functionality of welfare state growth: in an influential book Bacon and Eltis (1976) argued that the welfare state had unrecognized costs in reduced work motivation, in the growth of "unproductive" state employment, and in inflation. Implicitly, both left and right acknowledged that the security of the welfare state depended on a political consensus which might be shaken.

The sea-change that occurred in *political rhetoric* about government social spending in Britain in the mid-1970s has its origins in:

1. The collapse of economic growth and the world slump;
2. A deliberate government choice of favor of low inflation rather than low unemployment as a policy goal; and
3. Government arguments than when growth fell, the welfare state must suffer, and government arguments that its responsibility for the economy was very limited and that market forces should be left unfettered. Self-reliance should replace reliance on the state.

What is interesting is that the new political rhetoric has been accompanied by only minor changes in *public* attitudes to the welfare state (Taylor-Gooby, 1985: 26-33). The political consensus supporting the welfare state has proved much more resilient than the government expected. The level of spending on health and education are, for example, seen as potential election-losers for the Conservative government. This political consensus has hampered attempts to cut public spending.

The second theoretical debate concerns state structure. It is argued that a more centralized state structure makes it easier to initiate social reforms such as the welfare state but also easier to implement spending cuts. "Centralized" refers to the financial and policy control exercised by national government over local government. De Tocqueville was possibly the first to point out the connection between centralization and voluntary organizations. The argument developed by Rose (1954: ch. 4), is that the more centralized the state structure, the less the scope for local voluntary association activity. Rose claims support for the argument in the large number of voluntary associations in U.S., a less centralized state structure, and the lower number in France where state structure was more centralized. The logic here is one of "opportunity structure." The incentive to form voluntary associations is assumed greatest when local political institutions possess power and are hence a worthwhile target for pressure. (This argument applies to associations seeking to change policy, not to "expressive" associations.)

In attempting to apply this line of thinking to Britain, the initial problem is to know whether the state should be regarded as centralized. Nineteenth century writers, including de Tocqueville, characterized Britain as having decentralized administration (e.g., de Tocqueville, 1968: 1027). More recent scholars have argued that British administration is centralized compared with that of France (Ashford, 1982). The problem here is that centralization is measured by power to reform (often radically) the local government system. On *this* measure the slow pace of reform in France compared with the major changes in Britain supports the view of British government as centralized. However, if centralization is measured by the ability of national government to require local government to comply with day-to-day policy directives and financial controls, then the British state is, as I will show, less centralized than the French. British local government has vast spending powers and is a major employer. It possesses extensive technical expertise. French local government has less of both these characteristics. Hence central government in Britain has an arm's length relationship with local government, whereas in France it is a very close one. The result is that central day-to-day power and local resistance to reform are high in France and low in Britain. My hypothesis would be, therefore, that the incentives to voluntary organization formation at the local level are high in Britain (and the U.S.) and low in France.

The third theoretical debate concerns the degree of activism among voluntary organizations. One of the most influential theories of the 1970s, Castells' (1977) theory of urban movements, argued that as the state intervened increasingly in consumption, a whole new range of issues were politicized. "Collective consumption" became a new terrain of conflict in addition to the workplace. Castells envisaged the interventionist state triggering a new wave of demands by groups who felt they were not getting their share of resource redistribution. By underestimating obstacles to popular mobilization such as state strategies to contain conflict, Castells overestimated the degree of activism during the rise of the welfare state. Although he did not explicitly address the question of how groups accustomed to a certain level of public service benefits would respond to their contraction, implicitly he suggested cuts would provoke an active response.

In the remainder of the paper I shall outline the relation between the welfare state and the structure of government (Section I), the way the attack on public spending and local government has taken place (Section II), and the form taken by opposition (Section III). Finally, I shall draw out conclusions for the initial theoretical arguments.

THE WELFARE STATE AND LOCAL GOVERNMENT IN BRITAIN

The distribution of functions between elected levels of government (central/federal, regional/provincial/state, local) and between elected institutions and non-elected boards, agencies, and commissions varies greatly between countries. In general, in federal states local government has far fewer functions than in unitary states. One peculiarity of the British structure of government is that local governments have a very large number of functions. As a result major welfare state functions are carried out by local government. This is in addition to activities such as police and fire services, refuse collection, parks, libraries, roads, and car parking. While social security and the national health service are central government functions, local councils are responsible for all education spending for universities, for personal social services, and for part of housing spending. (The figures for 1973 and 1983 are shown in Table 1). Local government was responsible for 23% of welfare state

TABLE 1
Social Spending by Central and Local Government, 1973 and 1983 (£ Million)

	1973	1983
Central share	10319 (68.7%)	57332 (77.0%)
Social Security	5534	33741
National Health Service	2956	16016
Universities	498	1600
Housing (part) (est)	1331	5975
Local share	4699 (31.3%)	17159 (23.0%)
Education except universities	3133	11837
Personal social services	510	3028
Housing* (part) (est)	1076	2294
	15018 (100%)	74491 (100%)

Source: *Central Statistical Office, United Kingdom National Accounts 1984 edition.* Tables 7.2, 7.3, 8.2, 8.3, 9.4.
*The proceeds of council house sales have been added in.

spending in 1983 compared with 31.3% in 1973: this trend was largely due to the rapid growth of social security spending by central government.

The policy of cutting welfare state spending has, therefore, had a major effect on local government in Britain. The cuts introduced between 1976 and 1979 by Labour and continued since then by Conservative administrations have made local government the focus of unprecedented political controversy (Pickvance, 1986).

A second peculiarity of the British structure is that councils (the elected bodies which make local government policy) may only levy one local tax, a local property tax. The extent of welfare state functions of local government means that although central grants contribute substantially to council revenues, a considerable (and rising) proportion has to be collected through this local tax—hence its unpopularity and the various measures set out later to counter this.

Cutting welfare state spending is central to the New Right model of society being advanced by Conservative administrations. It has both rhetorical and "real" aspects. The former consist of simple slogans such as "not spending what you haven't earned," "the private sector as the locus of wealth creation," and the refusal to "throw money at the problems." The image is of a society where the role of government is minimal and where people's ability to pay for services determines what they can and should receive. Concealed in this rhetoric is that some types of public spending are positively encouraged—it is mainly welfare state spending which should be cut. For example, spending in the form of incentives to "wealth-creators" (tax reliefs and subsidies to high income earners, to owners of wealth and private firms)—what is sometimes called the "welfare state for the rich"—should remain undiminished.

Progress towards these new objectives has, in reality, been slow. Table 2 shows the evolution of central and local government spending from 1974 to 1983. While total central spending rose 2.1% per year in real terms, total local spending fell 1.6% per year. However, within local government spending only capital spending underwent a real fall (-7.6% per year); current spending managing a real increase even under the 1979-83 Conservative administration.

These trends can be interpreted in several ways. First, they do not correspond to budgetted spending since they are corrected for inflation: the high inflation of

TABLE 2
Trends in Central and Local Government Spending 1974-83

	1974 (£m)	1983 (£m)	CHANGE 1974-83 (1974 = 100)		SIMPLE ANNUAL GROWTH RATE			
			Money terms	Real[2] terms	Labour 1974-76	1976-79	Conservative 1979-83	1974-83 Whole period
1. GDP at factor cost	75641	257489	340	112	1.7	2.0	0.6	1.3
2. General government spending[1]	36997	137480	372	109	0.2	1.5	1.0	1.0
3. Central government spending	29721	120709	406	118	2.9	1.9	1.6	2.1
4. Local government spending	12859	37643	293	86	-2.1	-2.4	-1.0	-1.6
of which								
5. Capital spending[3]	3629	3951	109	32	-12.2	-11.5	-9.0	-7.6
6.	(3647)	(5555)	(149)	(44)	(-12.2)	(-9.4)	(-4.6)	(-6.3)
7. Current spending	9230	33692	365	107	1.9	0.2	0.5	0.7
8. Central grants to local authorities for current purposes	4683	18495	395	115	14.7	-4.3	0.6	1.7
9. Income from rates	3089	12456	403	118	-2.3	1.8	4.3	2.0

Source: Central Statistical Office, *United Kingdom National Accounts 1984 edition.* London: H.M.S.O.

Notes
1. General government spending nets out transfers between central and local government. It excludes spending by nationalized industries.
2. Columns 4-8 are calculated using the GDP factor cost deflator (row 1) and the general government deflator (rows 2-9).
3. Local government capital spending in row 5 is calculated net of receipts from council house sales. In 1983 these totalled £1604m. The figures in parentheses in row 6 include these receipts.

1974-76 helps explain the real cuts then, and the low inflation of 1982 and 1983 helps explain the higher than intended rate of increase then. Secondly, they represent a downward shift compared with the long-term spending plans of the mid-1970s: in that sense they show "cuts"—all the more so because expanding needs and the higher inflation rate of government spending mean that an increase in real terms is needed to provide a constant level of services to those eligible. Thirdly, they show that the cuts in spending have been less dramatic than political rhetoric would lead us to believe. This is partly because of the demand-related nature of social security spending (levels of benefit can be set, but the number of claimants cannot be predicted) and partly because of the political obstacles to controlling spending—for example, despite the rhetoric of cuts, central grant to local councils has in fact increased in real terms by 0.6% per year (1979-1983—see row 8).

To focus on local government spending and the government's problems in controlling it, one needs first to understand how British local government is organized and financed.

It is useful to think of two polar models of local government. In the *local autonomy model*, all of a local government's spending comes from local sources, and it is completely free to choose what services to provide. The consequence of such a model is that variation in service levels and taxation is extreme; there is also a built-in incentive to fragmentation of local government units since rich neighborhoods can thereby avoid paying for services used only by poorer groups.

The *welfare state model of* local government is diametrically opposed to the local autonomy model. All of a local government's spending is financed from national sources, for example, via a fixed share of a nationally collected tax, or by an annually calculated grant. The choice of services is made at the national level. Local government becomes an "agent" of central government, despite being an elected body. Local government units are large in size and boundaries can only be changed as part of nation-wide changes. This model has two advantages: uniform services can be provided across areas and central financing can be arranged so as to compensate areas with higher than average needs or costs of service provision, such as central cities, sparsely populated areas, or areas with large retired populations. A less extreme version of this model involves some local financing: in this case the wealth of the population can be compensated for by a central equalization grant. The drawback of this model is that local government almost loses its *raison d'etre*.

The point of setting out these models is not to claim that, say, the U.S. corresponds to the local autonomy model or the U.K. to the welfare state model. Both countries are some way from the two extremes: the U.S. because of the major role of federal financing (McKay, 1980) and the U.K. because of the presence of some local financing and some local control over service provision (Newton, 1980). The purpose of the models is rather to draw attention to a fundamental contradiction in local government systems: *local self-government and self-financing are incompatible with territorial justice as measured by equality in service provision and in tax burden.*

In the British case the growth of the welfare state has meant that the local government system has been driven towards the welfare state model but remains a considerable way from it. This distance can be measured in two ways. First, the share of central grant in the total of central grants and local property taxes ("rates") rose from 50% in 1945 to a peak of 67% in 1975 but has since fallen back to 48% (1984/5);[1] local councils until 1985 have been free to decide how much they received in rates—

their sole local tax source. Secondly, central controls on service provision in principle ensure that certain minimum standards are achieved in all areas. But these controls are rarely compulsory. More often they allow great leeway to councils as to *how* to provide compulsory services, and *whether* to provide noncompulsory services. As a result the degree of centralization is considerable but far from complete: only one third of all council current spending is centrally funded; rates and charges for services can be fixed locally (but see below); and there is considerable discretion over the allocation of current expenditure between services, and in the choice of capital projects. It is because of this important area of local discretion that the defence of "local autonomy" has been such a popular slogan in the battle over local government.

THE ATTACK ON LOCAL GOVERNMENT

Ever since 1975 when a Labour minister announced "the party's over" for council spending, successive national governments have sought to achieve control over local government council spending. The technical problem was that government has only controlled one of the sources of current income to councils: the central grant they receive (see Table 2, row 8). The two other sources of current income, rates, and fees and charges for services, were largely beyond central control. In 1975 the Labour government set a cash limit to this central grant: this was an innovation since previously the grant was set as a fixed percentage of councils' spending. This percentage varied between localities and was inversely proportional to the property wealth of the locality. (This meant that in areas such as impoverished Welsh mining valleys the percentage might be 85%, giving a high incentive to spend on services since only 15% of the cost had to be met from local sources—the defect from the government's viewpoint of a percentage grant.)

The technical problem immediately took on a political dimension. Councils were threatened collectively by the idea that central grant would no longer rise to keep pace with demands. Councils are organized into three national organizations: the Association of Metropolitan Authorities which includes upper-tier and lower-tier councils[2] in London and the six conurbations; the Association of County Councils which consists of upper-tier councils outside the conurbations; and the Association of District Councils which represents lower tier councils in the same areas. It is these organizations of councils which represent the councils' interests vis-a-vis the government—the AMA is Labour-dominated and the ACC and ADC Conservative-dominated. Together with national political party organizations and trade unions of local government employees they have taken a leading role in the defense of local government.

The key point here is that the ability of a government to control spending by local councils is politically constrained by the fact many of these councils are run by its own supporters, many of whom are more committed to their own towns and their councils than to party ideology. In other words a Conservative government that sought to cut central grant to councils would immediately face protests from Conservative councils and Conservative associations of councils (the ACC and ADC), as well as from Labour ones.

Table 2 shows that between 1976 and 1979 Labour made sharp cuts in local government spending (2.4% per annum in real terms), entirely by cutting capital spending. Since this primarily affected housing, which is mostly built for councils by private building firms, the main impact was on nonunionized workers, so political repercussions were avoided.

Turning to the Conservative period of office from 1979 one can see a continuation of the same trend: a (smaller) cut in the real level of local government spending (1% per annum) achieved through capital spending cuts while real growth in current spending was held down to under 1% per annum as under Labour. This shows that the radical rhetoric of the Conservative government has been less apparent in action.

During the period from 1979 four sets of initiatives to cut local government spending can be identified. Their sheer number indicates how complex it has proved to cut local government spending, and are evidence of the limited centralization of the British state structure.

(1) *Laissez faire*. For a brief period the national Conservative government relied on local electors to help control council spending. The argument was that no sane voter would support a council which set high rates to help finance spending judged "high" by the government. It thus discussed freeing councils from some central constraints, and obliged councils to produce annual reports on their activities which would be available on payment to electors. This failed to have the desired effect, since some councils continued to spend at "high" levels. Two conflicting explanations of this can be given: either "high" spending policies have popular support, or local election results in Britain depend largely on national party popularity thus insulating local councils from the influence of electors opposed to "high" spending (Dunleavy, 1980).

(2) *Spending targets and penalties*. A more interventive system was introduced in 1981. Two spending targets, for each council were set and a graduated system of penalties was applied to spending in excess of this. The penalty took the form of reduction in central grant, and ultimately of complete withdrawal of central grant. One spending target was a percentage increase over a previous year's spending (the "volume" target), and the other an absolute level. The absolute target was a deliberate response to the political problem mentioned above. Since Conservative councils tend to spend less, volume targets hit them sharply: a council whose spending has traditionally been low will find a real cut of 2% harder to achieve than a "high" spending council. Hence there was a loud outcry against volume targets from Conservative councils and in response the targets were not applied in 1981 and 1982. Absolute level targets had the advantage that they enabled traditionally higher spending Labour councils to be penalized: their protests were ignored for party political reasons. The partial abandonment of targets for political reasons helps explain why central grant continued to increase from 1979-83 (Table 2, row 8).

However, even spending targets and penalties failed to achieve their effect. This is because, as we have seen, central grant is only one source of councils' current income, and councils kept up their spending by raising rates to compensate for lower central grant. (This was particularly striking between 1979 and 1983 when rates income went up 4.3% per year in real terms—Table 2, row 9.) The best known case was the Greater London Council, which spent so much on subsidizing public transport as part of its cheap fares policy in 1981/2 that it was penalized by the removal of *all* of its central grant—and raised rates to make good the loss, much to the irritation of business ratepayers. This showed that the threat of penalities was not effective and led to the last two initiatives.

(3) *Rate-capping*. In 1984 an act was passed to give government control over the

level of rates councils can set. This was known as "rate-capping." The same act also obliged councils to consult the largest ratepayers in the area before passing a budget.

The origins of these measures goes back to the 1979 and 1983 election manifestos where the Conservatives pledged themselves to reexamine the rating system. But by 1983 all their efforts to abolish rates had foundered and they were under pressure to be seen to take action. This pressure was particularly exerted by business interests who claimed that rates were an unfair tax since they amounted to "taxation without representation": business ratepayers contribute about one third of all rates but have no vote in local elections (except as individual residents). In addition they claimed that high rates reduced profits and threatened employment. It is perfectly understandable that businessmen should prefer to pay less in taxes, but what was new was the attention given by the Conservative government to this special pleading. Once again it was apparent that the ideal of an "enterprise culture" with minimal state intervention *in practice* required massive state transfers to the "wealth creators"—perhaps better termed "wealth guzzlers."

The Rates Act is a response to this business-instigated pressure. The opposition to it was universal among councils. A council's right to fix local rates was a jealously guarded one. Removal of it would mean councils coming closer to being "agents" of central government—a term in fact used by Conservative ministers. As a concession the government announced it would not cap the rates of those councils which had spent within both their targets for the previous three years.[3]

In July 1984 the eighteen councils whose rates were to be capped were named. Subsequently the permitted increases they would be allowed were made public, and these varied greatly, reflecting the councils' varying levels of reserves, their use of "creative accounting" to conceal their real level of spending, and the government's intention to create divisions among them and weaken their unity. Sixteen of these councils were Labour and they announced a collective response of defiance. They said they would refuse to set a legal rate—which all local councils are obliged to set to meet the gap between other income and spending—thereby opening the councillors involved to surchage, dismissal, and imprisonment. In the event the defiance response was abandoned, the permitted increases were large enough for those opposing them to be branded as "confrontationists" who thus lost support. Nevertheless eight of the councils were late in making a legal rate, opening councillors fo the threat of bankruptcy and disqualification. In addition two councils which were not capped but which were set stringent targets also defied the government. They included Liverpool council which in 1984 was alone in defying the government and eventually succeeded in gaining some £50m worth of concessions (Pickvance, 1985). In the Liverpool case, the government has taken the councillors to court. This is the first government use of legal measures against councils since the Clay Cross rebellion in 1972 (Skinner and Langdon, 1974; Sklair, 1975) and is quite exceptional—the government prefers to rely on negotiation.

(4) *Abolition of the GLC and metropolitan county councils.* The final initiative is the most drastic of all: the outright abolition of the higher-tier authority in London and the six conurbations (West Midlands, Merseyside, West Yorkshire, South Yorkshire, Tyne and Wear, Greater Manchester). An act transferring the powers of these councils either to central government (as with London Transport) or to joint boards appointed by the lower-tier authorities in the area (e.g., for police, fire, refuse disposal) came into effect on 1 April 1986.

The rationale given by the government for this measure is lame. It was claimed that there was duplication of functions between the two tiers of councils leading to wasteful spending, and that the councils had been inventing new functions to justify their own existence. But no government estimates were made of savings, and the estimates commissioned by the six metropolitan councils show that under the proposed new arrangements their costs would be some £60m greater.

In fact even government supporters openly admitted that the aim of the abolition measure is party political. The seven councils involved are all Labour controlled and have been at the forefront of opposition to the government. Ken Livingstone, GLC leader, has explicitly said that the GLC is the "best redistributor of wealth we've ever been able to take control of, much better than any other council in the country. That's why I think the government is moving to abolish the GLC" (1984: 265). These councils have been prominent in exploitating the discretion allowed to them, e.g., via cheap fares policies, the setting up of Enterprise Boards and other employment-creation and protection initiatives, financial support for women's, black, and gay groups, etc.

As with the other government initiatives against local government there was opposition to the abolition proposals, but less than there was to the penalty system and rate-capping. There is traditionalist support for not abolishing elected bodies, particularly when this can be interpreted as due to a failure to win control of them democratically, but there was long-standing hostility to the upper-tier councils by the lower-tier councils, which also of course stood to gain by the abolition act.

In this section, we have outlined the Labour and Conservative measures aimed at local government which are also aimed at the welfare state: cash limits, reliance on electors to keep spending down, reliance on targets and penalties, rate-capping, and proposals to abolish the GLC and metropolitan councils. The recurrent theme has been that all the measures, except outright abolution, have failed in their aims. This reflects the degree of decentralized power enjoyed by the councils, and the opposition of both Labour and many Conservative councils.

What was the response to these attacks on the welfare state, in particular the role of voluntary organizations?

OPPOSING LOCAL GOVERNMENT CUTS: DEFENDING THE WELFARE STATE OR DEFENDING LOCAL AUTONOMY

The key point about the opposition to the measures against local government and the welfare state is that it has come from local government councils and not from voluntary associations. This section examines why this is and whether the interests defended by council are those of consumers too.

Consumer opposition to cuts in public services through voluntary associations has been limited and fragmented. A few protests against closures of small schools have taken place, but reduced spending levels on school equipment have more often prompted fund-raising by associations of parents than opposition to cuts. Only a few short-lived attempts have been made to set up "anticuts alliances." These have usually been limited to single issues and have been based on specific trade unions or political parties rather than general consumers.

The failure of consumers and voluntary associations to lead opposition to spending cuts can be explained in several ways. Most important in my view is the discouragement of public involvement or participation in local public services. In British tradition, central government is seen as "knowing best," reforms are implemented in a "top-down" direction, and good government requires maximum secrecy. The public is cast in the role of the grateful receiver of services—in some cases with a stigma attached for having failed to provide themselves through the market, as in council housing. Since the public is judged to lack expertise, the less it is involved in service provision the more the public interest is served. In contrast, in the U.S., it sometimes appears that the greater the attention given to vocal pressure groups the more the public interest is being served (Newton, 1976). The absence of structures of public participation due to the paternalist assumptions of service provision means that any consumer opposition to cuts cannot make use of existing structures and has to create new ones.

It is partly in recognition of this that some Labour councils (and some Conservative councils) have recently introduced decentralized administration of services such as rent collection and housing repairs.[4] Neighborhood offices are set up and some existing staff (both clerical and workers) transferred to them. The motives for this initiative are mixed. The most political is that decentralized services are more satisfactory and consumers are more likely to defend them. A frequent result is that the workload rises rapidly as the council's responsiveness to complaints increases. A more pragmatic motive is that decentralization can, by reducing administration, save money. An interesting observation in these cases of decentralization is that trade unions have been highly resistant (Seabrook, 1984). This is partly because of the disruption of work practices, but also because of the naivety of councillors in industrial relations matters (Pilkington, 1985). This shows the conflict of interest between the defense of local government in its present form as an end in itself and defense of local government as an element of the welfare state where the level of services, their quality and public commitment to them is essential.

A second explanation of the weakness of community action in defense of local government services is the spread of ideologies which see public provision as inferior to private provision. This belief is strongest in housing and transport, and weakest in education and health where cuts have been least severe. Taylor-Gooby (1985: 26-7) shows that there has been some shift in public attitudes between 1963 and 1979, though it has been far more limited than political rhetoric would suggest. He also shows that there is widespread support for most benefits and services—with restrictions on free access to those for "undeserving" minorities such as the unemployed and single parents—but that this coexists with dissatisfaction with their realities. Hence it is quite consistent, Taylor-Gooby argues, that of those preferring private health and education for themselves if costs were equal, 48% and 63% support higher spending on state provision (1985: 46). In the case of health this is linked to the belief that private provision is quicker (38%) and better (51%), and to dissatisfaction with the NHS (9%). Those preferring the national health service refer to favorable past experience (63%) and the need to support state services (36%) (1985: 41). It is risky to read too much into these data: if the 89% who prefer private provision do so on the basis of actual experience rather than belief and the 36% who choose the NHS for ideological reasons do so despite their experiences of it, the outlook for state provision is poor, but both these conditions are hypothetical as is the assumption that private and state health costs are the same.

It would be complacent to say that this limited shift in public attitudes has spread for no other reason than a change of government policy, i.e., that objectively public provision in housing and transport is as good as private. The deterioration in services and the exclusion of public involvement only serve to increase people's alienation from them. (See Saunders (1984) for an argument that private provision is intrinsically superior because of the greater control it affords.) It is perfectly understandable that some people respond to this by "exit" rather than "voice," to use Hirschman's (1970) terms. I would not agree, however, with the argument of LEWRG (1979) that paternalism and the exclusion of public involvement are inherent features of capitalist welfare provision. Overall I see attitudes to public services as less crucial to explaining consumer inaction than the lack of participatory structures, since there are clearly vastly more people with positive attitudes to those services than people actively defending them.

A third explanation for the failure of significant opposition to cuts points to more mundane but no less real features. In many cases the cuts in spending have been difficult to identify. They have also been gradual. Less frequent maintenance, reduced rate of council house-building, and reduction of staff by natural wastage all mean that cuts are not very visible. The transitory role of certain consumer statuses, such as public transport user, and the dependency of others (geriatric patients in hospitals) make consumer action less likely.

Overall, then, Castells' idea of a widespread movement of consumers of "collective consumption" is not borne out in the British case. But what kind of consumer opposition did mobilize, and were consumer interests paramount within it?

The major opposition to cuts in public spending has been by local government councils, their representative associations, and to a lesser extent trade unions. Government initiatives on local government spending were shaped and implemented in the light of representations by local councils, as the previous section here explained. The national government's ultimate failure to control local government spending is an index of the combined effect of Labour and especially Conservative council pressure. The single successful measure—the abolition of the GLC and metropolitan county councils—can be understood in terms of the earlier argument that drastic change is easier to achieve in the British system than day-to-day policy change which requires cooperation by the councils affected (see Pickvance, 1986).

The key feature of the opposition by councils is that it has focussed on the need to preserve *local autonomy*, the right of councils to run their own affairs rather than to maintain *spending levels*. The notion of local autonomy has considerable resonance in British local politics. Counter to the national centralist tradition, there is a localist tradition which asserts that councils are closely in touch with local needs, and that central policy control is inimical to proper local government. This was manifest in the last major inquiry into the organization of local government, the Layfield report (Cmnd. 6453, 1976), which recommended that services should be divided into those that were the responsibility of central government both in funding and policy terms, and those that were the responsibility of local government in funding and policy terms. This recommendation (which like the rest of the Report was never acted upon) would have allowed complete autonomy for local councils within their sphere of influence. It reflects the idea that local councils are entitled to run services as they choose since they are more closely in touch with local needs than central government.

The persistence of this idea in a local government system which tends towards the welfare state model, but which is not completely centralized, is interesting. However, the claimed sensitivity of councils to local needs is little more than a myth. In terms of linkages between electors and councils, British local government is notorious for the low level of voting turnout at local elections. Twenty-five percent is common, compared with 75% at general elections. There is widespread popular ignorance of what activities councils are responsible for and who local councillors are. At best the argument refers to the high degree of professionalization of local government where educational and other administrators try to keep in touch with local needs within the paternalist variant of the welfare state prevailing in Britain. Hence local autonomy is best seen as an ideology supported by those with professional interests in local government. These interests do not necessarily coincide with a high level of welfare state spending and more participatory services.

There is thus a *real contradiction between the defence of the national welfare state and the defence of local government which is concealed by the local autonomy slogan* (see also Cochrane, 1985). This can be seen clearly in the following news story. The story follows Neil Kinnock's discovery during the 1983 General Election campaign that the Labour party he led was not planning any press conferences on education policy:

> Kinnock . . . was furious at the failure to exploit the Tories' shocking neglect of primary and secondary schools . . . He had the idea of placing a statutory obligation on local authorities to ensure that all children were educated to a "national minimum standard" in the basic subjects . . . He wanted, by law, to stipulate the maximum size of class permitted and to guarantee nursery provision for all children whose parents wanted it. *The idea was killed in infancy by the powerful local government lobby within the [Labour] party who were worried at the threat to local autonomy* (Hugill, 1985, emphasis added).

Historically Britain has been ambivalent about state centralization. Traditionally Conservative governments have stated a preference for the local autonomy model of local government but have favored centralization to control spendthrift Labour councils. Labour governments favored the national welfare state model. They have sought centralization to ensure all councils provided at least a minimum level of services. The paradox is that since the attack on the welfare state started in the 1970s centralization has been used by both Labour as well as Conservative governments to *reduce* service provision. "Local autonomy" is now the battle cry both of Labour councils opposed to centrally imposed cuts, *and* of Conservative councils who feel they should be free to provide as few services as they wish. This is why there has been opposition to cuts in local government from both parties. It also suggests that this party convergence in defence of local autonomy is a short-term one, since each party has a quite different conception of what model of local government is desirable on the continuum from self-government to welfare state mentioned earlier.

In sum, the defense of local government conducted by councils and their representative organizations under the local autonomy banner has not coincided with the interests of consumers. It represents far more a defence of decision-making autonomy by professional groups working in local government. For this group a high level of spending imposed by central government is anathema. Trade unions have been primarily concerned about protecting members jobs, and only secondarily about service levels. Often this has meant accepting natural wastage and a gradual running down of services. Hence, like councils themselves they are a conservative force with no interest in more participatory forms of public service.

CONCLUSION

I have shown that the main opposition to the attack on local government and state social spending has been conducted by councils themselves (and their associations) with some support from trade unions, but with little from service consumers or through voluntary associations. This opposition has primarily been in the name of the highly ambiguous slogan of local autonomy rather than the defense of services. This reflects the institutional power of councils vis-a-vis trade unions and service consumers. The quotation referring to Neil Kinnock's vain attempt to defend education standards illustrated this.

Community action by voluntary associations has been a minor voice in the opposition due to 1) the lack of participatory structures which would facilitate the mobilization of opposition—this relates to the tradition of secret government and exclusion of public involvement, 2) the pattern of attitudes to public services which is a sophisticated balance of support for good quality services and concern for taxation levels, rather than outright support for public services whatever their quality or cost, and 3) difficulties of identifying spending cuts and their short-lived impact in some cases.

These explanations for the lack of voluntary association activity suggest that centralization of state structure is *not* the crucial determinant of this activity in defense of public service cuts. De Tocqueville and Rose argued that where the state was decentralized the incentive to mobilize at the local level was maximized. A key conclusion from the British experience is that it is not the *actual* degree of centralization (which I believe to be far from total) which is crucial but the *perceived* degree. As I have shown, local councils have continually protested their lack of autonomy over policy and finance. The effect of this has been to present central government as in total control of councils. This has the advantage for councils that it encourages protest to be deflected onto central government. In fact the public has directed some protest against local councils, but it is likely that the volume of protest has been lower because of the proclaimed impotence of councils. Hence it is the perceived rather than the actual degree of centralization of state structure which influences the pattern of protest.

Only by developing participatory public services and increasing the consumer's voice is the welfare state element of local government likely to be defended. This would increase awareness of the discretion possessed by local government despite its protestations, and help its proven opposition power to be more fruitfully redirected.

NOTES

1. This government grant is distributed between councils in a compensatory way so that councils with the least resources (in property wealth) and the greatest needs and costs of meeting them receive the largest grant percentages. For example, if on average the grant covers 50% of a council's spending, this might vary between, say, 20% for rich councils and 85% for poor councils.
2. Up to April 1986, every household in England and Wales lay within the jurisdiction of two councils: upper-tier (metropolitan or 'shire') county councils and lower-tier district councils. In London and the six conurbations the district councils have more functions than elsewhere since they are responsible for education and personal social services, but in other respects the split of functions between tiers is similar.
3. Only about one half of councils had kept within both targets—a measure of the ineffectiveness of the target and penalty system.
4. Outside the scope of this paper is the fact that decentralization initiatives by Labour councils have been

part of a small wave of radical council actions which are closely connected to *past* community action (Boddy and Fudge, 1984; Pickvance, 1985). The best known of these policies have been a) cheap fares: on London buses and tube by the GLC (1981-3) and by South Yorkshire metropolitan county council where bus fares were frozen at their 1975 level until 1986, and b) employment creation and protection of work conditions (by the GLC, Sheffield, West Midlands etc.). What is interesting is that those actively involved in these policies either as leading councillors or employees are the community activists of the 1960s and 1970s (Gyford, 1984). The demands they were making then for better services involving more participation have now become policy in a limited number of cases. Conversely Liverpool council which is run by Labour with the 'Militant' group very active, and which won its rebellion against the government in 1984, is seen as the 'black sheep' by ex-community action activists. Its roots are in the trade union movement—Liverpool council is the largest employer in the city and there is active council shop stewards involvement in branch Labour parties—and its policy of large-scale council housebuilding has been at the expense of support for housing cooperatives (which are an outgrowth of community action).

REFERENCES

Ashford, D.E. (ed.)
    1980   *Financing Urban Government in the Welfare State*, London: Croom Helm.
Ashford, D.E.
    1982   *British Dogmatism and French Pragmatism*, London: George Allen and Unwin.
Bacon, R. and Eltis, W.
    1976   *Britian's Economic Problem: Too Few Producers*, London: Macmillan.
Boddy, M. and Fudge, C. (eds.)
    1984   *Local Socialism?* London: Macmillan.
Castells, M.
    1977   *The Urban Question*, London: Edward Arnold.
Cmnd. 6453
    1976   *Local Government Finance: Report of the (Layfield) Committee of Enquiry*, London: HMSO.
Cochrane, A.
    1985   "The Attack on Local Government: What It Is and What It Isn't," Critical Social Policy 12: 44-62.
de Tocqueville, A.
    1968   *Democracy in America*, (2 vols.) London: Fontana.
Dunleavy, P.
    1980   *Urban Political Analysis*, London: Macmillan.
Ginsburg, N.
    1979   *Class, capital and social policy*, London: Macmillan.
Gough, I.
    1979   *The Political Economy of the Welfare State*, London: Macmillan.
Gyford, J.
    1984   "From Community Action to Local Socialism," Local Government Studies 10, 4: 5-10.
Hirschman, A.O.
    1970   *Exit, voice and loyalty*, Cambridge: Harvard U.P.
Hugill, B.
    1985   "New Champion of Parents' Rights" *New Statesman* 12 April 1985.
Le Grand, J.
    1982   *The Strategy of Equality* London: George Allen and Unwin.
Livingstone, K.
    1984   Interview in Boddy and Fudge (1984).
London Edinburgh Weekend Return Group
    1979   *In and Against the State* London: Publications Distribution Cooperative.
McKay, D.H.
    1980   "The Rise of the Topocratic State: US Intergovernmental Relations in the 1970s," in Ashford (1980).
Newton, K.
    1980   "Central Government Grants, Territorial Justice and Local Democracy in Post-war Britain," in Ashford (1980).
Pickvance, C.G.
    1982   *The State and Collective Consumption*, (course D202, Unit 24), Milton Keynes: Open University Press.
Pickvance, C.G.
    1985   "Les Politiques Municipales Socialistes en Grande-Bretagne," Revue Internationale d'Action Communautaire 13/53: 131-9.

Pickvance, C.G.
    1986   "The Crisis of Local Government in Britain: An Interpretation," in M. Gottdiener (ed.)
                Cities in Stress Beverly Hills: Sage.
Pilkington, J.
    1985   "Looking for New Friends," *New Statesman* 5 April 1985.
Rose, A.M.
    1954   *Theory and Methods of Social Sciences*, Minneapolis: University of Minnesota Press.
Saunders, P.
    1984   "Beyond Housing Classes: The Sociological Significance of Private Property Rights and
                Means of Consumption," International Journal of Urban and Regional Research 8:
                202-225.
Seabrook, J.
    1984   *The Idea of Neighbourhood*, London: Pluto.
Skinner, D. and Langdon, J.
    1974   *The Story of Clay Cross*, Nottingham: Spokesman.
Sklair, L.
    1975   "The Struggle Against the Housing Finance Act," Socialist Register 1975: 250-292.
Taylor-Gooby, P.
    1985   *Public Opinion, Ideology and Social Welfare*, London: Routledge and Kegan Paul.

Volunteering as Linkage
in the Three Sectors

Jacqueline DeLaat

The public, the for-profit market, and the nonprofit sectors are often viewed as separate and somewhat competitive segments of society. Voluntary efforts are most commonly associated exclusively with the nonprofit sector. This paper argues that it is not useful to view the three sectors as inviolately separate, nor as competitive. Rather, the author suggests that the sectors are linked in a variety of ways. In particular, the activities of volunteers in all three sectors link them. These voluntary activities also help to reduce competition between the three sectors. Several distinct types of volunteer activities are discussed in support of this argument. First, the author examines the wide range of volunteer activities that occur outside the nonprofit sector. Volunteer activities occur in the public sector, related to campaigns, policy planning, policy implementation, and policy evaluation. Volunteer activities also occur in the for-profit market sector, often in connection with paid work roles. Volunteer activity in connection with work may be an expansion of the work role, related to professional advancement, or a form of work. The latter suggests a reformulation of volunteering as a variant of work activity, rather than something apart from paid work roles. Occurrence of volunteering in all three sectors questions the notion of clear conceptual separation between them. Individuals move freely between the three sectors, in both paid and unpaid roles. These individuals perceive commonalities of interest among the sectors. They bring understanding of one sector into the other two. They can propose solutions to conflicts between the sectors, because they are part of all the sectors. They carry information from one sector into the others. In all these ways, individuals moving between the three sectors of society, in both paid and unpaid roles, contribute to closer linkage of the sectors and reduced competition between them.

It is the thesis of this paper that volunteering as a social activity can serve an integrative function for society by linking the public governmental sector, the private for-profit market sector, and the private nonprofit voluntary sector.[1] Much current activity in these sectors increasingly calls into question the often assumed dichotomy between the public and private sectors of society. Another common assumption—that the public and private sectors are or ought to be essentially competitive in their relationships—is also challenged by current developments. These two major strands in theories of the public and private sectors are challenged here.

In this paper the *individual* level of analysis is of primary concern.[2] The central question here is: What do the activities of individuals in volunteering and voluntary organizations suggest about the separation between the three sectors and about competition or cooperation among them? Several distinct types of activities will be discussed.

Jacqueline DeLaat, Politics and Public Policy, Bethany College, Bethany, WV 26032.

I examine volunteer activities *outside* the nonprofit sector, and suggest that volunteering occurs in both the public and the profitmaking sector, as well as in the traditional voluntary organizations of the nonprofit sector, thus blurring or reducing the importance of separation between the sectors. I also suggest that many individuals now combine or integrate volunteering with paid work, in a variety of ways. This implies increasing connections between organizations, whether public or private. The individuals combining paid work (in whatever sector) with volunteering (in whatever sector) are performing key linkage functions between two, or even all three, sectors. Through these linkages, individuals are likely to contribute to reduction of the levels of competition between the sectors. As the sectors are increasingly linked, viewing them competitively becomes less useful. The assessment of particular volunteering behaviors, then, is directly related to the theoretical assumptions of separation and competition between the sectors.

My argument proceeds by an initial analysis of prevalent theories of the public and private sectors as they relate to volunteering, examining the notions of separation and competition between the sectors. Subsequently, a number of current developments related to individuals and volunteering with particular relevance to these two theoretical positions are examined.

BACKGROUND: SEPARATION AND COMPETITION BETWEEN PUBLIC AND PRIVATE SECTORS

A wealth of literature describes the actual and ideal relationship between the public and private sectors in the contemporary United States. I am particularly concerned here with that work which includes reference to the "third" or voluntary sector. The starting point for almost all of this literature is the demarcation of at least two, and usually three, distinct sectors of activity: the public or governmental sphere; the commercial or profitmaking segment of the private sector, and the private nonprofit sector, all of which are of interest here.

Definitions of the sectors vary, with the greatest variation in delineating the third sector. The profitmaking sector is generally presumed to be relatively self-explanatory, consisting of those organizations, primarily firms, which are privately owned, largely privately controlled (within limitations of law), and concerned overwhelmingly with the generation of profits for their owners. Similarly, the public sector is defined as consisting primarily of governmentally operated, politically responsible and controlled organizations, whose primary purpose is to provide quality goods and services determined necessary for the good of the entire society.

The voluntary nonprofit sector is usually presented as having as its objective the serving of other people, often using unpaid volunteers. It may be defined as performing necessary functions not related to profitmaking, and not provided or mandated by government (Zurcher, 1978; Smith, 1981). Voluntary organizations are not in the business of making money for anyone. Volunteers participate freely, though for a variety of reasons. The objectives of the organization contain some element of service, and frequently the activities are seen as supplemental to those of government.

Using these broad definitions, much of the theoretical work related to these three sectors proceeds in a comparative fashion, attempting to specify how these sectors differ from or resemble each other. For example, much work has centered around comparisons of the incentives or motivations for individual behavior that are important in the various sectors. Some compare motivations of employees in public and private organizations (Clark and Wilson, 1961). Others suggest differences in the way public and private employees view work, and in job satisfaction (Smith and Nock, 1980). The importance of material rewards in the profitmaking and public sectors is debated in this literature (Newstrom, Reif and Monczka, 1976; Foss, 1979). Findings on the motivations for volunteerism also vary (Smith, 1981; Van Til, 1983; Jenner, 1981). Motivations include wanting to help people, career enhancement, and enjoyment of the work. There is as well, a body of literature that suggests that human motivations are basically the same, regardless of the organizational setting (Maslow, 1954; Herzberg, 1967; Thayer, 1981). This work does not, however, contradict the assumption of boundaries between the sectors, but merely views it as a tangential issue.

Others have compared organizations in two or more of the sectors on the dimension of decision-making and authority structures. Some findings include: differences between voluntary organizations and profitmaking firms in decentralization of power and participation in decision-making (Knoke and Prensky, 1984); more cumbersome decision-making mechanisms in the public sector than in profitmaking firms (Simon, 1976); and similarity of management in public and private organizations (Denhardt, 1984). "Generic" organizational theorists, again, maintain that these patterns are similar in all formal organizations (Scott and Hart, 1979; Thayer, 1981).

While the notion of some separation between the sectors is central to theories of the public and proprietary sectors and the role of the third or voluntary sector, in recent work on the provision of social services there is an awareness of the intermingling of the public and nonprofit sectors. Most notably, work on "private federalism," on direct national grants to nonprofit organizations (Gilbert, 1975), and analysis of the Reagan budget cuts on the nonprofits (Demone and Gibelman, 1984; Salamon and Abrahamson, 1982) and of the overall effects of nonprofit acceptance of major public funding (Kramer, 1979) all indicate sensitivity to the notion of blurring of the lines between the public and nonprofit sectors. In much of this recent work, the theoretical focus moves beyond dichotomous or trichotomous comparison and generally takes one of two other approaches; either the new desired goal becomes the clearer reseparation of the sectors; or it is seen as necessary to specify more precisely what the relationships between or among the sectors ought to be. The language of "public/private partnerships," for example, falls in this latter category and it is in this theoretical niche that the present paper is most closely located.

A second major strand in the theory of public and private sector relationships, following the first theme of separation, is the notion that the sectors are or ought to be essentially competitive in their relationships (cf. Gronjberg, 1983). The nature of the competition between the sectors is variously seen as in some way beneficial to society; or, alternatively, as hostile or negative competition that is not in the common good. Within this theme of competition, one or another sector is seen as a superior in comparison to the others. There is, for example, a substantial body of theory that advocates increased reliance on the profitmaking sector in the provision of public services. Terms such as "privatization" and "public choice," have been applied to this movement. Its advocates assume certain specified superiorities of the profitmaking sector in comparison to the public sector (Savas, 1977). In essence, the privatization movement argues that the profitmaking sector is dominated by competition between firms. This is seen as having numerous benefits, including the adopting of the most efficient technology, efficient managing of personnel, and maintaining the lowest possible costs. Profitmaking firms are also seen as being more flexible and freer to manage all resources efficiently, because they are not bound by many of the political constraints of the public sector. Profitmaking firms, it is further argued, attract personnel superior to that in the public sector (Foss, 1979). The consumer also is said to benefit from the competition, by having a choice of providers.

The use of the profitmaking sector for public service also has its critics. Competition for profits is seen as a negative factor for a variety of reasons. Competition may cause private firms to skimp on services, reducing service quality (Fisk, Kiesling, and Muller, 1978; Sharkansky, 1980). It may lead to unfair personnel practices, graft and/or corruption in the pursuit of profits. Conflict of interest issues may be raised. In some cases, private provision may actually result in *higher* costs of public services, if the community is "at the mercy" of one or several private providers. A loss of public accountability and difficulties in monitoring service quality are additional problems cited by critics of both profitmaking firms and nonprofit organization as public service providers. As in the case of those seeing profitmaking firms as superior to public organizations, the critics also center their arguments on comparisons between the profitmaking and public sectors. The two are seen as competitive here as well, but the public sector in this instance is viewed as "winning" the implied competition with the profitmaking sector.

The literature on the nonprofit sector also evidences a similar analysis of and disagreement about competition between this and the other sectors. Advocates of the nonprofit or voluntary sector generally see it as superior in some respects to both the profitmaking and the public sectors (Kramer, 1981). Currently much attention centers on the relationship between the nonprofit and public governmental sectors. Again, the two are often analyzed as competitive with each other. Some see the competition in strongly negative terms (Nisbet, 1962) with the state tending to establish a state monopoly over all nonprofit purposes and functions[3] (Berger and Neuhaus, 1977). Others fear that, as the nonprofits increasingly perform public services with public dollars, they become too dependent upon that funding, and excessively subject to public sector dictates (Thomas, 1980). Defenders of the public sector, in contrast, argue that over-reliance on the nonprofits for public services reduces accountability. Fragmentation of service provision and monitoring problems are also mentioned by public sector critics of the nonprofits (Fisk, Kiesling and Muller, 1978).

A quite different theoretical position is advanced by some, including the present author. That is, the public and private sectors need not necessarily be viewed as separate or as competitive (Kramer, 1981). Public-private partnerships or sharing of responsibilities are increasingly suggested (Salamon and Abramson, 1982). This view of public and private as partners is borne out by the following analysis. I now turn my attention to current developments and activities, specifically in the nature of volunteering, which support the breakdown of separation between the sectors and provide evidence of increased cooperation between them.

VOLUNTEERING OUTSIDE THE VOLUNTARY SECTOR: IN AND FOR GOVERNMENT

Not all volunteering takes place in the nonprofit or private "voluntary sector" and only a portion of what goes on in the nonprofit sector is actual volunteering. Many in the sector are paid workers, especially professional social workers in voluntary social service agencies.[4] To the extent that volunteering also occurs in the public governmental and private profitmaking sectors, the presumed "lines" between three sectors may become softened or erased. The degree and nature of such volunteering is the first issue to be considered here in some detail.

Volunteer activity in the public sector is substantial and well documented (Ferris, 1984; Whitaker, 1980). Such activity takes a variety of forms and occurs at all levels of government: local, state, and federal. Citizens, acting in a volunteer capacity, participate in activities related to the formulation or planning of public policy in a range of ways.

Almost all domestic, federally funded programs, for example, now require some form of citizen of "community" consultation and input (Yin, 1973). This is true of all three levels of government. The citizen contribution to policymaking is carried out in a variety of ways, including boards totally composed of citizens and community representatives, or joint government-citizen planning boards. Or, the legislature may simply mandate community hearings. Area Councils on Aging, zoning hearings in local communities, and open hearings on the use of federal revenue sharing funds are a few examples of such mechanisms. Paid staff of nonprofit and profitmaking organizations, as well as employees of the public sector, are often also involved in these activities. They are not exclusively volunteer in nature. However, many private citizens participate in them as well, on a nonpaid basis, as volunteers.

Less direct, but perhaps equally important, are the volunteer activities of private citizens in political campaigns. The connection between partisan volunteer activity and policymaking is not always a direct one, but the literature indicates that at least some substantial portion of those who volunteer in campaigns do so out of concern for public issues and a desire to bring about some specific public policy outcome[5] (Sorauf, 1984). These volunteers are also, then, contributing, or attempting to contribute, to the formulation of public policy, albeit indirectly.

Further, some volunteering activity that occurs formally in the nongovernmental nonprofit sector nonetheless makes a contribution to government's choice of policies. For example, volunteering for labor union or other interest groups has an underlying intent of influencing the direction of public policy (Truman, 1971; Verba & Nie, 1972). Social advocacy takes place in voluntary social service agencies. To the extent that such activity provides new information, or useful alternatives, to the public sector, it is thereby an indirect, voluntary contribution to formulating public policy.

Volunteer contributions to the public sector are not limited to policy formulation. Individual citizens and groups of volunteers also perform numerous activities which are a part of implementation or execution of governmental policy (Edwards, 1980; Spiegel, 1980; Washnis, 1976). Those include participation in services delivered totally by volunteer groups, assisting public servants in the delivery of services, and volunteer activity in self-help organizations which indirectly reduce the need for higher levels of public services. A brief discussion of each of these three types of activities follows.

Some public services, in some locations, are entirely conducted by volunteer groups. Perhaps the best known example is the volunteer fire department or ambulance service. Some refer to these as "off-loaded" services, or services which government is successfully able to pass to the voluntary sector. The service being provided, is however one which, in most communities, is deemed a public necessity.

The activity of the individual volunteers, then, is a direct contribution to the public sector, even if it is technically performed in the "third" or nongovernmental nonprofit sector.

Some individuals volunteer for private, nonprofit organizations that are under contract, or reimbursed, for providing public services. For example, volunteers may serve medicare and medicaid patients in hospitals, deliver "meals on wheels," serve on boards of local social service agencies with government contracts for day care services, and so on. Here again the volunteering is done in the nonprofit sector, technically, but one beneficiary is the public sector, for whom the service is either less costly, of higher quality, or both, due to the presence and contribution of individual volunteers.

Many citizens also assist public employees in the delivery of services, or else perform services that government would probably have to perform if private citizens did not. Sometimes this involves actual presence in the program, such as volunteer teacher's aids in public classrooms or volunteer counselors in prisons. Other times citizens may also do part of the work independently in the course of their daily lives, again reducing the workload on the public employee, such as carrying refuse to the curb, rather than requiring its pickup at a more remote location. Parental investment of time working with children on homework and studies, some would argue, constitutes a form of voluntary assistance to the teacher and the process of public education. One sizeable aspect of this kind of "volunteering" that has received some attention is that done in families, primarily by women. Some of this work relieves the public sector from providing essential services, such as care of elderly and physically and mentally handicapped. Neighbors and friends also do some of this work.

Voluntary participation with or for public employees, then, takes a wide variety of direct or indirect forms. In some policy, notably public safety, for example, it is even argued that successful policy implementation would be impossible *without* such voluntary citizen participation.

Some programs require citizen help in identifying the need for and targets of particular public programs. In some cases, such as social security and unemployment compensation, citizens must apply to receive benefits. Presumably, despite ever more sophisticated "outreach" services of public agencies, there are still citizens eligible for services who might not receive them without other citizens informing them, on a voluntary basis, of their potential eligibility. Here again, a citizen volunteer may be performing a valuable contribution to the delivery of public services.

Further, citizens' voluntary requests for services, whether available or not, may often contribute to the defining of a public agency's workload (Whitaker, 1980). That is, numerous requests for services may lead to a change in the program itself. In addition, such requests are often central to a public program's survival or expansion, as they are used to document need for it with the legislature and the public. Simply by requesting services, then, a citizen may be contributing to public services in one of these ways.

The voluntary actions of citizens may also contribute to the process of policy and evaluation and reformulation: for example, many local governments rely upon citizens voluntarily reporting difficulties with services as a major means of monitoring service performance, especially in situations where the service is contracted out to private providers (Fisk, Kiesling and Muller, 1978). Presumably such complaints contribute, then to the improvement of services for the entire community. In addition, Whitaker and others have described a process of "mutual adjustment" which occurs between "street level bureaucrats" and citizens (Whitaker, 1980). Here again, the voluntary communication of private citizens may prove important in influencing the ways in which services are delivered and their overall quality. Education and law enforcement are frequently cited as areas in which such "mutual adjustment" between public servants and citizens is important to service quality.

Volunteering already exists in the public sector and makes a valuable contribution to the formulation, implementation and evaluation of public policy. Volunteers contribute through consultation with public officials, participation in campaigns, lobbying, assisting in delivering services, identifying the *need* for various services, and evaluating programs.

Volunteering behavior occurs in connection with the private profit-making sector, as well as the public governmental sector. In most cases, this volunteering is related in some way to the individual's paid work role. It is to the complex linkages between paid work and volunteering that attention is now turned.

VOLUNTEERING OUTSIDE THE VOLUNTARY SECTOR: IN AND FOR THE MARKET

The relationships between primary work roles and volunteering activity are varied and complex. At least four possible ways of viewing the paid work-volunteering connection are suggested: 1) volunteering is supplemental to primary work roles, and often compensates for needs not met in the work role situation (Henderson, 1982); 2) volunteering is *instrumental* to primary work roles, or helps in the achievement of career objectives (Gidron, 1978; Jenner, 1981); 3) volunteering is a form of *expanding* the work role by doing additional, unpaid labor somehow related to the work role; or, 4) volunteering is, in itself, a conscious work activity (Jenner, 1981). These relationships are possible regardless of the sector in which the paid work and volunteering take place. How one conceptualizes the relationship between volunteering and work has direct implications for the relationship between the governmental, voluntary nonprofit, and profitmaking sectors.

First, it is suggested that volunteering is supplemental to the primary work role, and often compensatory in nature (Henderson, 1982). This proposition, a common one, strengthens the notion of volunteering as something "apart" from the individual's "main" work, whether that be a paid career, or unpaid homemaking. Indeed, it has frequently been argued that the "traditional volunteer," was a married woman between the ages of 25 and 45, not working, with children in school, who compensated for the lack of certain opportunities in the homemaking role by becoming active in the voluntary sector. This conceptualization tends to reinforce the ideas that volunteering is primarily in the nonprofit sector, and apart from "work."

A different formulation sees volunteering, at times, as instrumental in achieving career objectives, as a way to eventually move from unpaid household work to paid work, or as a way to "move up" in business or in a paid job in government. Recent research suggests that increasing numbers of women in particular may be using volunteering as a vehicle for maintaining work contacts during an interrupted career, or to explore the possibility of new, paid careers (Gidron, 1978; Loeser, 1974; Jenner, 1981). Similarly, the tendency of corporations and law firms to strongly encourage executives and other employees to participate in community volunteer efforts suggests the value of volunteering in career prestige or advancement. In such situations, "the employee gains leadership skills, community contacts, and experience in working with people in all types of jobs . . . and also learn to work under pressure" (Beattie, 1985:22). Loaned executive programs, common in private, profitmaking firms, fall into this category; these involve the extensive assignment, often at corporate expense, of corporate executives to work with nonprofit or public agencies. Notice that often, in this type of relationship between paid work and volunteering, the individual crosses "sector" lines; that is, his or her paid work role may occur in the profitmaking sector, while the volunteering activity occurs in one of the other two.

Closely related to the instrumental category is that conceptualization of volunteering activity as expansion of the work role. Usually, this is seen as the individual's work activity somehow "carrying over" into a form of community involvement, which is often similar or related to the primary work role (Zurcher, 1978).

It is also possible, however, to see unpaid labor *on the job* as a form of volunteering, to see job related work that is *undercompensated* as volunteering activity. Smith (1982:23) suggests, for example:

> Being a volunteer is a matter of degree in regards to compensation. A low skilled Peace Corps "volunteer" receiving both expenses and a stipend may indeed not be a volunteer at all, but merely a low paid worker. In contrast a law school professor who foregoes private practice, either totally or partially, because of dedication to teaching and research on the law may be viewed as a quasi-volunteer, assuming an average academic salary.

This view would suggest that expanding one's job, without compensation, or intentionally foregoing a more lucrative career choice, may constitute a form of volunteering. This may be especially common in the non-profit sector:

> There is a kind of quasi-volunteerism among paid-staff non-profit organizations in general, at least to the extent that the general employment situation in the country is sufficiently flexible to permit non-profit organization paid employees to find jobs in business or government should they desire to (Smith, 1972:28).

Gatewood and Lahiff support the idea of some significant element of volunteerism in the work of nonprofit employees (Gatewood and Lahiff, 1977). However, there is no conceptual reason why such a formulation of volunteering should be limited to the nonprofit sector. Any individual, in any job in any sector, can expand his or her work beyond that for which s/he is being compensated.

Finally, volunteering may itself be viewed as primary work activity. As Jenner (1981:307) writes:

> The element of consistency and accepted responsibility (among "primary" volunteers) is worklike . . . For many women, volunteer work is an element in the life-long progression of jobs that makes up a career.

If work is defined in a broad fashion as "exertion of effort to accomplish something," certainly the consistent, frequent, disciplined efforts of many volunteers qualify. As Astin (1984:119) suggests, "virtually all adults, male and female, engage in some form of work behavior, whether it be actual paid employment, volunteer work, or what I will term in this essay 'family work.'" Further, there is much common ground in the motivations behind much "volunteering" and "work," as well as in the satisfactions derived from the two. As Astin further argues, the needs of "survival, pleasure and contribution" can explain most work behavior. Even if, as in some definitions, one rules out "survival" oriented behavior as volunteering, clearly both "pleasure" and "contribution" needs can be satisfied through both what is typically referred to as "work" and volunteering activity.

This latter formulation is a useful one. If volunteering is seen as a *form* of work activity, rather than as something clearly apart from work, what becomes important is conceptualizing the conditions under which various types of work activity appear most appropriate for the individual. The organizational context, (governmental, profitmaking, nonprofit) does not then, *per se*, identify whether or not the activity is "work" or "pleasure/contribution" in its orientation. The nature of the linkage between paid work and volunteering changes, with volunteering seen, as homemaking has come to be, as a *variant* of work, rather than a form of nonwork. As such, then, volunteering serves the entire gamut of functions, and is capable of meeting the same needs, as work role behavior. Our entire perspective on it thus changes from that of an "extra" or separate activity, to one that is an integral part of the individual's worklife and/or career.

IMPLICATIONS

Much of the work on theories of the public and private sectors has stressed the concepts of separation and competition between the sectors. Increased institutional linkages between the sectors have been cited by some as evidence of the declining usefulness of the concept of clear separation between them. Calls for "partnerships" between or among the sectors, in a wide variety of endeavors, have also suggested the declining utility of the emphasis on competition.

The analysis here adds further weight to these arguments. Volunteering activity in the society increasingly occurs in all three sectors and, for the individual, volunteering is often directly linked with paid work roles or is itself a kind of work. Both of these trends have clear implications for separation and competition between the sectors.

Clear lines of separation between the three sectors seem to be contradicted by the occurrence of volunteering in all of them. Volunteering in all three sectors may contribute to the reduction of tensions and competition among or between the sectors. Individuals combining paid work and volunteering in more than one sector may help in this regard. These tensions may include a perception of the other sector as hostile, as is frequently clear in the communication of profitmaking individuals and firms about government, for example. Differences in values and goals, norms, and expectations, touched upon earlier, may also exist between organizations in the various sectors, creating some tension. Often there is fear or mistrust of the motives of the other sector, which is commonly a result of lack of information about or understanding of the other. All of these contribute to the impression of clear differences and separation between the sectors, and increase feelings of competition.

The occurrence of volunteering in all three sectors happens because the needs volunteering satisfies can be met in organizations in all three sectors. Motivations for volunteering, as mentioned earlier, vary tremendously between individuals and in various circumstances. However, it is clear that many of these motivations—desire to contribute, wanting to help others, career enhancement, enjoyment of the task it-self—can be met in governmental as well as profitmaking and "voluntary" organiza-tions. The notion of clear separation, then, based on the idea that one sector is for the public good or for making money and the third for helping others, collapses.

Individuals concerned about a particular issue in the society can contribute to its resolution or mitigation in all three sectors, whether in a paid or unpaid capacity. As an example, consider the person whose major concern is the improvement of educa-tion. He or she may work in a training, consulting, or personnel capacity as paid employment, in the profitmaking or the nonprofit sector and may expand his/her job through additional, unpaid efforts in the employer organization. The individual may also serve or the board of otherwise do unpaid volunteering in nonprofit com-munity organizations related in some way to education, such as scouting, YWCA, a day care center, and so on. In the public sector, the individual may be active in interest groups lobbying for educational change, work for political candidates who espouse education as a major issue, serve on a school board, or volunteer in some other capacity in a public school.

This individual is, in all these activities, focused on the same or similar concerns. All these organizations, in all three sectors, share some concern and involvement in the educational issue. The notion, then, of some commonality of interests between the public and private sectors emerges. The individual, perceiving this common ground, moves freely between the sectors. Thus, the occurrence of volunteering behavior in all three sectors reduces the clear lines of separation between them.

How, more specifically, do volunteers moving between the sectors, in paid and unpaid roles, help reduce these tensions? Likert's concept of "linking pins" and other work on transorganizational processes and overlapping memberships, is helpful here (Likert, 1967). The basic relevant notion is that individuals, through their overlapping memberships in profitmaking, nonprofit, and governmental organizations provide a variety of benefits that relate to the problems of hostility, mistrust, lack of informa-tion and understanding, and alienation or separation between the sectors discussed previously.

First, and most obviously, the individuals with roles in more than one sector, paid or unpaid, bring information about one sector into the other. This helps to defuse or belie the most common, often inaccurate, "myths" each sector may hold about the other. Suspicions that public servants are not hardworking, for example, or that private sector employees are concerned solely with profits, become less credible when one or more individuals have firsthand knowledge of the other sector. Such knowledge may reduce this kind of misconception in both groups, taking some of the feeling of the other as "enemy" or rival out of the interaction process.

As an example of how this works, consider the instance of a small, relatively isolated, liberal arts college, staffed by more or less "typical" academics, concerned primarily with teaching and their own disciplines. A group of corporate executives is formed, on a voluntary basis, from nearby cities, with two purposes: to participate in continuing education programs the college will provide on current issues in the society; and, secondly, to interact with faculty in this and other settings, providing up-to-date information about corporate activities. The corporate executives in this case bring firsthand experience of the profitmaking sector into the nonprofit (aca-demic) one. It will be unusual if the academic stereotypes of "corporate types" are not to some degree influenced by contact with the executives, and vice-versa. The corporate notion of academics as "ivory tower" individuals may well be defused by the relevance of the educational activities being provided. Valuable linkage is being provided by the corporate volunteers in this instance, one benefit of which is reduced levels of misinformation on both sides.[6]

Volunteers and paid workers moving between the sectors may also reduce the levels of conflict between and among them. which in turn affects the perception of the sectors as competitive. Coleman has noted that conflicts become most acute when issues become polarized, so that individuals or groups become identified with out of two opposing "sides," exactly as many theorists have pictured the separate, competitive relations between the public, profitmaking, and nonprofit sectors. If, however, there are many people moving between the sectors, these individuals experience the most conflict, since they are pressured from both directions. The common response of individuals in this situation is to try to reduce the conflicting pressures. In extreme cases, of course, the individual may "opt out" of one sector or the other, removing the cross pressures. More likely, especially if the individual wants to continue to participate in both sectors, is the attempt by the "linking" individual to suggest compromise or adjustment to one or both of the groups involved. When these are accepted, then, the degree of conflict and competition is lessened.

Thayer's work on transorganizational processes suggests an even more complete formulation of this type of possibility. He describes what has been called "creative bargaining" between groups, which contains these five elements:

1. Getting a sharply defined perception of the essential aspect of the conflict;
2. Developing a disturbing concern for the satisfaction of opposing interests;
3. Discovering new possible aims or interests, in which conflicting ones can be absorbed to the larger advantage of all;
4. Embodying the new aims in a practical program;
5. Expressing all ideas used throughout the process in ways which enable everyone to identify deficiencies in those ideas as they are now used (Thayer, 1981:137).

Imagine how this type of scenario occurs, being facilitated by the movement of individuals functioning in all three sectors, in a variety of paid and volunteer roles. Such individuals contribute to sharpened perceptions of the *true* areas of disagreement between the sectors, since they have firsthand knowledge of both. Experiencing cross-pressures from the two sectors, these individuals are very personally interested in satisfying the needs or demands of each. To do so reduces any personal value conflict arising out of multiple participation.

The third element, the discovery of new possible aims or interests that solve or reduce the conflict, is also facilitated by individuals moving among the sectors. Able to see (and indeed share) the values and expectations of *both* sectors in which s/he participates, the individual is more likely than those participating exclusively in one sector to see common, overriding interests and to point them out. Such linking individuals are also more apt to be practical and realistic, knowing the limitations, operating procedures, and capabilities of both sectors, and communicating these back and forth. Finally, the last point, the avoidance of outworn ideas, has already been suggested. Individuals moving among the sectors are unlikely to cling to or express outdated stereotypes or myths when their own experience suggests otherwise.

Such a process, with overlapping participation (paid and unpaid) between the public and private sectors at the heart, has much potential as a source of creativity and innovation. It brings to each sector heterogenous points of view and a variety of information and values. Volunteers moving among the sectors, and combining paid work and volunteering in all three sectors, are uniquely situated to link the sectors in this fashion. Indeed, the increasing occurrence of such behaviors as volunteering in all sectors and combining paid work and volunteering, in all sectors, may already be contributing to some of the literature cited earlier, that recognizes that it's not useful theoretically to view the sectors separately.

Some suggest that the quality of relations between any two groups may be expected to depend on the degree to which they have members in common (Cartwright and Zander, 1968). At one extreme is the condition of disjoint membership where no one is a member of both groups. When two such groups come into contact with each other, the possibilites of conflict, competition, and misinformation would seem to be almost limitless. At the other extreme, all members of one group are in the other, and relations between the two will depend to a considerable degree upon the position of the subgroup within the inclusive one. Between these extremes are the many cases in which groups share some unspecified proportion of members in common, such as have been discussed here.

The individual who moves between the governmental, profitmaking, and nonprofit sectors, then, potentially contributes substantially to reducing the degree of conflict and competition among them. More and more individuals are doing this. Such individuals carry with them the values and understandings common to each sector. In the event of real, as opposed to imagined, conflict between sectors, these individuals may uniquely contribute to reduction of tensions, hostility, and competition by contributing their understandings and experience of both "sides." The additional fact that both paid work and volunteering now occur in all three sectors also suggests that not only competition, but clear conceptual separation between the sectors is also of declining utility in understanding relations between public and private. The individual volunteer, then, make a potentially significant contribution to reduced tensions between the public and private sectors, and possibly, the improved performance of both.

NOTES

The author wishes to express her appreciation to Professor Susan Ostrander, for invaluable suggestions and helpful criticism through several drafts in preparation of this paper.

1. This thesis is similar to the commonly advanced "mediation thesis," or the idea that voluntary organizations connect the individual to the large, bureaucratic and often impersonal organizations of the market and of government. Voluntary organizations are seen as valuable partially because of the integrative function they may serve in the lives of individuals, who might otherwise be alienated from the other organizations which dominate their lives (Pollock, 1982).
2. There are many institutional linkages between the public and the profitmaking and nonprofit sectors. Increased reliance on both profitmaking and nonprofit organizations in the areas of public service provision is one example. Contracting out services to forprofit and nonprofit groups has expanded tremendously in recent years. Contracting is now used in all the social services, in addition to the traditional areas of defense contracting, construction, etc., and is also employed for many of the traditional "housekeeping" functions of local government. Contracting *between* governments is also on the increase. See, for example, Fisk, Kiesling and Muller (1976); Sharkansky (1980); and Savas (1977). Similarly, the turning over of formerly public functions completely to the private sector, with citizens choosing their own provider, is on the increase. Finally, proposed and actual "mixed" systems have received wide attention, provision systems in which both public and private services are available and

the client may choose among them. The literature in public choice and privatization of services argues that the private sector may be used as an *alternative* to direct public provision of services, offering consumer-clients a choice of providers; or that the private provider may *replace* the public sector in providing the service. For an introduction see Mueller (1979). Similarly, the linkages involved in the increased public funding of nonprofit organizations (and publically financed loans to profitmaking ones) signify new organizational connections among the three sectors. Resulting issues of accountability, independence, flexibility, and conflicting roles are relevant to the theoretical points addressed here, though are not the primary concern.

3. Some point out the tendency for twentieth century political leaders to advance this negative view of the state, as well. See Salamon and Abramson (1982) and Karl (1984).

4. The idea that the connection between volunteerism and pay is a complex one is discussed well by Smith (1981) and will be addressed more fully in a later section of the paper.

5. Motivations for political participation are as varied as those for volunteering in general. Among others see Sorauf (1982), especially Ch. 7; Angus Campbell et al. (1960), especially Ch. 6; and Verba and Nie (1972).

6. Such a group is the "Bethany College Leadership Center's Associates Council" at Bethany College in West Virginia.

REFERENCES

Astin, H.S.
    1984   "The Meaning of Work in Women's Lives," *Counselling Psychology* 12 (304): 117-26.
Beattie, L.E.
    1985   "The New Voluntarism." *Business and Economic Review* 31: 22-3.
Berger, P.L. and R.J. Neuhaus
    1977   *To Empower People.* Washington, D.C.: American Enterprise Institute.
Campbell, Angus, et al.
    1960   *The American Voter.* New York: Wiley & Sons.
Cartwright, Darwin and Alvin Zander
    1968   *Group Dynamics: Research and Theory.* New York: Harper & Row.
Clark, P.B. and J.Q. Wilson
    1961   "Incentive Systems: A Theory of Organizations." *Administrative Science Quarterly* 6(2): 129-66.
Demone, H.W. and M. Gibelman
           "Reaganomics: Its Impact on the Voluntary, Not-for Profit Sector." *Social Work* 29: 421-7.
Denhardt, Robert B.
    1984   *Theories of Public Organization.* Belmont, California: Brooks/Cole.
Edwards, G. C.
    1980   *Implementing Public Policy.* Washington, D.C.: Congressional Quarterly Press.
Ferris, J.M.
    1984   "Coprovision of Public Services." *Public Administration Review* 44: 324-33.
Fisk, D.D., H. Kiesling, and T. Muller
    1976   *Private Provision of Public Services: An Overview.* Washington, D.C.: Urban Institute.
Foss, G.C.
    1979   "The Compensation Treatment of Public Executives." *Public Personnel Management* 74-87.
Gatewood, R.G. and J. Lahiff
    1977   "Differences in Importance of Job Factors in Voluntary and Profit Organizations." *Journal of Voluntary Action Research* 6 (3-4): 133-138.
Gidron, B.
    1978   "Volunteer Work and Its Rewards." *Volunteer Administration* 11 (3): 18-32.
Gilbert, C.
    1975   "Welfare Policy." In *Policies and Policy Making: Handbook of Political Science.* F. Greenstein and N. Polsby (ed.). Reading, Mass. Addison Wesley Publishing Co.
Gronbjerg, K.A.
    1983   "Private Welfare: Its Future in the Welfare State." *American Behavioral Scientist* 26: 773-93.
Henderson, K.A.
    1982   "Motivations and Perceptions of Volunteerism as a Leisure Activity." *Journal of Leisure Research* 13: 208-18.
Herzberg, F.E. et. al.
    1967   *The Motivation to Work.* New York: John Wiley & Sons, Inc.
Jenner, J.R.
    1981   "Volunteerism as an Aspect of Women's Work Lives." *Journal of Vocational Behavior* 19 (3): 302-314.

Karl, B.D.
    1984   "Lo, the Poor Volunteer: An Essay on the Relation Between History and Myth." *Social Service Review* 58:493-522.
Knoke, D. and D. Prensky
                "What Relevance Do Organization Theories Have For Voluntary Organizations?" *Social Science Quarterly* 65: 3-20.
Kramer, R.M.
    1979   "Public Fiscal Policy and Voluntary Agencies in the Welfare State." *Social Service Review* 52: 1-14.
    1981   *Voluntary Agencies in the Welfare State.* Berkeley and Los Angeles, California: University of California Press, Ltd.
Likert, Rensis
    1967   *The Human Organization.* New York: McGraw-Hill
Loeser, H.
    1974   *Women, Work and Volunteering.* Boston: Beacon Press.
Maslow, A.
    1954   *Motivation and Personality.* New York: D. Van Nostrand.
Mueller, Dennis C.
    1979   *Public Choice.* Cambridge: The Cambridge University Publications.
Newstrom, J.W., W.E. Reif, and R.M. Monczka
    1976   "Motivating the Public Employee: Fact v. Fiction." *Public Personnel Management.*
Nisbet, R.A.
    1961   *Community and Power.* New York: Oxford University.
Pollock, P.H.
    1982   "Organizations and Alienation: The Mediation Hypothesis." *Sociological Quarterly* 23 (2): 143-55.
Salamon, L.B. and A.J. Abramson
    1982   "The Nonprofit Sector," in J.L. Palmer and I.V. Sawhill (eds.). *The Reagan Experiment.* Washington, D.C.: Urban Institute.
Savas, E.S.
    1977   "An Empirical Study of Competition in Municipal Service Delivery." *Public Administration Review* 717-24.
Scott, W.G. and D.K. Hart
    1979   *Organizational America.* Boston: Houghton Mifflin.
Sharkansky, Ira
    1980   "Policy-Making and Service Delivery on the Margins of Government: The Case of Contractors." *Public Administration Review* 40: 116-123.
Simon, H.A.
    1976   *Administrative Behavior,* 3rd ed. New York: The Free Press.
Smith, D.H.
    1981   "Altruism, Volunteers and Volunteerism." *Journal of Voluntary Action Research,* 101 (Jan.-Mar.) 21-36.
Smith, M.P. and S.L. Nock
    1980   "Social Class and the Quality of Work Life in Public and Private Organizations." Journal of Social Issues 36: 4.
Sorauf, F.C.
    1984   *Party Politics in America,* 5th Edition. Boston: Little Brown.
Spiegel, H.
    1980   "Volunteers in the Federal System: Who? What? Why?" *National Civil Review* 69: 185-90.
Thayer, F.C.
    1981   *An End to Hierarchy and Competition: Administration in the Post-Affluent World.* New York: Franklin Watts.
Thomas, William V.
    1980   "Volunteerism in the Eighties." *Editorial Research Reports,* p. 907-24.
Truman, D.B.
    1971   *The Governmental Process,* 2nd ed. New York: Alfred A. Knopf.
Van Til, J.
    1983   "Mixed Motives: Residues of Altruism in an Age of Narcissism." Pp. 383-400 in Independent Sector, Working Papers for The Spring Research Forum. Washington, D.C.: Independent Sector.
Verba, S. and N.H. Nie
    1972   *Participation in America.* New York: Harper & Row.
Washnis, G.
    1976   Citizen Involvement in Crime Prevention. Lexington, Mass.: D.C. Heath and Co.

Whitaker, G.
    1980   "Coproduction: Citizen Participation in Service Delivery." *Public Administration Review* 40: 240-246.
Yin, R.K., et al.
    1973   *Citizen Organization: Increasing Client Control Over Services.* Santa Monica, California: Rand Corporation.
Zurcher, L.A.
    1978   "Ephemeral Roles, Voluntary Action and Voluntary Associations." 73 (4): 65-74.

Privacy and Confidentiality as Obstacles to Interweaving Formal and Informal Social Care: The Boundaries of the Private Realm

Martin Bulmer

Community care provides a setting in which both public, formal social care and private, informal, social care have the potential to complement one another in meeting the needs of dependent persons. The theoretical implications of "interweaving" formal and informal care are considered in the light of concerns about privacy and confidentiality which may limit such potential collaboration. The obstacles to those working in welfare agencies tapping informal networks are highlighted. Empirical evidence from the study of neighbors and neighborhood care is presented to show that drawing boundaries around a private sphere belonging to the self and the family is universal and that various defences are erected against gossip and the local sharing of personal information. The implications of such privacy concerns for interweaving are considered in terms of balance theory, the substitutability of carers, the circumstances in which information may be shared with third parties, the use of natural leaders, and problems of professional responsibility. The need to rethink the boundaries of the private realm is suggested.

Social care may be provided in a variety of different ways. It may be provided by governmental agencies, by voluntary agencies run in a formal bureaucratic manner, by for-profit commercial enterprises, and by informal supporters, principally family members but also neighbors and friends. The care provided may be of varying types ranging from generalized social support, visiting at home, providing transport, doing shopping, to the more intimate personal "tending" of the dependent and immobile (cf. Parker, 1981). This article, drawing on British experience and research, considers the forms of the relationship between more formal and more informal types of social care and the implications for that relationship of considerations of personal privacy, which have been unduly neglected.

The theoretical issue addressed here concerns the division between informal (private) care and the various types of formal (public) care for groups such as the dependent elderly at home. "Public" care in this paper refers to formally provided bureaucratically organized services, both governmental and formal voluntary.[1] "Private" care refers to informal care provided by kin, neighbors, and friends. Though kin presently accounts for the majority of such care, if community care is to mean more than care by female kin (Abrams 1977:84), it must be able to mobilize informal networks which exist in the local community. More emphasis is therefore given here to informal care by neighbors and friends than by kin.

Martin Bulmer, London School of Economics and Political Science, Department of Social Science and Administration, Houghton Street, London WC2A 2AE, Great Britain.

The questions addressed here are: How is the boundary drawn between different types of caring? What are the implications for the drawing of boundaries for conceptions of the private realm (as defined here) and for the privacy of those being cared for and their families?

Community care is Britain is currently attracting increasing attention (cf. Walker, 1982). A major area of interest on which the discussion here centers concerns the care of the elderly and other dependent minorities such as the physically and mentally handicapped in their own homes in the community rather than in institutions. Approximately nineteen out of every twenty elderly persons over the age of 65 in Britain lives in their own home, so this type of care constitutes a very significant form of social support (For examples of work on caring and informal networks see Abrams, 1980; Bulmer, 1985 and 1986:88-96; Gottlieb, 1981; Price, 1981; Warren, 1981; and Wenger, 1984).

This paper is based on the premise that drawing on informal networks for social care is more problematic than has currently been recognized. Much of the current literature on the subject does not take sufficient account of the nature and integrity of informal care. (See for example, the 1982 British Barclay Report into the contemporary roles of social workers. See also Maguire, 1983). Other are more aware of the potential difficulties (such as Allan, 1983 and Darvill, 1985:258).

There is currently increasing interest in Britain in the possibilities of "interweaving" formal and informal care: by this is meant the scope for providing care through formal, governmental channels, through voluntary activity, and through the informal sector in ways which are complementary to one another. The metaphor of a "continuum" of care is commonly invoked, and it is argued that the provision of care at different points on the continuum, far from being mutually exclusive, tends to be mutually reinforcing (cf. Bayley 1973:343). Dissenting voices have pointed out that far from being complementary, there may be a "principled antithesis" between formal and informal care, with a particular tendency for the former to colonize the latter and in the process change its character. Maintaining the balance between public and private worlds is difficult, with a marked tendency for the public sphere to take over the private (cf. Abrams 1978; 1984; 1986, ch. 11. See also Froland 1980).

One major source of resistance to interweaving formal and informal care has been found to be the privacy concerns of networks of families, neighbors and friends (Robinson and Abrams, 1977; Robinson, 1981). That concern is the major focus of this paper.

PRIVACY IN INFORMATION EXCHANGE BETWEEN
FORMAL AND INFORMAL NETWORKS

Privacy may best be defined in terms of the control of information about oneself. It is the "claim of individuals, groups or institutions to determine for themselves when, how and to what extent information is communicated to others" (Westin 1970:7). This implies that there will be some disclosure of information, and the individual who provides it should decide the nature and extent of such disclosure, or indeed whether to make the disclosure at all. Privacy is thus an interactional concept—it refers to the privacy of individual or group vis-à-vis other individuals or groups, and to information transfer between them. Confidentiality, on the other hand, refers to the conditions under which such information, once communicated to another person, group, or institution, is held, assessed, and available to third parties. It refers to the conditions of use and disclosure of information, once it has been made known to another.

Most discussion of privacy and confidentiality in the professions has been concerned with the practical, moral, and ethical issues that arise, given that some sharing of information among professionals and other workers in public agencies about clients is almost unavoidable. Hospitals and GPs create medical records to which more than one person has access; social workers both create, file and hold records and conduct case conferences. If information is to be exchanged with other colleagues, there must be adequate safeguards (cf. Barclay 1982:183).

A dimension of privacy and confidentiality in social service provision and social care which has received little attention to date, and which is of major importance in relation to community care, is the passing of information between the person cared-for, staff of a public agency, and other members of the public with whom the person cared-for shares membership of a common primary group. ("Primary groups" refers to face-to-face, relatively permanent, informal social groupings without an instrumental purpose, of which kinship groups, friends and neighbors are the classic examples (Litwak and Szelenyi 1969).

The exchanges involved may be of four types: (1) between the person cared-for and an agency staff member, (2) between the person cared-for and a relation or a friend or a neighbor, without the agency staff member being involved, (3) between the agency staff member and a relation, or a friend or a neighbor of the client, without the person cared-for being involved, and (4) between all three parties, with the knowledge and involvement of all three. While the first clearly falls within the realm of formal care, and the second within the sphere of informal care, the third and fourth fall in between (or in *both* public and private spheres).

Privacy and confidentiality issues are of particular salience in relation to "interweaving" formal and informal care, yet appear to have received little attention. Their discussion in the social work literature, for example, is almost entirely on the conditions under which confidences between client and professional worker may be shared with other professionals either in the interests of the client or on a "need to know" basis (BASW 1971; Hill 1978; Wilson 1978). Less attention is paid to the integrity of the informal care network and the interests of its members.

EMPIRICAL EVIDENCE

Research on neighbors and neighborhood care

Where does the "private" informal network draw its boundaries? One entrée to the issue is provided by research on neighbors and neighborhood care, where there are research findings relevant to the impact of privacy concerns upon informal networks and primary groups. The long line of studies upon neighboring, neighborliness, and local social care (cf. Robinson and Abrams 1977; Robinson and Robinson 1981) shows in a number of cases that linking in to informal social networks is likely to run up against resistance due to privacy concerns.

An early study by Leo Kuper in Coventry (1953) paid particular attention to privacy among neighbors. One reason for desiring privacy was to restrain gossip about oneself and one's family. In the working-class council estate studied, gossip was (he suggested) a means of sociability, a way of regulating status reputation, and a form of social control, particularly through fear of what neighbors would say. Local residents emphasized that gossip could be malicious and improved in the telling, a source of local conflict, and a threat to privacy.

One of the chief findings was that respondents varied a great deal in their need for privacy. People in the area also distinguished between their neighbors, and were more reserved with some than with others, an important point in attempts to mobilize informal networks. There was also differential sensitivity to the privacy needs of others among neighbors. There was wide variation in the practice of popping in and out of each other's houses. Some saw visiting as a threat to privacy, through neighbors getting to know your business, or as likely to breed familiarity, which in turn threatened privacy. The men visited other houses much less than the women. There was reluctance among both men and women to form friendships with neighbors. All of these findings suggest the fine gradations of proximity and distance, familiarity and reserve, through which local social relationships are conducted.

Ten years later, H.E. Bracey's study of neighbors on new estates in Britain and the U.S. showed a similar concern with the preservation of privacy. English respondents asked to define a "good neighbor" placed definite limits upon the degree of friendliness that they would welcome. There was also resistance among working class respondents to the practice of calling into each other's houses, and particularly to the practice of borrowing small quantities of food or household items, as opposed to garden tools.

> English householders clearly recognised that neighbours constitute a threat to privacy . . . Although, in their new homes, the physical barriers were slender in the extreme, in most people the mental barrier which they had grown up with remained as robust as ever. . . . (T)hey fear 'noseyness' from neighbours, by which they mean that the neighbours might discover, by accident if not by design, information about the family way of life which they would not especially like communicated to others (Bracey 1964:80, 85).

The "Good Neighbor"

Studies of neighboring have shown that this emphasis on the family keeping itself to itself is a common element in definitions of a "good neighbor" and expectations about how neighbors should treat one another. Kuper (1953:64) elicited definitions such as "don't believe in going into each other's houses," "keep themselves to themselves," "respect your privacy," and "not nosey." A study of the social effects of planned rehousing by Vere Hole reached very similar conclusions.

> Discussion showed that tenants conceived the ideal neighbour in slightly contradictory terms. Great value was placed on helpfulness, such as practical assistance in times of illness, or keeping an eye on children when the mother was out. At the same time there was an almost equal emphasis on withdrawal. The ideal neighbour was neither too interfering nor too intimate and did not repeat confidences (Hole 1959:167).

This balance between the positive and negative sides of neighboring has obvious relevance to the question of to what extent informal networks can be mobilized to provide social care. Insufficient attention has been paid to what people see as the hazards of neighboring. As one Greenleigh respondent told Young and Willmott (1972:148), "The policy here is don't have a lot to do with each other (the neighbors) then there won't be any trouble." A study in Buxton, Derbyshire, carried out by Kingston Polytechnic in 1971, showed this clearly. A large proportion of respondents in both middle and working class areas agreed with the statement "It doesn't pay to get too friendly with neighbors," and disagreed with the statement "A neighbor is someone you can tell your troubles to." Definitions of a "good neighbor" balanced helpfulness and friendliness with respecting each other's privacy.

A small-scale study carried out by Colin and Mog Ball in the late 1970s in seven localities in England and Wales provides further evidence of the importance of recognizing the balance between involvement and reserve in contacts between neighbors. Specifically concerned with the scope for promoting neighborhood care, they emphasized the delicacy of the balance between the two.

> We did not interview one person who did not express a need for privacy and for control over 'their' territory. But at the same time a few yards from the front door is that shared territory—the garden path, the street, the corner shop—that belongs to no-one yet belongs to everyone. 'Neighbourliness' requires the preservation of a balance (Ball and Ball 1982:19).

The example shows very clearly how difficult it may be to draw on the resources offered by informal networks without changing those networks in the process.

Philip Abrams on Neighboring

The most substantial recent work in the area of neighborhood care is that of the late Philip Abrams (1977; 1978; 1980; 1984; 1985; Bulmer 1986). The first phase of this research was concerned with informal patterns of neighboring in six streets in different parts of the country. These studies provide ample evidence of the extent to which neighbors wish to keep themselves to themselves. Systematic evidence was gathered upon respondents' definitions of what they understood by a "good neighbor" in the informal sense of the word. A large proportion of responses referred to reserve or privacy as an element in their definition (Bulmer 1986:44-82). Reference to "nosey" and "interfering" neighbors, or those "always in and out" appeared in all the street studies. Relations with neighbors were understood as involving distance and privacy as much as friendliness or helpfulness.

Referring to "the guarded quality so characteristic of neighboring," Philip Abrams also emphasized the difference between friendliness—commonly cited as a characteristic of the good neighbor—and friendship. Friendliness is a desirable characteristic of casual interaction, involving a restricted conviviality which flourishes by carefully respecting each party's right to preserve the privacy of a "back stage" realm. Friendship involves much deeper commitment, and involves progressively breaking down the barriers of privacy so essential to mere friendliness and steadily increasing the "secrets" with which one is willing to trust the other. The longer a relationship is established the more likelihood there is of mutual confidence.

> Since a primary relationship involves the right of one person to invade the privacy of the other, most people will require some assurance that such a right will not be abused before

entering into such a relationship. This assurance is gained through experience with the person (Shulman 1967:60).

Between neighbors, this barrier of reserve may never be broken down.

So far as neighborliness was concerned, Abrams suggested that confidentiality was one of its cornerstones, and mutual respect for privacy the basis of tolerable neighboring. It was put in an extreme form by the respondent who wrote a note to the interviewer: "We don't want our neighbors talking about us so we're sorry we won't talk to you about them." Such instinctive feelings about the boundaries between neighbors, and the reserve which is an integral part of the relationship, deserves much closer attention when the scope of "interweaving" formal and informal services is being considered.

Gossip

These defenses erected between neighbors, to protect the privacy of the family, have considerable implications for the mobilization of informal networks in the way advocated by Barclay. Consider the social significance of gossip. Gossip is a phenomenon which Barclay does not discuss. It may be defined as informal personal talk about other people who are absent (Bok 1984:91), their conduct, and moral evaluation of that conduct (Bailey 1971:288). As anthropologists and psychologists have shown (cf. Gluckman 1963; Paine 1967; Rosnow and Fine 1976), gossip is a network of communication and a means of testing and reinforcing judgments about human nature. It helps to assimilate and interpret bits of information about the lives of others. It bridges the gap between the private and the public worlds, and reduces reliance upon what people themselves wish to reveal. Gossip is a feature of informal personal networks linking kin, neighbors or friends.

Historically, gossip between and about neighbors has been a potent social force, both as a form of communication between neighbors and a means of social control. Robert Roberts describes how in Edwardian Salford, the matriarchs in the community guarded the conscience of the local community.

> From early morning to an hour before midnight, little groups. . . . formed and faded, trading with goodwill, candour or cattishness the detailed gossip of a closed society. Over a period the health, honesty, conduct, history and connections of everyone in the neighbourhood would be examined. Each would be criticised, praised, censured openly or by hint and finally allotted by tacit consent a position on the social scale (Roberts 1973:42).

Much of the talk was practical and useful, not merely malicious and scandalmongering. But everyone's behavior was minutely watched. The Balls' research confirmed the continuing importance of gossip (1982:42).

Such traditional neighborhoods of strongly bonded, locally based networks based upon isolation, closure, and economic deprivation have virtually disappeared today. Philip Abrams, however, identified two contemporary survivals: close kinship relations between parents and children, and gossip, "the more or less idle, more or less benevolent or malicious talk in which people engage in their efforts to construct a known and comfortable socio-spatial setting for their own lives" (1980:18). The balance between helpfulness and reserve reflects in part the power of gossip. "Neighbors are called upon in times of trouble; but they possess a lot of potentially dangerous information, and they are not inhibited in the use of this information to the same degree as kinsmen. Neighbors are thus a present help and a potential danger" (Heppenstall 1971:151).

Increasing reliance upon informal networks to mobilize social care would have to take account of the existence of gossip, and the ways in which this might affect what people were willing to reveal. Sharing of personal information about oneself with others in the immediate neighborhood might be deemed an unacceptable price to pay for receiving care or support.

THE IMPLICATIONS FOR THE THEORY AND PRACTICE OF INTERWEAVING

These instances of the sensitivity of the private sphere relate primarily to neighbors as carers. They are an example of the type of boundary issues that can arise in the development of community care. Some of the more direct implications for a theory of interweaving public and private care will now will be considered. In the first place, distinctions have to be made between different types of informal network of support, between those linking the person cared-for with close kin, with more distant kin, with friends or with neighbors. Moreover, the term "care" needs examining more closely. Informal social networks may be better at providing some types of care than others. A more differentiated understanding of varieties of support and help is needed.

Balance Theory and Alternatives

Theoretically, more attention needs to be given to the ways in which the public and private sectors interact. An early formulation was Litwak and Meyer's (1966) balance theory of coordination between bureaucratic organizations and community primary groups. Recognizing that bureaucratic structures and informal groups differ markedly, social scientists have tended to emphasise the insulation and incompatibilities between at one extreme the Weberian ideal type of bureaucracy, at the other the warmth and intimacy of the family. Litwak and Meyer suggest that this antithesis has been exaggerated, and that there are in fact distinct complementarities between the two. If they are too isolated, they are likely to interfere with each other and reduce the contribution of one or the other in achieving a social goal. If they are brought too close together, their antithetical ethos is likely to disrupt one or both. If however, coordinating mechanisms can be developed which balance their relationships at a midpoint of social distance where formal and informal care are not too intimate and not too isolated from each other, an optimum situation can be achieved. Though this is a helpful ground-clearing exercise, the idea of complementarity is too unspecific and is redolent of a functionalism which postulates harmonious societal integration.

More useful are typologies which suggest different modes of relationship between the public and private sectors of care. Philip Abrams (1984) distinguished between colonization, conflict, and coexistence, the latter subdivided into domination, appropriation, and incorporation. A similar though slightly different classification distinguished between conflict, competition, cooptation, coexistence, and collaboration (Froland 1980:577-9). Such typologies focus usefully upon the organizational characteristics and power relationships found in attempts to link or interweave public and private forms of care. They make explicit the possibility that discontinuity as well as continuities may occur between different types of care.

Different Kinds of Carer

A further difficulty stems from the idea of a continuum of care, which underlies the concept of interweaving public and private care. This is the implication which is sometimes conveyed that different carers can be substituted for one another, for example that neighbors can provide certain forms of care if kin are absent or geographically distant. There is evidence from several studies that ties with neighbors are "weak" by comparison with ties with kin, and that the situations in which support can be looked for from neighbors are specific ones, principally crises requiring rapid action where the neighbor is the person best placed to assist (Litwak and Szelenyi, 1969:470). Most studies show that where longer-term care is required, kin are the principal source of support and failing them, statutory services. Neighbors tend to play a subsidiary role.

This reflects not only the weakness of the tie, but the desire to maintain distance in one's personal affairs. "No one else could cope with my mother" is a familiar phrase to would-be volunteers, but the social foundations of such suspicion and the tendency to privatize family problems are poorly understood. Are these tendencies similar to those which lead to the most dependent old people in residential homes being the ones who least welcome visits and help from outside volunteers (Parker 1981:24)? Does inadequacy seek to hide its head rather than share the pain and anguish? Is there a parallel with other types of household—one-parent families, or families with disabled children—who if they seek outside contacts, prefer self-help groups of those in a similar condition to themselves to contact with neighbors?

Finer distinctions are needed to distinguish what is meant by "care" in relation to the formal/informal divide. There is clear evidence that the more intimate forms of care—what Roy Parker terms "tending"—are not readily shared with the extended family or friends, let alone neighbors.

> 'Sharing' [care] has an attractive sound to it, it is commendable. That does not mean to say that it is easily realised. It may be hard to achieve emotionally, and practically, it may be exceedingly complicated to organise. We know, for instance, how difficult it is for the parent of the child in care to share that child's care in any meaningful fashion with residential care staff or with foster parents. Sharing care may mean sharing love or sharing anguish and pain. Not least, adults who have experienced independence may be reluctant to share their self-care with others. In fact, if one looks carefully at how tending is organised, the succession of responsibility is much more common than genuine sharing (Parker 1981:24).

Personal privacy, as the evidence quoted earlier shows, is an important consideration in determining who is appropriate to provide personal care for those who are dependent. Philip Abrams's research found that the community nurse was an acceptable person to provide more intimate care whereas neighbors or friends typically were not. In some situations there is clearly a kind of polarization. Either personal care is provided by a close relative (typically a spouse or daughter) or someone from the formal sector is preferred, who is a relative stranger not encumbered by the reciprocities of the informal network.

Central Figures

If informal networks are to be mobilized, who will be at their center and what implications does this have for the privacy of local residents? Certain key roles are likely to be particularly important. Collins and Pancoast's influential American essay on informal networks (1976) identified a number of roles whose occupants could be a "central figure," including meter readers, milkmen, shop assistants, hairdressers, and filling station attendants. They suggested that productive relationships between social care agency staff and these central figures could dramatically extend the effective reach of professional efforts. More attention needs to be given to the role of such "natural leaders" or "sociometric stars" in informal networks. What functions are they expected to perform, and how exactly will they act as a link between statutory voluntary and informal care? Who is expected to act as a "central figure"? And what are the privacy implications of the performance of such a role?

In Britain, such a role may be played by local shopkeepers, proprietors of public houses ("pubs"), and, in some areas, ministers of religion. Robert Roberts (1978:13-23) provides a vivid description of central role his mother's shop played in their Salford neighborhood. Today the corner shop may still play a significant role in a locality. Research in Kent into the informal economy revealed one shopkeeper who monitored the expenditure of his unemployed customers. If it appeared excessive, he reported them to the state welfare agency (Wallace 1984). Modern society is more segmented than the area of Salford in which Roberts grew up. Everyone does not know everyone else's business, but informal social control may still operate—"the enforcement of collective standards through gossip, stigma, ostracism, public complaint and an array of similar devices" (Abrams 1984:424).

Our knowledge of the negative as against the positive aspects of neighboring is still unsystematic, but the very existence of negative neighboring suggests that attempts to tap informal networks to provide care may run into difficulties. It is clear, however, that the preservation of privacy is still a major concern to many people, and well-meaning attempts to help, directly or indirectly, by "central figures" may fall on stony ground for that reason. More research is needed.

Professional Workers and Informal Networks

The implications of mobilizing local informal networks for the work of professionals such as social workers or district nurses also needs to be thought through much more carefully so far as the privacy implications are concerned. If informal networks are to be mobilized as channels of communication, how is information to be fed to professionals, and how are they to present themselves to clients or patients? In relation to neighborhood care, Abrams commented that "interesting, not to say alarming, ethical issues are raised, especially for professional social workers, by the possibility of building care on gossip" (1980:18). The Balls advocate openness about information being shared with neighbors, but this runs entirely counter to the ethos of confidentiality characteristic of the social worker-client relationship. It also runs counter to people's inclination to keep their own personal affairs to themselves. Three-way relationships pose yet more difficult questions. Should a doctor explain to a neighbor who is budgeting and caring for a sick neighbor what is wrong with them? To what extent should professionals *ask* neighbors for information about third parties? Can such inquiries be undertaken without upsetting the delicate balance of helpfulness and privacy characteristic of links between neighbors? When private information about a client is sought from or shared with a neighborhood caregiver who is part of a local network, entirely new problems are created about which there is currently little guidance.

Much more careful specification is required of the circumstances under which information can or can not reasonably be expected to be shared across the formal/ informal, public/private divide. There are clearly differences between different types of worker, between for example, a community worker trying to develop a local facility and a social case worker or home help dealing with an individual's problems, where privacy and confidentiality are much more salient. Different types of prob- lems also raise these issues to a different degree. Cases involving child abuse or neglect, mental illness or serious financial difficulty are usually treated as con- fidential, and the families involved would be unlikely to welcome the involvement of other primary group members in discussion of their difficulties, even in some cases members of the extended family. A survey of families with chronic practical and emotional difficulties, who were Family Service Unit clients, showed the unaccep- tability of "any notion of reliance on informal networks, family, friends or neigh- bours, their vivid fear of being victims of gossip, and the importance they attach to confidentiality" (Barclay 1982:168). On the other hand, delivery of support services to groups such as the elderly may be less sensitive. Even here, however, the privacy limits which the person cared-for establishes are important, and it cannot be as- sumed that the sharing of information, for example on degrees of dependency and need, with neighbors, friends, and kin will in all circumstances be welcomed. It is difficult to avoid the conclusion that the implications of openness and sharing of information about people's personal circumstances has not been thought through.

Professional Responsibility and Accountability

Major objections to the implementation of interweaving have been advanced on grounds of undermining or diluting the responsibility of the professional worker. Matters are diffucult enough among different kinds of professional worker. One of the objects of experimental, locally based systems of social service delivery evaluated in British studies such as Dinnington (Bayley 1984) or Normanton (Hadley and McGrath 1984) appears to be not just to bring formal provision closer to the recip- ients, but to break down some of the bureaucratic obstacles between different sectors such as health services and personal social services.

With attempts to bridge the formal/informal gap, the channels of accountability which provide guidance about how and with whom information about people being cared-for is shared, are disturbed. Staff of local government social service depart- ments are part of a local government structure in which they are subordinate to managers who themselves are answerable to the chief executive and committees of elected representatives. Though in practice they have quite a high degree of profes- sional autonomy, this answerability represents quite a major obstacle to experiments with money or people. It is perhaps significant that attempts to interweave formal and informal care have been concerned far more with the elderly, with whom social workers are much less involved, than with children, where they are. Indeed, apart from self-help in caring among mothers with young children (though cf. Finch 1984), the main form of intervention with children is statutory, within tightly drawn legal limits and within highly formalized procedures. Where the informal sector is involved, this is either on a payment basis, as with fostering, or responsibility is completely transferred over a period of time, as with adoption. In either case, strict rules of confidentiality apply, and it would not be good practice to discuss the care of an individual child with the relatives, friends, or neighbors of that child's caretaker.

CONCLUSION

Potentially, community care may provide a means of integrating the public and the private care systems. Yet what individuals conceptualize as "private"—how they draw boundaries around this private realm—has major implications for attempts to "interweave" public and private care. Empirically, much closer consideration is needed of the circumstances under which information is shared between the person cared for, agency workers, and third parties in the informal sector, with or without the knowledge of the person cared for. The conditions and circumstances under which such information exchanges can and should take place are at present little considered, yet they are central to the idea of tapping informal networks either to increase the effectiveness of, or substitute for, formal care. Privacy and confidentiality issues are particularly salient, and evidence quoted earlier suggests that the obstacles to such exchanges are much greater than is often recognized.

Special interest attaches, empirically and practically, to various attempts to bridge the gap between the formal and informal sectors by the use of waged "street wardens" drawn from the home help service (cf. Abrams *et al.* 1981:79-87), informal helpers paid small amounts to provide support for the elderly (Challis and Davies 1980), and different levels of financial support for "good neighbor" schemes which attempt to organize informal support at the neighborhood level on a voluntary basis (Abrams *et al.* 1981; Bulmer 1986). Such "bridging" initiatives are important experiments in bringing the formal and informal spheres into closer relationship. They are not cheap, and serve as a reminder that the costs of transferring care to the community are considerable. They also raise significant questions about whether the provision and delivery of care is more acceptable to the people cared-for if it is provided on some sort of paid, semiformal, basis, which overcomes concerns about personal privacy more effectively on that account.

Theoretically, there needs to be much more explicit recognition of a desire to preserve personal privacy as a possible inhibiting factor in attempts to interweave public and private care. Models of interweaving need to incorporate clients' personal privacy as a dimension in the theory, and to specify ways in which privacy obstacles may be overcome. One way to do so may be to develop typologies of acceptable alternative carers, so that there is some real sense of which types of care are substitutable rather than a tendency to assume that different types of necessarily are, as at present. A more radical claim would be to reconceptualize what is seen as private—not to be shared outside the private realm—in order to change people's everyday notion of what is public and what is private. An effective interweaving of informal and formal social support may necessitate such a change, if the implications of the ideas about a continuum of care are to be followed through. What is certain is that community care is potentially a field in which the public and the private, the formal and informal systems of care, may be brought together, but that the obstacles to such interweaving posed by privacy concerns are not inconsiderable and must be much more seriously incorporated into theory and practice.

NOTE

1. In discussing formal care, the main agencies referred to are those of the government and formal voluntary bodies. In Britain, local government Social Service Departments have statutory responsibility for care provision, including social work, residential homes, home helps, and various advisory functions. Voluntary organizations include the Women's Royal Voluntary Service, and Age Concern (cf. Mellor, 1985).

REFERENCES

Abrams, Philip
 1977   "Community care: some research problems and priorities." *Policy and Politics* 6(2):125-51.
Abrams, Philip
 1978   *Neighbourhood Care and Social Policy: a research perspective.* Berkhamsted, Herts.: The Volunteer Centre.
Abrams, Philip
 1980   "Social change, social networks and neighbourhood care." *Social Work Service* 22 (February):12-23.
Abrams, Philip and Sheila Abrams and Robin Humphrey and Ray Snaith
 1981   *Action for Care: a review of Good Neighbour Schemes in England.* Berkhamsted, Herts.: The Volunteer Centre.
Abrams, Philip
 1984   "Realities of neighbourhood care," *Policy and Politics* 12:413-29.
Abrams, Philip
 1985   "Policies to promote informal social care: some reflections on voluntary action, neighbourhood involvement and neighbourhood care." *Ageing & Society* 5:1-18.
Allan, Graham
 1983   "Informal networks of care: issues raised by Barclay." *British Journal of Social Work* 13:417-33.
Bailey, Frederick
 1971   *Gifts and Poison: the politics of reputation.* Oxford: Blackwell.
Ball, Colin and Mog Ball
 1982   *What the Neighbours Say: a report on a study of neighbours.* Berkhamsted, Herts.: The Volunteer Centre.
Barclay Report
 1982   *Social Workers: Their Role and Tasks.* London: Bedford Square Press for National Institute of Social Work.
British Association of Social Workers
 1971   *Confidentiality in Social Work.* London: British Association of Social Workers.
Bayley, Michael
 1973   *Mental Handicap and Community Care.* London: Routledge & Kegan Paul.
Bayley, Michael *et al.*
 1984   *Neighbourhood Services Project, Dinnington: Paper Series.* Sheffield: University of Sheffield, Department of Sociological Studies.
Bok, Sissela
 1984   *Secrets: on the ethics of concealment and revelation.* Oxford: Oxford University Press.
Bulmer, Martin
 1985   "The rejuvenation of community studies? Neighbours, networks and policy." *The Sociological Review* 33:430-48.
Bulmer, Martin
 1986   *Neighbours: the work of Philip Abrams.* Cambridge: Cambridge University Press.
Bracey, H.E.
 1964   *Neighbours.* London: Routledge & Kegan Paul.
Challis, David and Bleddyn Davies
 1980   "A new approach to community care of the elderly." *British Journal of Social Work* 10:1-18.
Collins, Alice H. and Diane L. Pancoast
 1976   *Natural Helping Networks: a strategy for prevention.* Washington, D.C.: National Association of Social Workers.

Darvill, Giles
    1983   "Shuttle diplomacy in the personal social services: interweaving statutory and informal
                care in a changing Britain" in D.L. Pancoast *et al.* 1983:239-60.
Finch, Janet
    1984   "The deceit of self-help: preschool playgroups and working class mothers." *Journal of Social
                Policy* 13:1-20.
Froland, Charles
    1980   "Formal and informal care: discontinuities on a continuum." *Social Service Review*
                54(4):572-87.
Froland, Charles, Paul Parker and Michael Bayley
    1980   "Relating formal and informal sources of care: reflections on initiatives in England and
                America." Conference Paper: University of Sheffield, mimeo.
Froland, Charles and Diane Pancoast and Nancy Chapman and Priscilla Kimboko
    1981   *Helping Networks and Human Services.* Beverly Hills: Sage.
Gluckman, Max
    1963   "Gossip and scandal." *Current Anthropology* 4:307-16.
Gottlieb, Benjamin H. (Ed.)
    1981   *Social Networks and Social Support.* Beverly Hills: Sage.
Hadley, Roger and Morag McGrath
    1984   *When Social Services are Local: the Normanton experience.* London: Allen & Unwin.
Heppenstall, M.A.
    1971   "Reputation, criticism and information in an Austrian village" in Bailey 1971:139-66.
Hill, Dilys M.
    1978   "Privacy and social welfare" in J.B. Young (ed.) *Privacy.* Chichester and New York: Wiley:
                155-76.
Hole, Vere
    1959   "Social effects of planned rehousing." *Town Planning Review* 30:166-73.
Kingston Polytechnic
    1972   *The Buxton Report.* Kingston-Upon-Thames, Surrey: Kingston Polytechnic School of Archi-
                tecture.
Kuper, Leo
    1953   "Blueprint for living together" in L. Kuper (ed.) *Living in Towns.* London: Cresset: 1-202.
Litwak, Eugene and H.J. Meyer
    1966   "A balance theory of coordination between bureaucratic organisation and community
                primary groups." *Administrative Science Quarterly* 11:31-58.
Litwak, Eugene and Ivan Szelenyi
    1969   "Primary group structures and their functions: kin, neighbors and friends." *American So-
                ciological Review* 34:465-81.
Maguire, Lambert
    1983   *Understanding Social Networks.* Beverly Hills: Sage.
Mellor, H.W.
    1985   *The Role of Voluntary Organisations in Social Welfare.* London: Croom Helm.
Paine, Robert
    1967   "What is gossip about? an alternative hypothesis." *Man* n.s. 2:278-85.
Pancoast, Diane and Paul Parker and Charles Froland (Eds.)
    1983   *Rediscovering Self-Help: its role in social care.* Beverly Hills, Sage.
Parker, Roy
    1981   "Tending and social policy" in E. Matilda Goldberg and Stephen Hatch (eds.). *A New Look
                at the Personal Social Services.* London: Policy Studies Institute Discussion Paper no.
                4:17-34.
Price, Frances
    1981   "Only connect: issues in charting social networks." *The Sociological Review* 29:283-312.
Roberts, Robert
    1973   *The Classic Slum: Salford life in the first quarter of the century.* Harmondsworth: Penguin.
Roberts, Robert
    1978   *A Ragged Schooling: growing up in the classic slum.* London: Fontana.
Robinson, Fred and Philip Abrams
    1977   *What We Know About The Neighbours.* Durham: University of Durham, Rowntree Research
                Unit.
Robinson, Fred and Suzanne Robinson
    1981   *Neighbourhood Care: an exploratory bibliography.* Berkhamsted, Herts.: The Volunteer Cen-
                tre.
Rosnow, R.L. and G.A. Fine
    1976   *Rumor and Gossip: the social psychology of hearsay.* New York: Elsevier.

Shulman, N.
1967   "Mutual aid and neighbouring patterns." *Anthropologica* 9:51-60.
Stevenson, Olive
1983   "The Barclay Report: some reflections." *Journal of Social Policy* 12:235-40.
Timms, E.
1983   "On the relevance of informal social networks to social work intervention." *British Journal of Social Work* 13:405-15.
Walker, Alan (Ed.)
1982   *Community Care: the family, the state and social policy.* Oxford: Blackwell.
Wallace, Claire
1984   *Informal Work in Two Neighbourhoods: Warden Bay and Rushenden.* Canterbury: University of Canterbury, Work Strategies Unit, Isle of Sheppey Research Studies.
Warren, Donald I.
1981   *Helping Networks: how people cope with problems in the urban community.* Notre Dame, Indiana: University of Notre Dame Press.
Wenger, G. Clare
1984   *The Supportive Network: coping with old age.* London: Allen & Unwin.
Westin, Alan F.
1970   *Privacy and Freedom.* London: Bodley Head.
Wilson, Suanna J.
1978   *Confidentiality in Social Work: issues and principles.* New York: Free Press.
Young, Michael and Peter Willmott
1972   *Family and Kinship in East London.* Harmondsworth: Penguin (first published 1957).

Toward Implications for Research, Theory, and Policy on Nonprofits and Voluntarism

Susan A. Ostrander

In addition to the broad conceptual themes laid out in the introduction, the papers here deserve some discussion of overall implications for research and theory development, and for policy. That is the aim of this brief concluding statement. My goal is not to consider all of the main points in these papers, nor is it to restate what the authors here have already said so well. I intend rather to begin to pull together some of the major themes they have sought to address, seeing this as a way to encourage discussion among scholars, activists, and policymakers in the field of voluntary action about their own ideas of the implications of these seven papers for research, theory, and policy. The authors of this collection may or may not agree with what I see as the implications of their work, and they ought not be held accountable for what are my own interpretations.

The themes considered in this collection can be grouped into four general categories, each building on the other in terms of stages of thinking and questioning, leading toward implications for policy and practice. Those four are:

1. Initial tasks toward more powerful theories of the nonprofit section and voluntarism;
2. Reconceptualizing voluntarism, government, and the corporate sector and the relations among them;
3. Developing a definitive role for nonprofits and voluntary activity; and
4. Toward policy implications for nonprofits.

This statement is organized in terms of these four general categories. Within each general category, more specific themes are considered.

INITIAL TASKS TOWARD MORE POWERFUL THEORIES OF THE NONPROFIT SECTOR AND VOLUNTARISM

Theory contributes to constructing reality. It defines what is visible and invisible. Theory in this view does more than simply reflect or explain reality. It takes part in actively creating it.

Conventional theory about nonprofits has, for example, conceptualized the nonprofit sector as "independent" from the other sectors. This conventional theory—challenged by the papers in this collection—has contributed to an antagonistic view of the relations between the voluntary sector and government that obscures the historic cooperation between them. (This point is made perhaps most explicitly by Salamon.) Conventional theories of the voluntary sector have also seen the sector as

Susan A. Ostrander, Department of Sociology, Tufts University, Medford MA 02155.

separate and distinct from society (from what Van Til called the political economy of society) and from history (a point made particularly by Hall). These views have obscured the specific patterns of how the voluntary sector is imbedded in relations between the state and capitalism, as Gronbjerg for example discusses them. Conventional theories have also obscured the ways in which people in everyday life move among the three sectors, linking them in ways yet to be specified, a point made especially by DeLaat. The active role of clients and others in creating the boundaries of the voluntary sector has also not been as central as seems useful, a point made by Bulmer. This view of nonprofits as outside active history obscures the changing dynamics of sector relations, and sees nonprofits as impervious to such change and as having no particular role to play as agents of change, a view challenged by Hall and others. The remainder of this section will specify some of the major initial tasks that seem essential in building an alternative to this conventional theory of nonprofits.

It seems initially necessary to *abandon the rhetoric of independence*, to *recognize that this conceptualization of nonprofits has actually been harmful to the development of the voluntary sector.* As the authors here show, nonprofits are in fact dependent on government for funds and for setting broad directions in policy, and government is dependent on nonprofits for carrying out its mandates. To claim otherwise is to weaken this mutual dependence which seems necessary for the development of both sectors and for the efficient and effective delivery of services to those who need them. In the current political context in the United States, the rhetoric of independence has been used by the administration in Washington to justify cuts in federal funding to nonprofits that take part in delivering welfare state services.

As we abandon our view of nonprofits as comprising as "independent sector," we must *develop an alternative conceptualization* that will *reflect current and historical realities of sector relations*, and that will *enhance cooperation and mutual development* of the sectors. This will require a definition of nonprofits that is *nonresidual, and nonderivative;* that is, a definition that characterizes nonprofits in terms of *what they are,* not only in terms of what they are not. This requires a definition that is positive and affirming, not one that rests only on what is left over after government and the corporate sector do their work.

Another criterion for useful theories of nonprofits seems to be that such theories *incorporate the diversity of perspectives in social science and in history.* To date, as Van Til and Hall suggest, scholarly work on nonprofits has derived from the more conventional unidisciplinary and ahistorical perspectives, emphasizing functionality, order and stability. Useful perspectives must be multidisciplinary, sensitive to history. Perspectives that seem especially absent are those reflecting a *Marxist or neo-Marxist perspective. Feminist theory*, with its central focus on uncovering and reconstructing public/private relations, should also be explored, a point on which DeLaat just begins to touch. An incorporation of the wide diversity of theory would also include *the humanistic* (and phenomenological) *visions of people in everyday life.* Bulmer and DeLaat demonstrate some ways in which this perspective points to aspects of voluntary sector relations that are not visible from other perspectives.

It is particularly evident from the papers here that a *central task of new nonprofit sector theory is to identify the particular patterns of relationships among the three sectors, relationships reflecting interdependence.* This task includes *specifying the conditions under which the various patterns occur and the processes through which they come about and change*. This view suggests that *no single pattern of relations can or should be established as the ideal*. It suggests that how voluntary organizations, the state, and the corporate sector relate with one another is and should be *historically and perhaps locally specific and embedded in socio-political-economic-cultural context and ongoing dynamics of change*. Gronbjerg is among those making these points most explicitly in the current collection. Salamon also begins to lay out the conditions under which voluntary action and governmental action seem most appropriate. Pickvance cautions us about assumptions that strong local government—a decentralized welfare state—may necessarily create conditions conducive to voluntary activity.

RECONCEPTUALIZING VOLUNTARISM, GOVERNMENT, AND THE CORPORATE SECTORS AND THE RELATIONS AMONG THEM

One essential aspect of developing new and more powerful theories of nonprofits is to also develop new theories of the welfare state that include state-nonprofit relations. Salamon focuses on this point. Pickvance sensitizes us to the complexity of the state itself by investigating the impact of the dynamics between national and local government on voluntary activity. Nonprofit theories must also incorporate the business sector, as Van Til and Gronbjerg emphasize.

Beyond this, the authors here are also suggesting a *profound rethinking of the divisions of public and private*. Notions of "public" as governmental and "private" as nongovernmental (and thus outside the realm of accountability) are challenged. Several of the authors (Van Til in particular) *redefine "public"* as *matters in any and all of the three sectors—nonprofit, corporate, or state—that are major in their consequences*. Issues that have important effects on significant numbers of people are public issues. Public concerns are those for which an appropriately identified organized *set of actors would be held responsible and accountable*. Bulmer implies an acceptance of this kind of redefinition of the "public" sector when he includes formal voluntary services in the realm of public rather than private care.

This is not, of course, a new idea. It has, however, been strongly resisted by those in the "private" voluntary sector and in "private" business who do not wish to be as accountable as this definition of "public" issues would make them. Salamon, for example, reminds us that the original designation of "public" as governmental and "private" as nongovernmental was a political effort to enable expansion of the private (business) sector in the late nineteenth century. In recent years, this socially and politically created division between public and private sectors has been used to justify challenges to the welfare state. It has provided a basis for ideologies seeking to replace government with voluntary efforts and corporate philanthropy. Voluntary action scholars—and many supporters, activitists and policymakers in the voluntary sector—have been virtually unanimous in their opposition to this reactionary political agenda. The data base created to challenge this reactionary version of what I have called "chauvinistic" voluntarism was the first systematic effort to research the actual circumstances of nonprofits, a point made here by Hall.

Just as rethinking the socially constructed divisions between public and private calls for a fundamental redefinition of "public," so must the *definition of "private" be reformulated*. Bulmer provides us here with one effort to begin this redefinition of the boundaries of the private. "Private" action is not simply all that goes on outside the governmental realm or beyond state mandate. "Private" relations or issues are those which are seen as deserving of personal privacy and confidentiality. Privacy involves the *ability (and right) to control information about oneself.* Confidentiality refers to *confidences being kept when private information is revealed to another.* "Private" relations are those whose *integrity is to be respected and either enhanced or left unchallenged.* The "primary group" social support networks formed voluntarily by individuals in neighborhoods and families discussed by Bulmer are examples of these. A task for future research and theory is to further define the boundaries of the private as they are important to societies, groups, and individuals.

The use of the term "voluntary" is itself problematic and in need of further specification. Authors here propose that *voluntarism be conceived as a form of activity and social relation that occurs—like public and private activity—in all three sectors,* not simply in what has been called the voluntary (nonprofit) sector. *Voluntarism, once defined, would then become visible in government and in the corporate sector and could be appropriately developed and maximized in those settings.* Van Til and DeLaat in particular make this point.

One way in which voluntarism exists as a generic activity is through the active involvement of individuals as volunteers in all three sectors. DeLaat argues that this activity has the *potential for affecting relations among the three sectors in positive ways, maximizing cooperation and mitigating conflict and nonproductive forms of competition.* As part of reconceptualizing sector relations, this *potential for individuals linking sectors needs to be further explored.* For example, how effective are volunteer board members of nonprofit social service agencies in influencing state policy by serving in an unpaid capacity on governmental commissions? When an employee of a corporate firm becomes involved as a volunteer at a family service agency, whether state or nonprofit, is s/he more willing to put in volunteer efforts on the job to propose an onsite child care center at the firm?

This effort to reconceptualize voluntarism as generic to all three sectors also includes a *redefinition* of *volunteering,* proposed by DeLaat. *Volunteering is unpaid work in any sector, or work in any sector that is underpaid or beyond the requirements of one's paid job.* Using this conceptualization of volunteering, what aspects of activity by people in government, in business, and in nonprofit organizations can we see that were previously hidden? How, for example, does the conventional monolithically positive image of voluntarism in the United States contribute to a negative exploitation of workers, in the sense that work beyond the requirements on one's paid job is expected? How does the opportunity for volunteer activity at one's place of employment allow for expressions of political and other interests in a way that democratizes and humanizes the work environment, whether in the corporate, state, or nonprofit sector? What, overall, are the contributions (both positive and negative) of voluntarism as a generic activity in all three sectors?

DEVELOPING A DEFINITIVE ROLE FOR NONPROFITS AND VOLUNTARY ACTIVITY

Existing efforts to formulate a definitive role for nonprofits are based largely on mythical representations of the voluntary sector that are not reflective of social, economic, and political realities. Current definitions of a role for nonprofits tend to be derivative or residual—that is, they say more about what the voluntary sector is *not* than what it *is.*

One important role of voluntary organizations and voluntary activity that is not simply derivative or residual is that of a mediating structure. Van Til and DeLaat suggest, for example, that the *voluntary sector mediates or links the other two sectors with one another*. Van Til sees the voluntary sector as the locus of societal mediating structures. He defines *mediating* as *bridging the two sides of the political economy, the state and the marketplace or corporate sector*. DeLaat sees this mediating or linking role of voluntarism as individuals acting as volunteers in all three sectors, thus *spanning and bringing together the sectors in potentially cooperative ways*. Others have seen voluntary activity as integrating the otherwise alienated individual with large-scale institutions in society, particularly government.

Another aspect of this mediating function, implied by DeLaat, is the integration for the individual of what has been defined as "public" and "private" life. Traditional divisions in classical liberal thought between public and private have segmented individual experience in artificial and alienating ways. If individuals as volunteers can act on an issue of interest to them at their place of employment, in a citizen activist group in their neighborhood or through local government, in churches and other voluntary associations, this may serve to integrate the various aspects of their lives in satisfying ways. It may also serve to empower these individuals and to organize them. *These different meanings of mediation as a definitive role for nonprofits need to be further distinguished and specified.*

Meanwhile, some of the residual and derivative definitions of the role of non-profits considered here provide some clearer directions, moving us further toward specifying a definitive role. The authors seem agreed that it is not the primary function of the voluntary sector to fill in gaps left by current efforts in Washington to cut back the welfare state, that *voluntarism cannot be and ought not be a substitute for government services*. They are also agreed that the *voluntary sector ought not be defined in such a way that it is in competition with or opposition to the welfare state*.

Salamon's proposal of two theories of the voluntary sector in its relation to government is useful in specifying a definitive role for voluntarism in society. He poses a view of *nonprofits as "third party government,"* as *nongovernmental agencies used by the state to deliver needed services without increasing the size of the state apparatus*. He suggests an image of a *"public presence without a monstrous public bureaucracy."* Salamon's second theory of the nonprofit sector is what he calls *"voluntary failure theory."* Turning on its head the notion that the voluntary sector does best what government fails to do, the theory poses rather that *government must do what non-profits fail to do or do well*. Salamon suggests that *nonprofits do poorly in four areas*: where large scale resources are necessary to meet enormous needs; where there are gaps in voluntary services due to the particularistic focus of nonprofits; where democratic, nonelitist decision-making structures are needed and where equity is of importance; and where voluntary services lack experience, such as in serving the poor.

One other point made by the authors points toward an important, unrealized role for nonprofits, though not a new one. *The dependence of government on nonprofits for the delivery of mandated services gives nonprofits a substantial power base for political action that has yet to be fully developed.* It seems important to *identify the circumstances under which political action, and other forms of nonprofit activity, seem most appropriate and most likely to achieve their goals*. Pickvance's paper makes some contribution here. That is discussed further in the next section.

TOWARD POLICY IMPLICATIONS FOR NONPROFITS

Nonprofit organizations, like other organizations, have choices to make about what kinds of activities they wish to prioritize and how they wish to carry them out. The papers here have implications for developing criteria by which such choices might be made. Given that these papers seem to agree that interdependence among the three sectors is likely to increase, the impact of differing forms of relationships among the sectors on activities of nonprofits seems a useful focus in developing implications for policy and practice.

Several of the authors in this collection urge greater attention to the fact that a form of relationship characterized as public-private partnerships (that is, nonprofits and government working cooperatively in mutually reinforcing and beneficial ways) have existed for a long time in the United States. This historical reality has not been as clearly recognized as it needs to be, particularly in a political context where government is seen (incorrectly) as weakening the nonprofit sector and where voluntarism is often defined in opposition to the state. The authors also call attention to the fact that particular circumstances in the society and in the political economy impede and enable relationships between and among the three sectors. These circumstances need to be spelled out as a way of facilitating these relationships or "partnerships" when they are most beneficial to human welfare. It is essential to this task that more attention be paid to the role of the for-profit sector in affecting nonprofits and voluntary action. Gronbjerg states, for example, that while the role of government in weakening the voluntary sector has been exaggerated, the role of the proprietary organizations in this regard has been minimized. In the context of American capitalism, when proprietary organizations enter the field, they are (Gronbjerg argues) likely to dominate—weakening both government and nonprofits.

These are the points from which I will draw most directly to suggest implications for nonprofits and voluntary activity. The implications that follow derive most directly from the paper by Gronbjerg, who finds that cooperation between government and nonprofits ("public-private partnerships") occurs most readily in service areas where for-profit organizations have not become heavily involved. Both government and nonprofits need to be alerted to this dynamic as for-profit services increase, else relations become antagonistic and/or opportunistic rather than focused primarily on serving the needs of clientele. Nonprofits and government may wish to explore what action if any they might take together to either circumscribe for-profits, or to solidify public-private cooperation in the face of this potential threat from for-profit expansion. This finding by Gronbjerg also alerts us, it seems to me, to the potential negative consequences for nonprofits of engaging in for-profit activities, a point to be further addressed here.

Gronbjerg also finds that nonprofits find it difficult to act on their own initiative when both government and the proprietary sector are extensively involved in a service area. Given that service delivery may not be an option for the nonprofit sector in this circumstance, might this be a situation where focusing on the mediating role might be most effective and appropriate? Might, for example, nonprofits bring governmental officials and for-profit administrators together in forums designed to educate them about the community's needs in the particular service area? Might nonprofit forums and other activities encourage cooperation between government and for-profits? Might board members of nonprofit agencies seek to become appointed to the boards for for-profit and/or governmental organizations working in the same service areas? Might staff and volunteers in nonprofits testify at public hearings as to the appropriateness of licensure of for-profit agencies, and might they seek to be appointed to governmental commissions making such decisions? These seem to be only a few examples of the multiple ways in which nonprofit organizations and individuals from them might create mediating structures when for-profits and government may be headed for nonproductive competition.

Where government does not currently rely on nonprofits to deliver mandated services—and where there is no sizable proprietary involvement—nonprofits and government (according to Gronbjerg) are put in a situation where they are actively competing for clients. Competition requires expenditures on nonservice activities, on public relations, advertising or quasi-advertising, and on fundraising to attract both clients and support for activities. How productive are such expenditures in terms of the nonprofit sector's goals and purposes? Are such expenditures justified when the service is genuinely needed in the community (and not provided by either government or by nonprofits), but not justified if governmental services seem sufficient to meet the need? How might such needs be best determined? Might nonprofit expenditures on public relations and similar nonservice activities be justified if paying clients will buy attractive (though not necessarily essential) services, and if the revenue can then be used by the agency to support services for clients who cannot pay for essential services? These and other questions seem important for nonprofits to consider when placed in a competitive situation with for-profit organizations.

Where government does not make extensive use of nonprofits and where the proprietary sector is dominant is one situation where nonprofits might seize the opportunity to play an advocacy role. Nonprofits might encourage government to increase its involvement where the service area is deemed important, but not appropriate or not feasible for nonprofits to take on. The circumstances under which it is most productive for the voluntary sector to make political and social advocacy a priority need to be much more clearly and definitively spelled out.

CONCLUSION

This collection of papers aims to shift the terms of the current debate on the role of the voluntary sector. It is clear from the new theoretical conceptualizations proposed and developed in these papers that the future of the "private" voluntary sector is one of mutual interdependence with the "public" welfare state. The voluntary sector is neither independent from nor opposed to nor a substitute for government. It is clear further that the for-profit corporate sector needs to be incorporated into this conceptualization of interdependence. Its role in affecting—in negative and positive ways—the voluntary sector-governmental sector dynamic needs to be recognized and further specified.

New theories of the voluntary sector and of the welfare state and of capitalism will need to address the ways in which these sectors are imbedded in one another and how their relations emerge and change. This will require a profound reformulation of our notions of public and private realms in society, rendering voluntary organizations and corporations more publicly accountable, and establishing clearer boundaries of private control for individuals and groups. Voluntarism will come to be defined as a generic activity that occurs in all three sectors and serves as the locus of mediating structures that link them, and links the individual to the larger society in more empowering and less alienating ways than is presently the case.

The implications of this new theoretical vision of the voluntary sector for policy and practice have barely begun here. That is a task for future ongoing discussion in which the authors of this collection will most assuredly be active participants.

Envoi: Developing Nonprofit Theory

Stuart Langton

*The essays in this volume point to the need for reconstruction and further develop-
ment of theories about the role of nonprofit institutions in the contemporary welfare
state. This epilogue reflects upon the implications of this challenge by examining
what it means to develop "theory" and some of the practical difficulties involved in
this task. Acknowledging that "theory" may mean different things to different people, scholars and practitioners alike, it discusses the different types, functions, and
evaluative criteria of theory. Recognizing that the area of nonprofit studies is a
relatively new area of intellectual inquiry, it suggests a number of distinctions and
needs that are relevant to future theoretical development in regard to better understanding and prescribing roles for nonprofit institutions in our society.*

The 1970s and 1980s have been a period of unprecedented development and
change in the nonprofit sector. During the 1970s public appreciation of the value of
these institutions grew dramatically. Elsewhere (Langton, 1981), it has been suggested that this appreciation grew out of a sense of discontent and displeasure with
business and government. By contrast, there was a rise in "sector consciousness" of
the unique values and special social contributions of nonprofit institutions. This new
sector consciousness was reflected tangibly in the creation of organizations to study
and promote sector interests (e.g., Association of Voluntary Action Scholars, Volunteer, Independent Sector, et al.), the establishment of a national commission on
philanthropy (the Filer Commission), a substantial amount of new research and
publications, and the establishment of many government policies to make greater
use of nonprofit institutions in delivering services supported by government.

THE GROWING RATIONALIZATION OF THE NONPROFIT SECTOR

During the 1980s there has been no diminution of the development of attention to
and appreciation of the nonprofit sector. What has occurred has been a growth in the
rationalization and formalization of nonprofit sector interests. This growth has occurred primarily in the areas of policy, professional development, and research.

For example, the organization Independent Sector has emerged as a substantial
national institution to advance educational, research, and policy interests in the
nonprofit sector. Dozens of new graduate programs in nonprofit management have
been created during the 1980s.

A nonprofit management association has been formed, and several newsletters

Stuart Langton, Executive Director, Lincoln Filene Center for Citizenship and Public Affairs &
Lincoln Filene Professor of Citizenship and Public Affairs, Tufts University, Medford, MA
02155.

and many books on nonprofit management have been published. A number of projects have been undertaken to develop taxonomy to classify the various types of nonprofit groups (Sumariwalla, 1986). Major research programs and projects have been established including those at Yale University, the Urban Institute, and the Internal Revenue Service. A presidential task force on "Private Sector Initiatives" was created. The first statistical copendium of the nonprofit sector was published (Hodgkinson and Weitzman, 1984). Several data bases describing the programs of nonprofit institutions have been developed. Software packages have been created for nonprofit groups, and national surveys have been conducted to identify the nature and extent of public support for the nonprofit sector.

As a result of these, and many similar developments, the new sector consciousness of the 1970s has been institutionalized increasingly during the 1980s. The general interest and appreciation of the role of nonprofit institutions as a "sector" has become more formalized, legitimized, and advanced by institutional recognition and support. Within a decade America's rediscovery of the nonprofit "sector" has become codified and rationalized within our national consciousness and institutional life. We now more naturally and easily think about this "sector" and have developed a substantial capacity for attending to and advancing its interests.

THE RISE OF INTERSECTOR CONSCIOUSNESS

There has been, and is, a second trend in thinking about the nonprofit sector in the 1980s. Whereas, during the 1970s, much was written and said about the uniqueness and independence of the nonprofit sector, a major theme of the 1980s has been how much interdependence and duplication there is between the sectors. This growth in intersector consciousness, as the essays in this volume demonstrate, has focused on the negative, positive, and uncertain implications of the interrelations between sectors. As a consequence of this thinking about relations between sectors, awareness has increased concerning many issues of policy, practice, and theory in intersector relations.

But thinking about intersector relations has been incomplete, uncertain, and ambivalent. It has seemed to move in two directions at once. On the one hand, there has been great interest in the potentially positive benefits of such forms of interrelationship as public-private partnerships, coproduction, and mediation. On the other hand, there has been considerable concern, particularly about the negative impacts of federal budgetary policy (Salamon & Abramson, 1982; DeMone and Gibelman, 1984; Salamon, Musselwhite, and DeVito, 1986), and tax policy (Clotfelter and Salamon, 1986).

This has led to, or been accompanied by, two critical judgments. The first is a common recognition of the inadequacy of public policies in relation to nonprofit institutions. As Schooler (1983:436) noted, "The nonprofit sector has been addressed in public policymaking only in an ad hoc, relatively noncoherent, fragmented, segmented, and often contradictory fashion." This raises a fundamental question whether or not we should have a coherent government policy and follow the conclusion of Waldemar Nielsen (1979:213) that the nonprofit sector "must become the object of active protection and affirmative reinforcement by government." This may appeal as a clear and attractive option were it not for a more trenchant critical judgment that has emerged among a number of scholars and practitioners that the popularly accepted paradigm of triadic sectors in which the nonprofit sector is conceived as relatively special and independent is inadequate. This judgment is one that I share and will address later in this essay in raising the question of whether or not the sector metaphor should be abandoned. This judgment is also a concern of the authors of this volume who acknowledge that the degree of overlap and interpretation between the sectors demands a reexamination of popular and commonly accepted theory about the nature and role of nonprofit institutions.

But what does a reexamination of theory mean, and more particularly, what does it mean to reexamine, construct, or reconstruct a theory about the nature and role of nonprofit institutions?

This is no simple question since people mean different things when they refer to theory, and they want different things from it. Theory might mean better answers, better rules, better definitions, better research, better philosophy, or more of one or all of these things, or more integration between some or all of these things. This variation of meanings and intent is inevitable in popular culture, but among the community of scholars, values of reflective consciousness and parsimony invite greater clarity of meaning and purpose. For this reason, it seems that a reexamination of nonprofit theory might be aided and abetted by a discussion of the meaning of theory and how distinctions about aspects of theorizing may promote the development of theory concerning nonprofit institutions. This is the purpose of this essay.

WHAT IS THEORY?

The term "theory" is at once general, rich, and vague. As Anatol Rapoport (1966:3) has observed: "Theory has not only many uses but many meanings." This is evident in both the historical development of "theoria" in Hellenic culture and in the modern analysis of theory in the philosophy of science and even more particularly in the social sciences. To the Greeks, theory took on multiple uses and meanings, including concentrated identification, observation, speculation, and study (Cornford, 1957; Russell, 1945; Toulmin, 1982; and Wheelwright, 1951). In Aristotle, the notion of "theoria" was used to refer to both general reflection and to more precise scientific study. The study of the philosophy of science, especially since Thomas Kuhn's *The Structure of Scientific Revolutions* in 1962, has been almost completely preoccupied with different explanations of origin and change in theoretical development. This "metatheoretical" consideration of theory illustrates that examination of the meaning of "theory" is both controversial and complex.

This historical development suggests that any consideration of the development of a theory of nonprofit organizations cannot be casual. Clearly, theorizing is no easy or simple task, and yet it is a growing practical interest among those who share a common belief that there is something about nonprofit institutions and their role in the social order that begs more scrutiny and elaboration. This is the theoretical challenge. When scholars and practitioners of a given community ask for or recommend more or improved theory, they are both asserting that something is important (of value) and that we (our society) do not seem to understand enough about that "thing." Thus our call or recall to theory is both a normative preference as well as an invitation to more scientific inquiry and analysis. In this sense, the call to theorizing is both normatively based (we think something is or may be important or good) and objectively more neutral (we want challenge, or elaboration). Accordingly, the roots of theory are both normative and objective. We want both normative confirmation and extension as well as objective scrutiny. Theory is the process of appealing to these two dimensions of our consciousness.[1]

This is a lot to ask and that is why theorizing is so complex and controversial. We come to it with bias (normative preferences) and yet intend to be objective. We cannot escape this dilemma because we feel, prefer, want, and also believe that we can appropriate understanding, truth, and knowledge. We attempt to integrate these dimensions of our human condition by developing theories. A theory is therefore both self-justifying and self-examining. It seeks to confirm or alter our conception of reality. Depending upon our theoretical attitude, both of these results are possibilities to a greater or lesser extent.

To answer the question "what is theory?" this way is quite different from telling or describing how people engage in theorizing (or particularly scientific theorizing). Instead it suggests that building theory is not a pure single act of intention. Our motives in theorizing are mixed and this is both the blessing and the curse of theory, since those who theorize are influenced by their constellation of values and their intent to be as rational and objective as possible. This is why, as Rapoport suggests, theories have different uses and meanings. It also suggests the great potential and limitations of all theories and the need to seek out the purpose and assumptions of a theory and to scrutinize and appreciate its balance of subjective and objective character.

FUNCTIONS OR PURPOSES OF THEORY

Because theories grow out of different interests, values, and purposes, the very definition one gives to the term "theory" may reflect the different perspective, interest, or purpose of the theoretician. This is why, I suspect, that so many definitions of theory use instrumental language to refer to theories as "tools," "instruments," "products," "vehicles," etc. It is also why most definitions of theory usually refer to the different functions or purposes that theory serve. For example, Hoover (1976:64) defines theory as "a set of related propositions that attempt to explain, and sometimes predict, a set of events"; and Argyris and Schön (1974:5) go further by saying, "Theories are vehicles for explanation, prediction, and control."

A critical question for social science in general, and nonprofit theory in particular, is: What are the common functions that theory can serve? The functions proposed by Argyris and Schön point the way but, in my opinion, do not go far enough in differentiating the types of functions that meet the analytical and policy needs of theoretical effort in relation to the social sciences and nonprofit institutions. Because much of the pressing need for nonprofit theory has to do with making decisions about policies (micro and macro) concerning the behavior and role of nonprofit institutions, it is not surprising that a most helpful classification is available in a work that examines the elements of decision-making. John O'Shaughnessy's book, *Inquiry and Decision: A Methodology for Management and the Social Sciences* (1973) is relevant in this regard. O'Shaughnessy identifies five types of decision areas that I would propose are equivalent to the functions of theory in the social sciences in general and for nonprofit organizations in particular: description, explanation, prediction, evaluation, and prescription. Adopting his categories, I would propose that theories perform the following functions:

> DESCRIPTION: Theory describes what is meant and how things can be defined and ordered. What is the reality we are describing?
> EXPLANATION: Theory describes how and why things happen. What are causes and what are effects?
> PREDICTION: Theory proposes what might or will happen. What is likely to happen in the future?
> EVALUATION: Theory proposes the conditions or alternatives that are likely to make one or more things happen or not happen. What are alternatives and their consequences?
> PRESCRIPTION: Theory proposes what should happen in the future. What ends and means are preferable?

O'Shaughnessy points out that decision-making is a cumulative process that requires that each of these functions be served adequately.[2] I would stress, and I will later, that the fundamental building block in theoretical development is the first state or function of describing and that one of our greatest stumbling blocks in constructing nonprofit theory is the inadequacies of the concepts and definitions we use.

GENERAL TYPES OF THEORIES

As theories may differ in their function, they may also differ in their type and style. What may be taken for theory by one person may be viewed as gobbledygook by another, or what one person might call theory, another might reject as opinion. In this sense, the nature and extent of theory varies according to the types of theorizing we do. For example, we can draw distinctions between *casual theories* such as those we develop to explain something that interests us without a great deal of rigorous examination, *popular assumed* theories that we readily accept and respond to because they strike us as correct (such as the positions of political candidates); *micro-scientific* theories that rigorously examine a limited subject or phenomenon; *macro-scientific* theories that systematically examine many aspects of a subject, phenomenon, or field; and *grand theory* (Skinner: 1985) which provides a very broad and generally integrative explanation of reality.[3]

These distinctions are not trivial, as I will attempt to demonstrate below in discussing issues related to building theory about the nature and role of nonprofit institutions. What these distinctions do make clear is that any judgment about the value, validity, or adequacy of theory requires reference to both the function and type of theory with which we are concerned. Therefore, when we inquire as to what is a good or adequate theory we should be clear about the nature of theorizing under consideration. Otherwise, we may be negligent or too narrow in our inquiry, a danger that Jon Van Til has described in his earlier essay. We may harshly judge or reject other types or functions of theorizing because we are so preoccupied with our own theoretical frame of reference. This denies an opportunity to possibly learn something about the nature of other types of theorizing and the limits of our own. It also undermines the possibility of sympathetically integrating a feature (strategy or method) from one approach of theorizing to another. We may also impose our theoretical frame of reference and overcome, drive out, undermine, and deny other theoretical approaches. This is unfortunate because not only do we lose the opportunity for learning but we may also subvert theoretical development simply because it may differ from our own. I suspect that much of the discontent that accompanies social scientific inquiry today is fueled by these not uncommon practices. One can only hope that in the future of nonprofit theoretical development that these tendencies can be avoided and that mutual tolerance, if not constructive interest, will prevail among scholars from different disciplines.

WHAT IS GOOD THEORY?

To acknowledge that there are different functions and types of theory helps us to understand that there may be opinions about the worth of any singular theoretical effort or theorizing in general in a given field. So, when it is said that a theory is good or bad, or adequate or inadequate, the judgment may mean many different things. It might mean that the theory does or does not serve the appropriate function, is or is not of the right type, or addresses well or poorly a certain element of the theory itself. Therefore, a theory may be found wanting for what it fails to do or what it may do in excess, as well as for some quality it may lack. For these reasons it is unreasonable to expect that any theory can be absolutely good or bad. As Manheim and Rich (1986:17) observe, "Theories are neither true nor false in any absolute sense, only more or less useful. Just as there is more than one way to make a hammer, there are many ways to develop theories."

To say that theories are more or less useful is not to suggest a solipsistic conclusion that there are no standards for theory except those of each person who engages in theorizing. The very notion of "useful" suggests some kind of standards implied in utility. In this regard, the two dimensions of theory noted earlier are instructive. Theory may be relative in an existential sense because the intent and assumptions of each theory may differ. But this does not deny the objective dimension of theorizing. It only begs that those who engage in theory be clear and acknowledge their intent and assumptions. To acknowledge one's preformed intent and use of theory is to appeal to and confirm some common understanding of what is useful. Therefore, the critical question is: Are there some common qualities or standards of usefulness?

This question can be addressed in a more general phenomenological manner as well as from a more particular disciplinary perspective. That is to say we can inquire into what are the qualities of usefulness that are common in all types of theory (e.g., clarity, order, coherence, and logical consistency) or we can consider the qualities of usefulness that are common in a disciplinary field.[4] Since this essay is concerned with theoretical development in relation to nonprofit institutions, consideration will be given to the qualities of utility that are common in the social sciences.

Although there is no one single set of accepted criteria for assessing the value of the usefulness of a theory in the social sciences, a number of similar and overlapping terms have been used to prescribe useful qualities. As examples, such qualitative terms have been used as: "fruitfulness, clarity, power" (Meehan, 1968:115); "scope, precision, power, reliability and simplicity" (Rudner, 1966:41); "simplicity, predictive accuracy, and importance" (Shively, 1974:16); "generality, relevance, consistency, completeness, testability, centrality, and simplicity" (Argyris & Schön, 1979:4, 197, 198); and "testable, logically sound, communicable, general, and parsimonious" (Manheim & Rich, 1986:19, 20).

Among these lists of qualitative criteria, I prefer and will adopt (in a modified form

TABLE 1
Criteria for Theoretical Usefulness

Quality	Description	Evaluative Question
1. Breadth	Sufficiently general in scope	Is it extensive enough?
2. Depth	Sufficiently detailed in its level of examination	Is it intensive enough?
3. Relevance	Germane to recognizable need	Is it important?
4. Consistency	Reasonably justified propositions	Is it logical?
5. Clarity	Clear language and structure	Is it understandable?
6. Coherence	The elements fit together	Is it unified?
7. Testability	Propositions can be confirmed	Is it proveable?
8. Integrativeness	Draws upon and considers other relevant theoretical efforts and concerns	Is it complementary?

and with different terms) that of Argyris and Schön because they include the criteria that are suggested by others as well as other commonly accepted values in the social sciences. Accordingly, I would propose eight criteria of theoretical utility: breadth, depth, relevance, consistency, clarity, coherence, testability, and integrativeness. These criteria are briefly described in Table 1 which also includes accompanying evaluative questions. The table includes three terms used by Argyris and Schön: relevance, consistency, and testability. It replaces four terms: breadth for generality, depth for completeness, coherence for centrality, and clarity for simplicity. It also adds an eighth criterion, integrativeness, which differs from coherence. The latter suggests that a theory is useful when its internal parts are unified rather than being disjointed. Integrativeness, on the other hand, is concerned with external linkage with other relevant theoretical efforts and interests. In this sense integrativeness is of disciplinary and interdisciplinary use. It is somewhat like breadth, but it differs in that breadth is concerned with how far we go in examining a phenomenon. Integrativeness, on the other hand, is how far we go in considering the relation of other theories and concerns to ours and the potential implications of our theories to others. This criterion is useful because of the high degree of specialization that exists in the social sciences, and it is particularly useful in considering an interdisciplinary subject such as the nature and role of nonprofit institutions. This value seems very relevant as an antidote to the unfortunate intellectual practices of exclusion or intolerance described above. It is the lack of integrativeness, as Salamon has suggested in his essay in this volume, that has been a shortcoming of modern theories of the welfare state and that have failed to give adequate consideration to the role of nonprofit institutions.

EVALUATING NONPROFIT THEORY

The identification of qualities of theoretical usefulness may be helpful to theory building about nonprofit institutions in several ways. First, it provides some criteria to use in assessing theories about nonprofit institutions, and it may suggest to those who theorize some valued qualities to others that might be undervalued, overlooked, or avoided by them as they engage in theoretical effort. Secondly, consideration of these qualities of usefulness in relation to the various functions served by theory also provides a general tool for describing and assessing theoretical development in a

FIGURE 1
Evaluative Matrix of Functional Theoretical Development

Functions of Theory

DESIRED QUALITIES OF THEORY	Description	Explanation	Prediction	Evaluation	Prescription
Breadth					
Depth					
Relevance					
Consistency					
Clarity					
Coherence					
Testability					
Integrativeness					

field of inquiry (macro), subfield, or subject matter area (micro). As the matrix which follows illustrates (Figure 1), it is possible to identify many areas (40 in this instance) of functional theoretical development in the field of inquiry. Distinguishing between these "areas of functional theoretical development" can be particularly helpful in determining more accurately where theoretical development is inadequate, incomplete, or incorrect.[5] In this way, we can be clearer about theoretical gaps, strengths, and research opportunities in a field, subfield, or subject matter area.

Although no attempt will be made here to assess the theoretical development of nonprofit theory according to these areas in a systematic manner, three general observations are offered.[6] The first is that the field of nonprofit theory is not very well developed but it is not undeveloped. It is neither pre-paradigmatic, nor, to use Kuhn's notion, paradigmatic, but quasi-paradigmatic. It doesn't contain a wide and fully developed range of theoretical positions which cohere in any substantial way, yet there are a limited number of thoughtful and thorough theoretical efforts that serve as a touchstone for additional theoretical development. The fact that there are no well-clarified and accepted subdisciplinary areas or any great classics in the field is an indication of its theoretical adolescence.

Secondly, the great bulk of theoretical work in the field are efforts to explain and predict. There have been only few efforts to develop evaluative or prescriptive theory except in a more popularized fashion, and the qualities of testability and integrativeness, the most advanced qualities of theoretical development, have been the least present.

Thirdly, the general immaturity in the field of nonprofit theory is evident particularly in relation to the most fundamental theoretical function description. One example of this is that there is still no commonly accepted way to refer to the types of institutions which are the focii of the field. It is still a matter of considerable opinion and preference whether or not the institutional entities that are the subject of the study in this field are called voluntary, nonprofit, or third or independent sector. This need for descriptive development is illustrated even further in relation to the issue of the role of nonprofit institutions in the contemporary welfare state. The fact of the matter is that we do not have adequate language to describe the actual roles and preferred relationships between nonprofit and other institutions. As Ralph Kramer (1985:2) has acknowledged, "We do not have the conception and models to reflect this new reality in which there is a mingling of private funds and functions." Above all, this calls into question the most essential concept that has been used to describe and distinguish nonprofit institutions—the metaphor of sectors. The unavoidable theoretical question is: if there is so much overlap, interpenetration, and blurring between government, business, and nonprofit institutions, should we abandon the concept of three sectors?

SHOULD THE THREE-SECTOR METAPHOR BE ABANDONED?

The idea of differentiating between types of institutions is deeply rooted in Western intellectual tradition. Distinctions between the state and commerce and government are longstanding and abundant; for instance, the acknowledgement of associations including institutions other than churches described (as "lesser commonwealths") by Hobbes in the 17th century (especially in Chapters 22 and 29 of *The Leviathan*). Yet, a clear tripartite definition of social institutions is more recent. Most observers attribute the three-sector metaphor to Theodore Levitt (1973) and the Filer Commission, although there are other modern antecedents (c.f. MacIver & Page, 1949).

Beyond tradition and popular acceptance, however, the practical question is whether or not this typological description is adequate in representing the complex roles and dynamic relations among contemporary social institutions.

The limitation of the sector metaphor is that there appear to be anomalies or exceptions to a pure triadic classification of social institutions. The obvious fact is that there are many instances in which one type of institution is so influenced by or duplicative of an institution from another sector that it raises a fundamental question or the accuracy or reliability of the triadic-sector metaphor. However, these observations do not demonstrate, despite the extent or intensity of intersector relations, that the basic nature of most institutions within a sector is no longer the same. Although a nonprofit institution may be substantially affected by, and even change some of its behavior because of the influence of government, this does not make the nonprofit institution a government or business institution. Conceptually, the nonprofit institution is still a nonprofit, though perhaps somewhat more like a business or government as a result of its interaction with them. As Ernst Cassirer has observed in discussing metaphors, "Every concept has a certain 'area' that belongs to it and whereby it is distinguished from other conceptual spheres. No matter how much these areas may overlap, cover each other, or interpenetrate—each one maintains its definitely bounded location in conceptual space." (Cassirer, 1946: 90).

The discovery of an overlap or connection between conceptual spheres is not necessarily a reason to abandon them. Otherwise, most categorizations would be impossible. For example, we do not abandon the classifications of the roles of husband, wife, and child because they join in the concept of "family." Nor does a son become exclusively a "husband" when he marries. The alternative, in the practice of rational inquiry, leads in quite another direction. First, it makes clear that our conceptual areas need further clarification to explain the most common types of differences within an area and the most common types of relations between areas. Secondly, based upon this further analysis, normative questions emerge as to which types and relations are preferable. These questions constitute the core of any agenda to clarify the actual and preferred roles of nonprofit institutions in the welfare state. While these questions do not suggest that a triadic description of institutional forms is inaccurate, they do suggest that it is incomplete and of limited utility if not analyzed further.

Certainly, as many observers have noted, the complexity of the universe of institutional arrangements is not adequately reflected in the triadic representation. As Geoffrey Vickers has suggested, "We must often choose between the simplification which makes the problem manageable but gravely unrealistic and the more complex representation which makes it realistic but gravely unmanageable" (Vickers, 1972: 201, 202). The simplification of the three sectors is practically established and is an adequate initial framework, but only for further analysis. The triadic metaphor is not untrue, but it is not true enough. Because the sector metaphor is not true enough, or does not go far enough in describing significant differences and relations, it must be supplemented with additional concepts.

Accounting for Anomalies

The greatest problem with the three-sector metaphor is that is does not easily account for boundary change and penetration. These phenomena must be understood if we are to have a nonprofit theory that is accurate in describing reality and helpful in prescribing policy. Segmented ties between nonprofit institutions and government and business are both elastic and porous, and we need to consider why they do and should or should not expand or open.

The theoretical challenge in recognizing the anomalies to the sector metaphor due to boundary change and penetration is to determine and describe any common types of anomalies. What this requires is to clarify the "exceptions" to our general rules of theoretical classification in a systematic way so that they can become a part of a revised theoretical classification. If the exceptions are too numerous in quantity, it will most likely require a replacement in theory. If one or several of the exceptions is extensive, it will most likely require a major revision in theory.

Although a thorough examination of these types of anomalies is beyond the scope of this essay, I will suggest and describe very briefly four common types: hybridization, functional overlapping, trait absorption, and impingement.

Hybridization: Increasingly, we see instances of organizations that are not essentially government, business, or nonprofit, but some combination of them. These include businesses that are established by nonprofit entrepreneurs to create jobs or social change rather than profits, and nonprofit corporations created by former government administrators to receive government contracts. Not only do we have inadequate language to describe these kinds of organizations, but we do not have much information about how many there are, how fast they are growing in number, or how effective they are in achieving their objectives.

Functional Overlapping: As several of the essays in this volume have described, there are many fields (i.e., health services, education, day care) in which direct services are provided by nonprofit, government, and business institutions. It has been noted that the relationships within various fields and geographical settings may vary among different types of institutions. For example, as Gronbjerg points out in her article, the relationships between nonprofits and government or business institutions that have overlapping functions can be competitive. Although some economists have developed some very useful theoretical explanations of the market forces that influence this phenomenon (Hansmann, 1986; Weisbrod, 1986), there is a paucity of attention to prescriptive issues. The underlying macrotheoretical question, and what I believe is a critical concern that has given rise to this volume, is: To what extent and in what ways should we encourage or regulate the entry of and competition between different types of institutions in any given field?

Trait Absorption: As several of the authors of this volume have observed, institutions from one sector often absorb or adopt features, qualities, or activities associated with another. For example, nonprofits may adopt various business practices, governments may use volunteers, or a business may provide a voluntary service to the community unrelated to their profit-making objectives or activities. Although this may make institutions from different sectors more or less like each other in some ways, it is not clear whether this is necessarily good or bad. Some of our authors have praised some types of trait absorption, and some have questioned the value of others.

Impingement: The Latin *impingere* means to strike, or for one thing to forcefully impact against another. Such forceful impact between institutions within one sector on those in another can be described as a kind of impingement. The result of impingement is that the organization that is impinged upon will react and change to some extent or degree because of the outside force. For example, the federal government's budget, tax, or regulatory policy may impinge upon various nonprofit institutions. Likewise, the lobbying efforts of various nonprofit institutions may impinge upon government. The question of the effects of the force becomes very much a normative matter.

These typological distinctions are not assumed to be definitive since there may well be other anomalies that have been overlooked, and clearly, the ones summarized here could be defined and described more elegantly. The major point here is fourfold:

First, if the basic paradigm of institutional sectors is to have theoretical meaning, it is necessary to create new concepts to explain anomalies. This is the "yes-but" stage that transforms initial working theories into more mature ones. We are, it seems, at the threshold of this stage in the development of nonprofit theory.

Secondly, this new style of development suggests a very substantial research program (Lakatos and Musgrave, 1970). This is suggested graphically in the matrix in Figure 2, which illustrates the many areas for theoretical development that are possible if we are to address the various functional uses (or needs) of theory according to major types of anomalies.

Thirdly, this brings us back to the initial discussion of "what is theory" in which the normative dimensions of theory were discussed. If the kind of program of theoretical advance suggested above is undertaken, it will require that normative assumptions about any special qualities and role of nonprofit institutions be accepted as hypotheses to examine rather than a priori principles to demonstrate. It may well be that hybridization, overlapping, trait absorption, and impingement are good or bad, or good or bad in different fields, or good or bad according to the extent of some relevant quality being present or absent.

Finally, and perhaps most importantly, any assessment of anomalies regarding the tripartite-sector metaphor demands more functional analysis of the behavior and role of nonprofit institutions from field to field according to areas of social need. We

FIGURE 2
Areas of Potential Theoretical Analysis in Relation to Sector Metaphor Anomalies

Types of Anomalies

Theoretical Uses/Needs	Hybrid	Overlapping	Trait Absorption	Impingement
Describe				
Explain				
Predict				
Evaluate				
Prescribe				

cannot assume that the economic, sociological, and political role of nonprofit institutions is similar or preferred in each field or subfield (e.g., education, health services, day care). It may well be that in some fields or areas of social need it is preferable to seek a hegemonic role for nonprofit institutions. In other areas a duplicative, competitive, or cooperative presence may be preferred, and in still other areas, nonprofits should play other roles, such as advocacy or mediation. In this regard, stipulating an especial role for nonprofit, government, or business institutions requires a continuous assessment of the needs and factors and forces at work in each field or area of need. In this sense, nonprofit public policy is multifaceted and dynamic, requiring continued evaluation and readjustment according to the realities of social conditions and change. This is why, as has been suggested by Lester Salamon in this volume, it is important that any theory of the welfare state clearly distinguish between the role of government as the principal provider of direction and funds or the provider of direct services. And, as Susan Ostrander has noted in her previous essay, there is no pattern that should be accepted uncritically as an ideal in this regard.

CONCLUSION

If there is any substantial conclusion to this essay aside from clarifying what theory means and offering some tools for addressing theory building in relation to nonprofit institutions, it is this: the basic (and paradigmatic) conceptual building block of nonprofit theory is in question, and any normative assumptions about the preferential role of nonprofit institutions in the welfare state is a matter to be justified. What this means in practical terms is that the commonly accepted metaphor of tripartite sectors cannot be accepted without explication, and any assumption that nonprofit sector is better at performing various social functions than government or business is a matter to be proven rather than assumed. In Kramer's terms, it may be that *"how* is more critical than who" (1985:10).

These two positions represent a fundamental challenge to nonprofit theory by questioning the paradigmatic metaphor that guides thinking about nonprofit institutions and the common normative assumption that nonprofit institutions have either a unique or exclusive social role to play. This challenge is not a rejection of these dominant concepts, as I have tried to show, but it is rather a call to examine and alter them substantially and to strengthen their theoretical foundation.

NOTES

1. This discussion of the normative dimensions of theory is more than a reflection of the extentialist critique of the notion of objectivity. It is also: 1) a challenge to the "hyperrationalism" of disciplinary specialists and an acknowledgement of the value of knowledge through nonscientific sources (Lindblom & Cohen, 1979); 2) an acknowledgement that our capacity to control social events via policy derived from theory is limited (MacIntyre, 1981: Ch. 8); and 3) a recognition of the need for a more integrative and interdisciplinary approach to social problem-solving (Toulmin, 1982: 255f.).

2. O'Shaughnessy's model suggests an approach to theoretical development that is similar to what Kuhn suggests as "normal science": a cumulative development through a series of stages of description, explanation, prediction, etc. Although I believe this is a good way to work at building theory, I would not suggest it is the *only* way. It is possible that while proceeding with "normal scientific" development, a theorist could introduce a revolutionary new paradigm that totally reorients or "restarts" the theoretical process. This is one of several possible paths of theoretical change implied in Kuhn's theory (see Stegmuller, 1976).

3. The terms casual, popular, micro, macro, and grand theory suggest a progression from individual opinion through scientific development to a more metascientific synthesis. In regard to theoretical development regarding issues of nonprofit theory, I would suggest that micro-theories are concerned with such issues as organizational behavior in nonprofit institutions, volunteer motivation, the origins and functions of philanthropy, etc. A macro-theory would attempt to integrate these various considerations about nonprofit institutions. A grand theory would go a step further in considering the role of nonprofit institutions in terms of their psychological, sociological, and political meaning in a synthetic social theory. The issue of the role of the nonprofit sector in the welfare state, it seems to me, must ultimately be a part of a grand theory that confronts broader ideological considerations of neoconservative, pragmatic, feminist, and Marxist ideologies. Utilizing a more general theory of the role of the nonprofit sector in the welfare state must be imbedded in a broader political theory. A major issue that may serve as a critical link between nonprofit theory and general theory is the issue of citizen participation.

4. A phenomenological analysis of usefulness according to all types of theorizing, I suspect, would be much more compact than the eight items I identify. For example, breadth and depth may not be very useful in casual or popular theory. Further, it may well be that there is a different weighting of criteria of usefulness according to different types of theories. Breadth may be quite high in grand theory but quite low in casual or popular theory.

5. The matrix is not intended as a set of criteria for any individual theorist unless she or he so chooses. It is rather a tool to evaluate the extent of theoretical development in a given period of time in a given field or area of inquiry.

6. This discussion does not lean toward either an inductive or deductive method of theoretical development. Both methods are appreciated for the type of contributions to knowledge they can make.

REFERENCES

Argyris, Chris and Donald Schön
    1974   *Theory in Practice: Increasing Professional Effectiveness*. San Francisco, California: Jossey-
                Bass.
Buehrig, Edward (ed.)
    1966   *Essays in Political Science*. Bloomington, Indiana: Indiana University Press.
Cassirer, Ernst
    1946   *Language & Myth*. Mineola, New York: Dover Publications.
Clotfelter, Charles T. and Lester M. Salamon
    1986   "The Impact of the 1981 Tax Act on Individual Giving," in Rose-Ackerman, *The Economics
                of Nonprofit Institutions*. Oxford University Press, 207-223.
Cornford, F.M.
    1957   *From Religion to Philosophy*. New York: Harper Bros., Inc.
DeMone, H.W. and M. Gibelman
    1984   "Reagonomics: The Impact of the Voluntary Not-for-Profit-Sector." *Social Work*. 29:5.
Hodgkinson, Virginia and Murray S. Weitzman
    1985   *Dimensions of the Independent Sector: A Statistical Profile*. Washington: Independent Sector.

Etzioni, Amitai
    1968   *The Active Society*. New York: The Free Press.
Hansmann, Henry
    1968   "The Role of Nonprofit Enterprise," in Rose-Ackerman, *The Economics of Nonprofit Institutions*. Oxford University Press, 57-84.
Hoover, Kenneth
    1976   *The Elements of Social Scientific Thinking*. New York: St. Martins Press.
Kramer, Ralph
    1985   "The Voluntary Agency in a Mixed Economy: Dilemmas of Entrepreneurialism & Vendorism." Working Paper No. 85. Program on Nonprofit Organizations, Institution for Social and Policy Studies, Yale University, New Haven, Connecticut.
Kuhn, Thomas
    1962   *The Structure of Scientific Revolutions* (Vol. 2). Chicago, Illinois: University of Chicago Press.
Lakatos, Imre and Alan Musgrave
    1970   *Criticism and the Growth of Knowledge*. Cambridge, Massachusetts: The University Press.
Langton, Stuart
    1981   "The New Voluntarism," *Journal of Voluntary Action Research* (Vol. 10, No. 1). January 1981.
Levitt, Theodore
    1973   *The Third Sector: New Tactics for a Responsive Society*. New York: Amacom.
Lindbloom, Charles and David Cohen
    1979   *Usable Knowledge: Social Science and Social Problem-Solving*. New Haven, Connecticut: Yale University Press.
MacIntyre, Alasdair
    1981   *After Virtue: A Study of Moral Theory*. Notre Dame, Indiana: University of Notre Dame Press.
MacIver, Robert and Charles Page
    1928   *Community*. New York: The Macmillan Co.
Manheim, Jarol and Richard Rich
    1986   *Empirical Political Analysis, Research Methods in Political Science*. New York: Longman, Inc.
Meehan, Eugene
    1968   *Explanation in Social Science*. Homewood, Illinois: The Dorsey Press.
Nielsen, Waldemar
    1979   *The Endangered Sector*. New York: Columbia University Press.
O'Shaughnessy, John
    1973   *Inquiry and Decision: A Methodology for Management and the Social Sciences*. New York: Harper & Row.
    1986   *Philanthropy, Voluntary Action, and the Public Good: 1986 Spring Research Forum*. Working Papers. Independent Sector and United Way Institute.
Rapoport, Anatol
    1966   "The Use of Theory in the Study of Politics," in Buehrig, Edward (ed.), *Essays in Political Science*. Bloomington, Indiana: Indiana University Press.
Reynolds, Paul
    1971   *A Primer in Theory Construction*. Indianapolis, Indiana: Bobbs-Merrill Co.
Rudner, Richard
    1966   *Philosophy of Social Science*. Englewood Cliffs, New Jersey: Prentice-Hall, Inc.
Russell, Bertrand
    1945   *A History of Western Philosophy*. New York: Simon and Schuster.
Rose-Ackerman, Susan (ed.)
    1986   *The Economics of Nonprofit Institutions: Studies in Structure and Policy*. New York: Oxford University Press.
Rose, Arnold
    1954   *Theory and Method in the Social Sciences*. Minneapolis, Minnesota: The University of Minnesota Press.
Salamon, Lester and Allan J. Abramson
           The Federal Budget and the Nonprofit Sector. Washington, D.C.: The Urban Institute Press.
Salamon, Lester, James Musselwhite, Jr., and Carol DeVita
    1986   "Partners in Public Service Government and the Nonprofit Sector in the American Welfare State," in *Philanthropy, Voluntary Action, and the Public Good*, op. cit.
Schooler, Dean
    1983   "Policy Directions and the Nonprofit Sector: Elements of an Integrated, Comprehensive Agenda," *Policy Studies Journal* (Vol. II, No. 3). March 1983.
Shively, W. Phillips
    1974   *The Craft of Political Research*. Englewood Cliffs, New Jersey: Prentice-Hall, Inc.

Skinner, Quentin
    1985   *The Return of Grand Theory in the Human Sciences.* Cambridge: Cambridge University
                Press.
Stegmuller, Wolfgang
    1976   *The Structure and Dynamics of Theories.* New York: Springer-Verlag.
Sumariwalla, Russy
    1986   "Toward a National Taxonomy of Exempt Entities," in *Philanthropy, Voluntary Action, and
                the Public Good,* op. cit.
Toulmin, Stephen
    1982   *The Return to Cosmology: Postmodern Science and the Theology of Nature.* Berkeley, Califor-
                nia: University of California Press.
Vickers, Geoffrey
    1972   *Freedom in a Rocky Boat: Changing Values in an Unstable Society.* Middlesex, England:
                Penguin Books.
Wheelwright, Phillip (ed.)
    1951   *Aristotle.* New York: The Odyssey Press.
Weisbrod, Burton
    1986   "Toward a Theory of the Voluntary Nonprofit Sector in a Three-Sector Economy, in Rose-
                Ackerman, *The Economics of Nonprofit Institutions.* Oxford University Press, 21-44.
Wildavsky, Aaron
    1979   *Speaking Truth to Power: The Art and Craft of Policy Analysis.* Boston, Massachusetts: Little,
                Brown & Co.